T0330821

ROUTLEDGE LIBRARY EDITIONS: COLONIALISM AND IMPERIALISM

Volume 12

CAPITALISM AND COLONIAL PRODUCTION

CAPITALISM AND COLONIAL PRODUCTION

HAMZA ALAVI, P. L. BURNS, G. R. KNIGHT,
P. B. MAYER and DOUG McEACHERN

Routledge
Taylor & Francis Group

LONDON AND NEW YORK

First published in 1982 by Croom Helm Ltd

This edition first published in 2023
by Routledge
4 Park Square, Milton Park, Abingdon, Oxon OX14 4RN

and by Routledge
605 Third Avenue, New York, NY 10158

Routledge is an imprint of the Taylor & Francis Group, an informa business

British Library Cataloguing in Publication Data
A catalogue record for this book is available from the British Library

ISBN: 978-1-032-41054-8 (Set)
ISBN: 978-1-032-44522-9 (Volume 12) (hbk)
ISBN: 978-1-032-44523-6 (Volume 12) (pbk)
ISBN: 978-1-003-37258-5 (Volume 12) (ebk)

DOI: 10.4324/9781003372585

Publisher's Note
The publisher has gone to great lengths to ensure the quality of this reprint but points out that some imperfections in the original copies may be apparent.

Disclaimer
The publisher has made every effort to trace copyright holders and would welcome correspondence from those they have been unable to trace.

Capitalism
and Colonial Production

HAMZA ALAVI, P.L. BURNS, G.R. KNIGHT,
P.B. MAYER AND DOUG McEACHERN

CROOM HELM
London & Canberra

© 1982 Hamza Alavi, P.L. Burns, G.R. Knight, P.B. Mayer and Doug McEachern
Croom Helm Ltd, 2-10 St John's Road, London SW11

British Library Cataloguing in Publication Data

Capitalism and colonial production.
   1. Imperialism - Economic aspects
   I. Alavi, Hamza
   382.1   HC59
   ISBN 0-7099-0634-X

Printed and bound in Great Britain by
Biddles Ltd, Guildford and King's Lynn

CONTENTS

LIST OF MAPS

PREFACE

The link between colonialism and capitalism has been
frequently debated, and from many different perspectives.
Frank's work on Latin America initiated a significant
discussion of the nature of capitalism as it was created in
Third World countries subject to imperialist trade and, in
his terms, to incorporation into a capitalist world market.
Though Frank did discuss the numerous changes that followed
this process of incorporation, he was never precise about
their capitalist character, except to note that the surplus
extracted fed into the process of global capitalist
accumulation. This provided scope for a subsequent debate
about class and mode of production which sought to be more
precise about the nature and significance of the changes
engendered by imperialism or colonial subjugation.
Unfortunately, this concern rapidly degenerated, being
followed by numerous, simple schemes of 'conceptual
clarification' (which frequently concealed the many
complexities of historical development), the proliferation of
identified and imagined modes of production and the
development of a fascinating intellectual game whose object
was the description of the ways in which non-capitalist and
capitalist modes of production 'articulated' with one
another. Most often this blurring of focus was engendered by
a lack of concern with the precise nature of the capitalist
mode of production, a too close identification of the
capitalist mode of production with the labour process that
characterised the industrial factory and a lack of attention
to the complexities of the historical transformations that
accompanied both the industrialisation of capitalism in
Europe and the colonisation of the Third World. In this
volume we have sought to advance the debate by reconsidering
the problems involved in identifying pre-colonial modes of
production and by paying close attention to the precise
details of the changes wrought by colonial domination. It is
our hope that this book will stand as an invitation to others
to reconsider the whole character of the colonial
transformation and the process of capitalist development.

Initial versions of the papers by Alavi, Burns, Knight and Mayer were presented to the Third National Conference of the Asian Studies Association of Australia, Griffith University,Brisbane, August 1980. A version of Alavi's essay has appeared in the <u>Journal of Contemporary Asia</u>, Vol. 10, No. 4 (1980).

H.A., P.L.B., G.R.K., P.B.M., D.McE.

Chapter 1

CAPITALISM AND COLONIAL PRODUCTION: AN INTRODUCTION

Doug McEachern

In recent years, a number of attempts have been made to
analyse the way in which colonialism transformed the
societies which it dominated. From the path-breaking work of
Andre Gunder Frank and Immanuel Wallerstein onwards, there
have been moves to characterise the changes in production and
the new modes of production created. In these attempts and
in the critiques and formulations of counter views, a number
of different positions have been taken. Each position has
expressed a characteristic error; a blind spot, ommission,
over-emphasis or lack of precision. Frank's initial work on
Latin America was concerned to establish the penetration of
capitalism into the societies of that continent and to show
how they were all incorporated, and transformed by that
incorporation, into a global system of capital accumulation
and centralisation.[1] In showing the ways in which this
process occurred, Frank did not need to be precise about the
definitions of feudalism and capitalism, or the analytical
distinctions between modes of production. It was enough to
refute the dualist conception of an economy divided between a
traditional and a modern sector, to show that all areas of
the economy had been changed by the process of penetration
and incorporation. This, in itself, was a major
achievement. Laclau's celebrated critique of Frank's
argument concentrated on the conceptual inadequacies of
Frank's characterisation of various modes of production.[2]
Whilst Laclau successfully exposes the weaknesses in Frank's
usage, he does not provide a consistent statement of what a
mode of production is, nor how changes in modes of production
are to be established in a rigorous analytical manner. When
he comes to characterise the modes of production which exist
in Latin American societies, Laclau relies on obvious
features of the labour process, basically the absence of free
wage-labour relations, to show that capitalism does not exist
in the countryside.
    In the space between these two positions and their
associated and overlapping problems, many others have sought

to find terms to describe the processes and consequences of colonial transformation. Hamza Alavi's work has provided the most consistent attempt to link up developing arguments about the characterisation of modes of production with an analysis of what happened as a result of colonial domination. Alavi started from an analysis of what he described as 'the post-colonial state' but was forced to consider the social groups which he identified as the dominant classes of post colonial society.[3] It was necessary to clarify the way in which these classes, and the relations between them, had been developed by colonial and imperialist domination. To be precise about these class questions it was also necessary to consider the most appropriate characterisation of the mode of production produced by colonial domination. Alavi initiated the line of enquiry which forms the substance of this volume. To pose the question of the character of the classes produced by colonialism, Alavi summarised a debate on capitalism and agriculture which appeared in the influential Indian journal, the Economic and Political Weekly[4] and proposed a substantial reinterpretation of the problem. As its centre, this reinterpretation sought to show that the analysis of the nature of the relations of production was an essential part of the identification of the classes present in colonial society. It was not enough to treat the link between them as being self-evident. Alavi claimed that even if the character of the relations of production had not been changed by colonialism, it was not axiomatic that the class relations in the countryside remained unaltered. The changed context, colonialism, a system of imperial exchange, and the dominance of capitalism, was enough to impart a new meaning and significance to unchanged relations of production. More directly, though share-cropping existed in both pre-colonial and colonial India, it did not mean that the same mode of production prevailed. Rather that the class meaning of the share-cropping relationship needed to be probed. The end point of Alavi's interpretation was to suggest that colonialism brought into being a new mode of production that shared many of the attributes of capitalism but whose lack of dynamic was to be explained by the colony's place in an imperial system. It was to identify this aspect of the process that Alavi introduced the term 'colonial mode of production'.[5] By developing the argument in this manner, Alavi opened up many important dimensions for the analysis of the impact of colonial domination. His approach forced to the fore the question of the mode of production that preceded colonialism, since it was important to know the circumstances that were changed by colonialism; the changes instituted by colonialism and the characterisation of the class character of agrarian rent relations. At the same time, those associated with Review of African Political Economy, were trying to find adequate concepts to deal with the relationship between the African 'peasantry' and the forces

2

of capitalism that apparently impinged on that world without transforming the class and production relations upon which it was based. The work of Pierre Philipe Rey and Claude Meillassoux generated a number of differently conceived modes of production and relations of articulation as a response to this problem.[6] Henry Bernstein found the best solution, so far, in his treatment of commodity production in the African peasantry.[7] In the midst of all this there has been a proliferation of terms to describe the mode of production created by colonialism and the present day societies of the Third World. Colonial modes of production, tributory, linear, and even hybrid modes have been identified. Such a profusion of terms might indicate a variety of different situations being analysed. The real problem lies in the fact that these are all attempts to deal with the one situation, the transformation of non-capitalist societies by the domination of capitalism in the form of a process of colonial rule.

It is within this variety of terms and approaches that this book is cast. It is an attempt to solve the analytical problems of treating this process of social transformation and to illustrate that solution by reference to a number of different examples of colonial and capitalist transformations of what are now considered to be Third World societies. Again this argument is located within a debate about modes of production - but where others have settled for new terms to account for the complex situation, we have sought to show that colonialism created a distinctive form of capitalism in these societies. They are not dual economies; there is not feudalism or semi-feudalism in the countryside. There is, in fact, capitalism, but of a different form, in all parts of the economy. As such, the argument seeks to confront those traditional historians of colonialism who are unable to assess the consequences except in the sterile terms of a contrast between modern and traditional societies. It seeks to overturn the position which finds the reenforcement of non-capitalist relations in the agrarian sector or the creation of a dual economy. Also, it seeks to establish an effective basis for understanding how and why these societies develop in the ways that they have.

To prepare the basis for the arguments about how capitalism comes to be established in these circumstances, it is necessary to confront directly a number of important and disputed issues. Firstly, there is the question of how modes of production are to be characterised and how the passage from one mode of production to another is to be established. What kinds of relations characterise different modes of production? How are the changes in these relations to be identified in given historical contexts? Secondly, how are feudalism and other non-capitalist modes of production to be characterised? Assuming that an adequate characterisation of a capitalist mode of production is more common, it is important to consider the possible varieties of non-capitalist modes of production and the potential ways in which they can be transformed. Thirdly, and this is perhaps the most central problem, there is the question of how to analyse the class relations that exist in agricultural production. The class basis of the labour process and of the surplus extraction process are neither self-evident nor easy to unravel. It is vital to examine the problem of how to analyse the class relations that are present in rent and tax relations in rural societies.

Fourthly (and finally), is the process being analysed here only an example of a limited social transformation undertaken by merchant capital, in the sphere of circulation? Is the transformation confined to the sphere of circulation or does it affect the sphere of production? Is the subsequent limited development of these societies to be explained by the distorted transformation engendered by merchant capital or by the place of these capitalist economies within a global structure of capitalist economies? On the basis of considering these four problem areas, it is possible to give an overall sketch of what is at stake in the argument about the colonial transformation of production in these countries.

The Characterisation of Modes of Production

There are numerous theoretical and analytical problems involved in the characterisation of modes of production. At a theoretical level there is the question of what relations constitute a mode of production, whether the ingredients are invariant, and whether the tendencies for change are inherent in the given structure of a mode of production. At the analytical level the problem is slightly different. Given that the concepts of modes of production are abstract in character and express the essence of historical situations, how is the mode of production (or combinations of modes of production) present in an historically conditioned and constituted society to be recognised? By what means is it possible to decode the complications of production relations and patterns of class exploitation? As will be seen, the obvious features of the labour process, its organisation or its links with a process of surplus extraction do not help to simplify this problem. Despite the difficulties associated with characterising and identifying different modes of production, the effort is necessary to provide an adequate basis for an effective analysis of colonial transformation. It is only through a consideration of modes of production that it is possible to identify the major classes of a society and to explain the dynamics that lie embedded in the structure of their relations to each other.

In recent years there has been a marked attempt to provide an adequate theoretical elaboration of the concept

4

'mode of production'. The major focus of this conceptual 'clarification' has been a debate amongst those like Balibar, Althusser and Poulantzas in France and Hindess, Hirst, Cutler and Hussein in Britain who worked within a quasi-structuralist framework.[8] It is not necessary to follow the contorted path of conceptual proposition and refinement over the notion of a mode of a production. Nor to trace the path followed by Hindess and Hirst in their gradual rejection of its usefulness.[9] It suffices to indicate that the debate concerned the identification of the elements that make up a mode of production and the nature of the different ways in which these elements are combined within different modes of production.

For our purposes, it is sufficient to recognise that the term 'mode of production' refers to those relations that exist at the heart of a given society, identifies the major classes of that society and indicates the inherent logic of the relations and conflicts between those classes. In all societies we may identify means of production, direct producers and a relevant class of non-producers that combine in a process of social production. Production is also surplus production and surplus extraction; that is, the process of production also constitutes a process of class exploitation. The relations generated in the production process assume a different character in societies dominated by different modes of production. The problem is to suggest the different character of these relevant direct producers and non-producers and the forms of the relationships between them.

The different modes of production cannot be generated by theoretical reflection on the ways in which these three elements can be combined in the dual aspects of a labour process and a process of surplus extraction. It is useful to consider the historical sketches provided by Marx in that section of the Grundrisse extracted and published under the title Pre-Capitalist Economic Formations.[10] In this section of the Grundrisse, Marx suggests a map of the development of society from a form of primitive communalism to capitalism. The transformation is seen as the passage from a society in which the direct producers own and control, or dominate the means of production to one in which the direct producers are separated from the means of production which becomes the property of a class of non-producers who now dominate access to those means of production. Marx indicates a variety of technical changes (in the techniques of production) and class struggles that provide the means by which these modes of production are transformed. The logic of that argument is not relevant here, though later its implication for the argument about colonialism as the setting for a process of transformation needs to be considered.

The modes of production identified by Marx can be codified as follows. Primitive Communism is a mode of

production in which means of production (low level means of
hunting and agriculture) are dominated by some form of
communal institutions which organise production and
distribute the surplus. Feudalism is a mode of production in
which there is a partial separation of the direct producers
from the means of production (largely the basis of
agricultural production, land and the means to work that
land). Capitalism is a form of society in which the direct
producers have been separated from the means of production.
These now exist as the private property of a class of
non-producers. These outlines do not indicate all the
ingredients of the modes of production. It is also necessary
to show the way in which the various classes relate to each
other through their relations to the means of production in
the processes of production and surplus extraction. In
primitive communism the problem is less obvious. Through
membership of the community one has access to the means of
production and the production process. On that basis, means
of survival are acquired. Under feudalism, the situation of
divided ownership, but with a dominant position (especially
over the ownership of land) going to the non-producers,
production and surplus extraction is organised through rent
and tax relations. (It is incorrect to see a division
between the process of surplus extraction and the domination
of the means of production. The direct producers do not
control the production process and the surplus is not
extracted by external, essentially non-economic relations.
But more on this below.) Under capitalism, the form of
association is through wage-labour and surplus is extracted
through surplus value relations based on the separation of
the direct producer from the means of production. Further,
each mode of production has a characteristic state form.
Primitive communism is a society without classes and without
a state as such, though state-like functions are performed by
other means. In feudalism the state and the process of
surplus extraction are closely interconnected; the state is
involved both at a national level and in the local process of
production and accumulation. Under capitalism, the state is
formally separated from the economy, centralised,
bureaucratic and concerned with relating (mediating?) the
relations between the economic and political spheres of
society. Though different state forms appear to coincide
with different modes of production, it is open to dispute
whether the form of state is part of what constitutes a mode
of production.

Feudalism and Non-Capitalist Modes of Production

In the literature on colonialism and its associated
transformation there is a tendency to characterise some parts
of the economy as either feudal or semi-feudal. Such a
designation implies that the societies of the colonies are,

6

in essential regards, the same as the societies of Europe in the years preceding the transition to capitalism. More than that there is an attempt to harness the explanatory power of Marx's arguments about the transition to the analysis of these Third World countries. Just as feudalism contained embryonic capitalist production relations and provided an environment within which these could mature, so greater capitalist penetration will release growth and dynamism in the Third World setting. It is implied that the barriers to economic development lie in the nature or form of the production relations within the colony: it denies the importance of the place of the Third World capitalist country within a structured system of capitalist relations as part of the explanation for the problems of growth and development. At its most sophisticated designation, the development or the persistence of feudal or semi-feudal relations is treated as the result of the actions of capitalism (or, in some versions, of merchant capital) and thus combines both the internal and external logic of context. Whatever the reasoning, it is necessary to question both the accuracy and the adequacy of characterising Third World countries as having, or having had, feudal modes of production.

The characterisation of a feudal mode of production is no easy matter. Its basic features have been the subject of several protracted and complicated disputes.[11] Hamza Alavi, in the chapter included in this volume, provides a clear example of how this characterisation of feudalism works.[12] Alavi outlines five characteristics of feudalism. These are presented with explicit contrasts to the characteristics of capitalism, already framing the approach to transition. These 'components' are: unfree labour, extra-economic coercion in the extraction of surplus; fusion of economic and political power at the point of production; a self-sufficient or subsistence economy; an economy based on simple reproduction, that is a situation where the surplus is consumed and not accumulated in the form of expanded production. Alavi's characterisation of feudalism is derived from an orthodox reading of Marx. There are problems in treating this as an adequate, theoretical/analytical characterisation of the feudal mode of production. In places it shades into a general description of the elements common to many non-capitalist modes of production. This can be seen in the general level of these points, for example, extra-economic coercion can take a variety of forms. The specific character of such coercion may well distinguish different non-capitalist modes of production. The particular way in which these attributes are combined is also left unspecified. It would be difficult, were it not for the prevailing conventional assumptions about the problem, to generate a scheme of class and production relations, or to recognise something about the tensions and 'laws of motion' of a society based on such a mode of production.

Though there is much that is inadequate and perverse about Hindess and Hirst's approach to the question of modes of production, on the nature of the feudal mode of production their remarks have great force.[13] Hindess and Hirst assert that the characterisation of feudalism on the basis of extra-economic coercion in the process of surplus production misunderstands the essential feature of the organisation of the production process in feudal society. They argue that feudalism is a situation in which ownership and possession of the means of production are divided between a class of direct producers and a landed class which plays a necessary and vital part in initiating and organising production. It is on that basis that the rent and revenue relations that are so characteristic of feudalism are generated. They could not appear if the extraction process was largely based on 'extra-economic coercion', even if it were concealed custom and usage. This argument is important as it relates the process of surplus extraction to the organisation of the production process; it overcomes the separation of the process of production from the process of extraction. Now, this does not mean that a situation in which surplus is accumulated by extra-economic means does not exist. Nor that the process of production may not be separated from a crude process of surplus extraction by force or law backed by force. Simply, that where this exists, it would be inappropriate to designate such a situation as characteristic of a feudal mode of production.

If we were to schematise the feudal mode of production it would appear like this. Under feudalism, the ownership of the means of production is divided between the direct producers and a landed ruling class. The direct producers enter into a relationship with the means of production, take part in the production process on the basis of rent relations with the landed class. Surplus production is taken by the landed class in the form of rent in either labour time, produce or money. Such rent relations may be enshrined in custom and law and backed by religious argument or legitimation, though the basis for the extraction lies in the situation of divided possession and control of the means of production. Such a characterisation would give us a two class model of feudal society and would provide a way to understand the tensions that exist between the landed class and the direct producers.

For the analysis of the situation in Third World countries, especially in the conditions that prevailed in the period prior to colonial domination, it is necessary to be exceedingly cautious about characterising any part of it as feudal. The situation will almost always be characterised by a non-capitalist mode of production but it is necessary and important to establish the kind of non-capitalist mode of production it actually is. They are not all the same. The

8

shape of the pre-colonial mode of production needs to be known if the analysis of the impact of colonialism is to proceed effectively. On the whole, I am opposed to a proliferation of concepts of modes of production. However, with the prevailing lack of argument about the actual modes of production that existed in various countries and districts prior to colonialism, it may be necessary to witness a flowering of many ghastly apparitions; many differently characterised non-capitalist modes of production, before it is possible to identify broadly similar non-capitalist modes of production. But it is far better to confront such an agonising spectacle than to dissolve the problem by the too broad application of the term 'feudal'. Of the non-capitalist modes of production that precede colonialism, very little of a general nature can be said. On the basis of the above discussion of feudalism, and the previous observations on Marx's typology provided in the Grundrisse, it is possible to suggest one thing. Non-capitalist modes of production of this type will be characterised by various degrees of separation of the direct producers from the possession and control of the means of production. The forms of surplus extraction may vary, as can the character of the production process, but both will be based in an incomplete process of separation. The separation of direct producers from the means of production is the necessary basis for the development of capitalist relations of production and the capitalist mode of production. Colonialism may be one way in which the prehistory of capitalist development is completed: a transformation of non-capitalist modes of production, not a transition from feudal ones.

Agrarian Production and the Mode of Production

The real problems that are confronted in the attempt to identify the mode of production which exists in given historical circumstances is nowhere more obviously difficult than in the attempt to characterise the class relations generated in the process of agricultural production. It is possible to simplify the process by which modes of production are identified so much so that all problems disappear. This is done by treating the obvious features of how production is organised as the key to the identification of the mode of production. In other words, if the mode of production is identified solely on the basis of the appearance of the labour process, the organisation of work and the obvious features of the contractual basis of production, then the non-capitalist character of agricultural production is easily established. Nonetheless, in most Third World countries it is clear that there is some connection between what goes on in the agricultural sector and in the more obviously capitalist industrial sector, or in the relationship between agricultural production and some international market system of a distinctly capitalist character. The problem remains to account for the character of that relationship; of that connection between the agrarian and non-agrarian sectors in an apparently unified economy.

Many different solutions have been proposed to this analytical problem. Some have sought to dissolve the dilemma in the notion of capitalist penetration and incorporation in a world capitalist market system of surplus extraction, centralisation and accumulation. Others took refuge in conceptualising various 'articulations' between modes of production: that is, they sought to show how non-capitalist relations could contain and express capitalist relations and allow a process of capital accumulation to be fulfilled through them. Henry Bernstein's "Notes on Capital and Peasantry" comes closest to finding a solution to this problem.[14] Writing of the situation in Africa, and with assumptions about peasant household production and the destruction of a natural economy by the imposition of commodity production, Bernstein seeks to argue that the problem is best approached by avoiding notions of articulation and concentrating instead on "...the relations between peasant households and capital rather than by invoking modes of production other than the capitalist mode".[15] It is on such a basis that he is able to propose that "...the exchange of labour power may be concealed by forms of payment other than money-wages, and may be disguised by ostensibly 'traditional' forms of cooperation and reciprocity".[16] Despite this recognition, Bernstein is unwilling to extend this point and to treat the relations in agriculture as variants of capitalist relations of production. In fact he directly rejects this solution to the problem.

> No definitive solutions have been offered but the position taken here is that peasants have to be located in their relations with capital and the state, in other words, within capitalist relations of production mediated through forms of household production which are the site of a struggle for effective possession and control between the producers and capital/state. It may be inferred that in this way peasants are posed as 'wage-labour equivalents'...but in a relative sense that limits the subjugation and real subsumption of household labour by capital to the extent that the producers are not fully expropriated not dependent for their reproduction on the sale of labour-power through the wage-form.[17]

Working from a different set of assumptions and from a different debate, we have found an alternative solution to the problem of classes in agrarian production, one which gives substance to the suggestion of 'peasants' as 'wage-labour equivalents'. The debate on the character of agriculture in India as a result of the capital investment in technology and the green revolution, threw into relief the major issues concerning the capitalist or non-capitalist character of the production relations in agriculture.[18] At the heart of the exchanges was a concern with the empirical and obvious features about the organisation of agricultural production prior to the introduction of tractors and other forms of capital investment. The labour process, the organisation of work, in the agricultural sector did not conform with commonly held assumptions about the character of distinctly capitalist production. In a sense the two sides in the debate differed in their assessment of the significance of the labour process in the identification and characterisation of a capitalist mode of production. There were those who treated the levels of investment, technology and forms of tenancy as proof that the capitalist mode of production had not 'really' come to dominate in the agricultural sector.[19] On the other side, there were those who argued that these features were not sufficient, in themselves, to characterise the mode of production, the identification of which depended on the class relations of production and exploitation upon which agriculture was based.

Those who wished to argue that capitalism had come to dominate class relations in the countryside, had to confront a number of important assumptions about what would indicate capitalist class relations in agriculture. First, there was the question of the level of investment in agrarian production. Some assumed that if surplus was extracted from the agrarian sector and not reinvested (accumulated) in technology and improved production, then the mode of exploitation would not be capitalist. This position confuses the notion of capitalist accumulation by believing that the accumulation must occur in the same sector of the economy (enterprise, farm?) in which the surplus was produced. This need not be the case. The surplus can be accumulated in other spheres, or, given a structure of imperial relations, in other countries. Even if this position avoided theoretical problems, in empirical terms it can be shown that there had been forms of capital investment in agriculture on the basis of the changes introduced through colonial domination, land ownership and revenue reform. Capital investment and the improvements in production technique, the industrialisation of agriculture, may occur on the basis of a prior transformation of the class and production relations. The increased investment may simply make more visible the capitalist basis upon which that process proceeds by making the categories of capital and wage-labour more obvious in the agrarian sector.

Second, there was the important problem revealed by inadequate and inappropriate models for the analysis of class relations in agricultural production. Often it appeared as if the situation in agriculture was being contrasted with the situation in the factories of industrialised capitalism, or with the extensive farming sector of the American economy. There was little awareness of the nature of class relations in agrarian production in European countries in the long periods of capitalist development through the 19th and the first part of the 20th centuries. For example, if the situation in rural France and Germany was compared with the class situation in the Indian countryside (or in agricultural production of many non-tribal areas of the Third World) then the problem would not have seemed so simply solved.

Third, there was the question of the obvious features of the organisation of agrarian production. It was assumed that if capital/wage labour relations were either absent from, or only a minor part of, the agrarian scene, then it could not be treated as forming part of a capitalist mode of production. Indeed, it was on the basis of the forms of contract and rent relations that various non-capitalist designations were applied to classes in agrarian production. Some detected in these forms of unfreedom evidence of feudal or semi-feudal arrangements. Others saw these as evidence for the existence of pre-colonial forms of exploitation that may have been intensified or even created by colonial domination and the penetration of capitalism.

These positions all failed to deal adequately with the changes that occurred as a result of colonial domination and the transformation of agrarian relations. The significance of the increased role of commodity production was not assessed for its implications for the characterisation of the class relations evident in agrarian production. It is not just that widespread commodity production (that is, production of goods for sale rather than immediate use) is incompatible with the designation of feudal or unchanged class and production relations, it is also that such an occurrence is only possible on the basis of a reorganisation of production and the generation of a new set of class relations. With that in mind, it is possible to see the different ways in which contractual and rent relations and other ways of organising agrarian production for the regular supply of commodities occurs in forms that are compatible with capitalist relations of production, forms of those relations or capital/wage-labour relations in a direct sense.

Let us leave aside the obviously capitalist character of wage labour in the countryside and concentrate on the remaining two categories. The peasant household as such, that is, the household where the family owns the means of production (land) and works it with family labour, forms a class relationship that may exist in more than one mode of production. It can be the relationship of self-ownership and self-exploitation of the petit-bourgeoisie within capitalist society. The mode of production can not be read out from this set of relations. Rather the character of this household is determined on the basis of the wider, encapsulating mode of production. Such a class position, or such class relations, are compatible with a capitalist mode of production even where no significant quantity of surplus is extracted from it. In the situation of agricultural production in the Third World, such households do produce commodities and enter into market relations with the rest of the economic system. But the question of self-owning and exploitation is not the difficult one. The real problems concern the way in which rent relationships are interpreted, both as ways of organising the production process and in extracting surpluses from the direct producers.

Several points need to be made clear about the social basis of rent relationships before their place in modes of production can be analysed. For a rent relationship to exist, it is necessary for the direct producer to have been either separated from the major means of production (land) or to share control over the means of production necessary to initiate and complete production. Thus rent can exist on the basis of partial or complete separation of the direct producer from the means of production, in both cases it depends on the direct producer being separated from the primary means of agricultural production, land. It is only on the basis of such a separation that a rent relationship can operate; it is only through the rent relationship that the direct producer comes into a relationship to the means of production. In Third World countries, share-cropping is the most common form of rent relationship. Here the surplus is transferred to the landowner as a defined portion of the crop. Such a process works on the assumption that that proportion of crop can be traded for other goods and for money.

If we are to understand the relationship between rent relations and the identification of the mode of production, it is necessary to be aware of a number of problems. Since rent relations form the basis of the feudal mode of production it is tempting to interpret rent relationships as the defining characteristic of that mode. Many have succumbed to the temptation and describe agricultural production based on rent as feudal or semi-feudal. This is to overlook the way in which rent relations may persist under conditions of capitalism and the distance between rent under feudalism and rent as created and maintained in Third World societies. Rent under feudalism is based on the divided ownership of the means of production and the economic and political role of the dominant class towards the production process and the organisation of production and the extraction of surplus. In the Third World, rent relations work on the basis of the separation of the direct producer from the basic means of production. With the added recognition that commodity production has replaced production for use/subsistence with a small commodity surplus, it is possible to reinterpret the link between rent relations in agriculture and the recognition of the mode of production. Here it is argued that rent relations have become a distorted form of the wage-labour/capital relationship and that the relations of production can be interpreted in that way. This is not to assert that wage-labour and rent relations are identical. They are not. The form of the rent relationship engenders a different experience of production and class society. The assumption is, however, that the rent relations in the Third World are forms of wage-labour relationships and that, over time, will be transformed into wage labour relationships. The introduction of improved technologies and greater investment in agriculture will make manifest the capitalist basis upon which agricultural production already rests. The logic of that development was not created by the capital investment of the green revolution but the capital investment was possible on the basis of the prior transformation of the production relations as a result of colonial domination and economic policy.

Built into this assumption about rent relations and the problems in identifying the defining mode of production, is an assumption about the analysis of different forms of labour and the evident/obvious features of the labour process. Modes of production cannot be defined on the basis of the appearance of 'forms of labour' or the labour process. Forms of labour or the nature of the labour process, need to be interpreted on the basis of the argument about the mode of production. The mode of production cannot be derived, deduced or imputed from the obvious features of the labour process. The labour process, or the actual form of labour, is subordinate to the mode of production in which it exists. It does not determine or define the mode of production. To establish the mode of production we need to be able to identify, what is produced (commodities or not), who produces it, how they are related to the means of production as well as the mechanisms of the process by which surplus is extracted. In stark terms then, labour separated from the means of production, producing commodities with a surplus extracting and accumulating process based on that separation of the direct producer from the means of production constitutes labour undertaken within a capitalist mode of production. The form taken by that labour in its recruitment or mobilisation can then be interpreted as forms of the capital-wage labour relationship which is the essential character of labour within the capitalist mode of production.

Thus, on this basis, it is possible to resolve the problems in the analysis of agricultural production in Third World countries and to go beyond Bernstein's observations by giving substance to the claim that 'peasants' may be treated as wage-labour equivalents. The notion of a peasantry needs to be dissolved into its component sets of class relations and these linked up with the processes of capitalist class

14

relations. Those that own their own land and work it with
household or family labour form a rural petit-bourgeoisie.
Those that rent land and work it with hired-labour constitute
part of a class of capital. They parallel those that own
land and work it with hired-labour. The rent in the first
instance has become capitalist ground rent. Those that own
land and who rent it out to tenants on the basis of share
cropping are also capitalists, accumulating their surpluses
on the basis of the separation of the direct producers from
the means of production. The three positions are not the
same, the differences between them may, in certain
circumstances be significant but they all rest on the same
basis and embody the same class and production relations,
though these assume different forms and may be transformed
into each other. Given the dominance of the capitalist
relations of production it is presumed that rent forms will,
more commonly, be changed into wage-labour forms.

The Problem of Merchant Capitalism

Studies of the impact of colonialism can hardly avoid the
role of merchants. Colonial domination was closely related
to the activities of merchants seeking goods to ship to the
industrialising economies in Europe. Since the publication
of Geoffrey Kay's influential, Development and
Underdevelopment, it is difficult to ignore the problem of
merchant capital and the part it played in creating a
distorted form of economic development.[20] Shifting
attention from merchants to merchant capital affects the
analysis of what colonialism does to the organisation of
production. It raises the supposition that capital can exist
in the sphere of circulation without transforming the process
of production itself. Such a separation of the spheres of
circulation and production links up with a separation of two
fractions of capital; merchant and industrial capital.
Merchant capital is based in the sphere of circulation;
industrial capital in the sphere of production. It is
assumed that if industrial capital dominates, then a process
of growth and dynamism will be unleashed. If merchant
capital predominates, its parasitic role will leave the
cannibalised non-capitalist mode of production changed in
ways that will engender non-growth, stagnation and relative
economic backwardness. This approach to the question of
economic development in colonised countries has been treated
as a solution to the problems posed in the analysis of
colonial domination. It is for this reason that this issue
needs to be discussed.
    Some of the weaknesses of the approach stem from errors
in Kay's basic assumptions about method. Kay is very
effective in using the arguments of Marx to approach the
question of economic development. Even so, it is in his use
of Marx's analytical categories that the basic problem is to

be found. Kay takes the circuits of capital, which were essential for Marx's argument about the nature of surplus value production and capitalist accumulation, and gives them a real world existence. Of itself, this is not too serious. The difficulties arise when Kay takes the logic of the argument about the analytical significance of a particular circuit of capital and claims that these limitations are replicated in the historical process being examined in Third World countries. For example, Kay's discussion of the role of merchant capital in the development of Third World countries, stresses the indifference of this form of capitalism to the modes of production from which it derives commodities to trade. The actions of merchants are then treated only in so far as they conform to this argument about merchant capitalism. If the actions of merchants go beyond these limits and become involved in reorganising production, then they drop from view as this is no longer part of the role of merchants qua merchant capital.[21] But in treating the matter like this, Kay conceals the way in which it is through merchants going beyond the limits of the sphere of circulation that the colonial transformation of production is at its most potent. By focussing solely on the sphere of circulation, the circuit of merchant capital, the activities of merchants are substantially misinterpreted. While it remains true that merchant capital, in the sphere of circulation is indifferent to the origins of the commodities produced, this does not exhaust the analysis of the role of merchants. The argument derives its power from Marx's account of the role of merchants in dissolving the social relations of the feudal mode of production. But the logic of the argument does not translate easily from that situation to the circumstances of colonial domination.

Kay's approach to merchants in the sphere of circulation indicates that the process of profiting from the purchases and sale of goods will give merchants a set of concerns with important social consequences. Merchants will seek to monopolise trade, thereby enabling them to increase their profits. One way to gain such a monopoly, to gain a trade advantage, is to regularise the way in which commodities come into their hands. In colonial practice this entailed the setting up of 'factories' to centralise the storage of goods. The actions of merchants are more significant when they use various means to become involved in the sphere of production, and promote the regular and systematic production of commodities. In doing so, they do 'revolutionise' production. It is here that the analysis of the role of merchant capital has created most problems. It has been concerned to say that commodity production can be extended without transforming the mode of production; that the existence of commodities in the sphere of circulation is possible without commodity production in the sphere of production. For the merchant to operate it doesn't matter

16

how the commodities came into existence. It is another matter to claim that the general presence of commodities in the sphere of circulation cannot be used to reveal something about changes in the sphere of production. The existence of commodities need not indicate anything; in the circumstances of the colonised country it usually does indicate something. The fact that changes were often initiated by merchants, or to meet the requirements of merchanting activities, should not be used to devalue the significance of these changes.

In a general way, the role of merchant capital is only concerned with the buying and selling of goods, generating its profits from the difference between purchasing price and selling price. Nonetheless, trading coupled with the development of colonial domination, backed by the edicts of the colonial state, can have wide repercussions for the character of the production relations in that society subject to the process of colonial domination. It is not merchant capital, or capital in the sphere of circulation, that transforms the pre-colonial production relations. Rather it is merchant capital, capital in the sphere of circulation and the colonial state which provides a potent context within which pressures to transform production relations become effective. The moves to increase the quantities of goods that take the form of commodities have an important impact on the social arrangements of production that previously did not generate commodities as the end product of the production process. Capital moves from the sphere of circulation into the sphere of production. This is revealed by a number of changes and the development of large scale ('generalised') production of commodities. The most significant changes are those that see the means of production transformed into commodities that can be bought and sold; that is, can appear as a commodity in the sphere of circulation. The general separation of the direct producers ˙ from the means of production is signified by the appearance of hired labour and the development and transformation of forms of rental agreements so that they are based on that separation of the direct producers and the production of commodities. On the basis of these changes, it is possible for the surplus extracted from agricultural production to be capitalised, that is, accumulated in the process of capitalist production. It is the nature of the imperial dimension, rather than just the presence of merchant capital that enables the pattern of accumulation to be geographically split, and for the bulk of accumulation to occur in another sector of the economy. Further, the role of merchant capital in setting the framework within which capital 'penetrates' the sphere of production does not provide the explanation for the limited dynamic of the form of capitalism created in the agrarian sector of these countries subject to colonial domination. Rather, this is to be explained by the international dimension, the imperial connection and the global pattern of surplus extraction and accumulation. It should not be assumed that all the surplus is extracted from agricultural production, or from the country concerned. Some of that surplus is accumulated, either in the form of basic industrial production, in the generation of the necessary social infrastructure for commodity production or in improvements in the productivity in agricultural production. Just because the level of investment is low, or concentrated in some areas rather than others and does not lead to full scale mechanised and industrialised techniques of production, does not mean that accumulation has not occurred.

Conclusion

On the basis of the above arguments, it is possible to construct a set of procedures for analysing the impact of colonial domination. It is not that these procedures supplant other approaches, rather they provide an alternative way to understand why colonialism should have been the vehicle for the development of capitalism in countries where it would not otherwise have appeared. These procedures develop out of a concern to establish the classes and class forces that accompanied the colonial transformation of these societies. For this task to be performed effectively it is necessary to pay some attention to the character of the modes of production and the ways in which colonial policy and the actions of capital in the colonial environment transform the basic defining features of the mode of production.

For the analysis to work, to be able to be more precise about the character of the society established by colonialism, it is necessary to start with the difficult question of the characteristics of the society that existed before colonial domination. In this context it is useful to try to identify the way in which production is carried out: the class relations that are generated by that pattern of production. In short, it is important to try to characterise the mode of production in the pre-colonial setting. To make such an attempt relevant to the wider project, it is necessary to consider the identification of the major means of production and to consider who has access and domination of these means of production. Which groups control the production process? On what basis does this control rest? Who are the direct producers? On what basis do they have access to the means of production? What is produced? What is the form of production, for use or for exchange? Finally, what is the character of the surplus, how is it extracted and in what ways is the surplus consumed? The answers to these questions, especially if they are combined to give a schematic and systematic portrait of the pre-colonial setting, provides the basis for an account of what is changed by colonialism.

After establishing the details of the mode of production

that exists in the pre-colonial context, it is then possible to describe the ways in which the basic relations are affected by colonial domination and policy. For example, it is possible to recognise the way in which the form of production is changed by the increased role of commodities in the society. Further, it is possible to see how the pattern of access to the means of production is transformed, the relations of the direct producers to those that control the process of production are altered and the whole character of the surplus produced and the nature of the process of surplus extraction takes on a new significance. In typical circumstances we can expect to find a rise in commodity production and a transformed character of surplus and surplus extraction. Further, this increase in commodity production is not based on an unchanged mode of production. Rather, the very mode of production has necessarily been reconstituted so that generalised production of commodities occurs as the basic expression of the character and logic of this mode of production.

Having established the pattern of changes engendered by colonial policy and domination, then comes the vexed problem of how to assess the significance of these identified changes and, on that basis, to determine the character of the mode of production that now exists. As argued above, this cannot proceed on the basis of the simple and obvious features that appear. In agriculture, for example, the existence of rent or share-cropping relations cannot be taken to prove that the class basis of production embodies a mode of production other than that of a capitalist one. It was argued that it is possible for rent relations in agriculture, in a situation transformed by capitalism in a colonial setting, to be forms of the wage-labour/capital relations. Hence, the character of agrarian production may conform to the logic of the capitalist mode of production and provide the basis for a subsequent industrialisation of agrarian technique.

Whether this is what has happened in particular colonised countries can not be established by theoretical discussion or analytical fiat. What is required is an examination of those particular instances to see whether the arguments advanced in this introduction can be applied in such a way that they illuminate the character and consequences of colonial domination.

NOTES

1.   A.G. Frank, Capitalism and Underdevelopment in Latin America: Historical Studies of Chile and Brazil (Monthly Review Press, New York, 1969).
2.   E. Laclau, "Feudalism and Capitalism in Latin America", New Left Review, No. 61 (1971).
3.   H. Alavi, "The State in Post Colonial Societies:

Pakistan and Bangladesh" in K. Gough and H.P. Sharma (eds.), Imperialism and Revolution in South Asia (Monthly Review Press, New York, 1973).

4.	H. Alavi, "India and the Colonial Mode of Production", Socialist Register, 1975. See also D. McEachern, "The Mode of Production in India", Journal of Contemporary Asia, Vol. 6, No. 4, 1976.

5.	For an full assessment of Alavi's contribution to these arguments see D. McEachern, Colonialism and Colonial Modes of Production, Working Paper 9, Centre for Asian Studies, University of Adelaide, 1979.

5.	This debate is surveyed in H. Alavi, "India and the Colonial Mode of Production" and in D. McEachern, "The Mode of Production in India", Journal of Contemporary Asia, Vol. 7, No. 4, 1976.

6.	For a collection that includes several important pieces by Meillassoux and Rey see D. Seddon (ed.), Relations of Production: Marxist Approaches to Economic Anthropology (Frank Cass, London, 1978). For a survey of these contributions see A. Foster-Carter, "The Mode of Production Debate", New Left Review, No. 109, 1978.

7.	H. Bernstein, "Notes on Capital and the Peasantry", Review of African Political Economy, No. 10, 1977.

8.	Major texts in the discussion were E. Balibar, "The Basic Concepts of Historical Materialism" in E. Balibar, and L. Althusser, Reading Capital (New Left Books, London, 1975). N. Poulantzas, Political Power and Social Classes (New Left Review, London, 1975). B. Hindness and P. Hirst, Pre-Capitalist Modes of Production (Routledge and Kegan Paul, London, 1975) and Modes of Production and Social Formation: an Auto-Critique (Macmillan, London, 1976). Also see H. Wolpe (ed.), The Articulation of Modes of Production: Essays from Economy and Society (Routledge Kegan Paul, London, 1979).

9.	B. Hindness and P. Hirst, Modes of Production and Social Formations: An Auto-Critique.

11.	R. Hilton (ed.), The Transition from Feudalism to Capitalism (Verso, London, 1976)

12.	H. Alavi, "The Colonial Transformation of India", Ch. 2, pp. 28-42.

13.	Hindess and Hirst, Pre-capitalist Modes of Production, where they make telling use of Vinogradoff's historiography to reveal the inadequacies of many current arguments about feudalism as a mode of production.

14.	H. Bernstein, "Notes..."

15.	ibid., p. 68.

16.	Ibid., p. 68.

17.	Ibid., p. 73.

18.	D. McEachern, "Mode of Production in India".

19.	These observations parallel, but were not based upon, a confusion that can arise from the distinction between a 'formal' and a 'real' 'subsumption' of labour to capital. This distinction is made in Marx's draft "Results of the

Immediate Process of Production" published as an appendix in the Penguin translation of Volume One of Capital (Penguin Books in association with New Left Review. Translated by Ben Fowles. The appendix was translated by Rodney Livingstone.) In this piece, written for an earlier draft of Capital and published by neither Marx nor Engels, Marx is concerned to establish the transformation of labour processes by the capitalist mode of production. The stage of a 'formal subsumption' of labour refers to a period in which existing labour processes are taken over by capitalist mode of production. This subsumption becomes 'real' when the nature of the labour process is transformed by the logic of the capitalist mode of production and becomes a distinctly capitalist labour process. It is important to note that this draft is not concerned with the identification of demarcation points between modes of production - nor with the identification of the point at which the capitalist mode of production 'really' comes into being. The 'formal subsumption of labour' occurs within a capitalist mode of production. The passage to what in this text is described as a 'real subsumption' occurs on that basis. For an example of how this has been used in the analysis of the development of capitalism in a colonial context see K. Gough, "Modes of Production in Southern India", Economic and Political Weekly, Vol. XV, Nos. 5, 6 & 7 (Annual Number, 1980).

20.   G. Kay, Development and Underdevelopment: A Marxist Analysis (Macmillan, London, 1975).
21.   Ibid., Ch. 5.

Chapter 2

INDIA: TRANSITION TO COLONIAL CAPITALISM

Hamza Alavi

Colonisation and Peripheralization

An examination of the history of India since the beginning of
British conquest a little over two hundred years ago, raises
questions not only about the precise nature of the structural
changes that were brought about in the course of the colonial
transformation, but incidentally, some questions also about
the role of British relationships with India in the
initiation of the Industrial Revolution in England itself,
that great watershed in human history. It is the former set
of questions which will be my primary concern in this paper
and I do not propose to embark here on a search for the
causes of the Industrial Revolution in England.
Nevertheless, issues do arise in that connection too;
and they are of some importance. I feel therefore that I
must depart a little from the conventional approach to
problems in this area whereby the colony it is that is
transformed but not the metropolis.

    Was British rule in India and the new relationships that
were forged in the context of the colonial transformation a
significant factor, or even a uniquely critical factor, in
the progress of the Industrial Revolution in England? Such a
question is not usually posed in studies of the Industrial
Revolution or the transition from feudalism to capitalism in
England just as they are not in the study of the colonial
transformation. Marxist as well as non-Marxist scholars
alike, have laboured in this problem area essentially within
the narrowed context of Western Europe. To make this point,
we may, for example refer to Wallerstein's perspective on
these developments for, more emphatically than any other
scholar, he rejects the restricted matrix of 'national
development' and proposes instead concepts of 'world
economies' and 'world systems' as the proper entities in
terms of which such historical developments may adequately be
understood, the entities being denoted by networks of close
trading relationships that establish a 'unit with a single

division of labour', which may embrace territories without a common political structure or a common culture, the latter being thus treated as epiphenomenal in that vision.

For Wallerstein the 'core area' of the 'modern world system' is North-West Europe; Mediterranean Europe being a semi-peripheral area and Eastern Europe and the Western Hemisphere the periphery. In the first instance, therefore, he specifically excludes from that configuration the 'Indian Ocean Area' as well as Russia, the Ottoman Empire and East Asia. And Western Europe of course remains the core of this system. He then speaks of stages in the development of this Euro-centered World System. It is only after the 'third stage' is realised of the development of that 'modern world system', namely the Industrial Revolution and the rise of industrial capitalism, that, as a consequence, we have "further geographic expansion of the European world economy, now to include the whole of the globe". The 'Indian ocean area', hitherto itself a 'proto-world-economy' together with other 'world economies', and 'minisystems' of isolated and involuted simple agricultural hunting or gathering societies, are dissolved; and they are incorporated into the expanding Euro-centered modern world system as new peripheries.[1]

In such a perspective the role of Britain's relationship with India in the creation of the process that led to the rise of industrial capitalism, or at least in having played a significant, not to say decisive part in it, does not arise; its part in the development of the Euro-centered modern world system arises only as a consequence of the emergence of Industrial Revolution. Now it is not my present purpose to initiate a discussion of the concepts and the theoretical system that Wallerstein has proposed for analysis of this development. I have referred to him only to make the point that his expressed aim is to go beyond the frame of reference of most historiologists (if one may coin the term) by searching for a wider context than the national one, for analysis of the rise of industrial capitalism. Even so, he shares the scholarly consensus, it seems, in searching for the dynamics of capitalist development in England essentially within a European context, peripherally taking in Europe's relationship with Latin America but not recognising any specific, not to say crucial, role of England's relationship with India in it. A closer examination of that relationship, I would suggest, brings into focus large questions about the dynamics of development that are implicit in the conception of an autochthonous development of a Euro-centered modern world-system, the core, that subsequently expanded to incorporate India as a periphery. I propose in this paper to examine the structure of pre-colonial Indian society and the way in which it was transformed under the colonial impact. The issues about their effects on the industrial capitalism in England will be raised in the course of that analysis.

24

Stereotypes of Pre-colonial India

There is a conventional view of pre-colonial India that is widely shared; that of a static 'traditional society', primarily rural and agricultural, founded on self-contained corporate village communities bound down by the caste system and engaged mainly in subsistence production, superimposed on which was a parasitic state apparatus. That society lacked any endogenous dynamic for development and progress. It followed therefore that it was only the shattering impact of colonial domination that broke open that closed society and generated new forces of change.

That certainly was the view of colonialist historiography; and it constituted also the legitimating ideology of colonial rule. The contemporary ideas of colonial officials and their masters thought of British rule as the bearer of a new enlightenment for the natives. In theory at any rate colonial social and economic policy is supposed to have been informed by the liberal social philosophy, the orthodoxy of the day, firmly grounded in the teachings of Adam Smith and the classical system of political economy. In that light the market was the most efficient allocator of resources and the liberating function of the colonial regime was to remove obstacles to the free play of the market, and to establish the institutional structure that was a precondition for its proper functioning; capitalist private property, bourgeois laws and a judicial and administrative system that would enforce the rule of that law. Laissez faire was to be the order of the day. But, it was conceded that the colonial state would intervene to extend the infra-structure for the extension of the market, by building roads and railways and ports and all those facilities that were properly provided by public agency for the extension of commodity circulation. Subject to that, it was held that the welfare and well-being of the Indian people would depend upon their capacity to take advantage of the opportunities that were being provided by the widening of the market economy for engaging in trade and commodity production and, abandoning their 'otherworldly' attitudes and overcoming their traditional lack of enterprise, adopting the individualistic acquisitive ethos of capitalism. These were the self-legitimating ideas of colonial domination that still find occasional echoes in contemporary writings, in which there is no hint or acknowledgment of the destructive role of the colonial impact in India nor of the fact that doctrinal commitments did not inhibit the colonial regime from undertaking measures of state intervention which were inimical to indigenous development and others which promoted the colonial enterprise.

Marx's view of the nature of the pre-colonial Indian economy and society was not substantially different. His view of the colonial regime was, of course, less benign. But capitalist development had a dynamic of its own which transcended the purposes and actions of the colonial regime itself. Given the destruction of the stultifying pre-capitalist mode of production in India and the injection of the dynamism of capitalist development his vision of the future was essentially an optimistic one. "England", he wrote, "has to fulfill a double mission in India: one destructive, the other regenerating - the annihilation of the old Asiatic society and the laying of the material foundations of Western Society in Asia."[2] The colonial impact on India was cruel and devastating. But it had initiated a re-structuration of Indian society along capitalist lines. This new process of development was breaking up the self-sufficiency and inertia of the Indian village communities. It was establishing new means of communication that would draw the Indian people into wider intercourse and greatly extend the sphere of commodity circulation and with it, bring production under the rule of industrial capital. "All the English bourgeoisie may be forced to do will neither emancipate nor materially mend the social conditions of the mass of the people, depending not only on the development of the productive powers, but on their appropriation by the people. But what they will not fail to do is lay down the material premises for both", he wrote. The future of India depended neither on the goodwill nor the malevolence of the colonial regime. It was being decided by the objective conditions of capitalist development that was set in motion, a stage of development which, however, would in turn generate forces for the destruction of capitalism itself and open the way for an advance towards socialism.

Indian nationalist writing, likewise, shared the view that the old order was static and inimical to progress and had to go. Most of the classical nationalist writing was by men who had been brought up on liberal social theory and worked within the general framework of that theoretical system. Their main complaint was two-fold. One was about the unrequited drain of resources from India that had led and was continuing to impoverish India. The other was that the colonial regime was doing little to promote indigenous industrial enterprise and was doing a good deal to resist it. It was the ruthless pursuit of laissez faire that was, in their eyes, the main cause of Indian backwardness. They found justification for protection for infant Indian industries not only in the works of Frederik List but, above all in their great teacher himself, John Stuart Mill, who did recognise the legitimacy of protection of infant industries and did not advocate unqualified pursuit of laissez faire.

The nationalists' vision, therefore, was not always backward looking and nostalgic, although myths of a golden past often intruded into their rhetoric. As Bipan Chandra pointed out in an exchange with Morris: "From R.C. Dutt,

26

Dadabhai Naorojee and Ranade down to Jawaharlal Nehru and R.P. Dutt, the anti-imperialist writers have not used the word 'economic decay' to mean decay of handicrafts but to signify the arrested nature of India's industrialisation and modernisation. None of them have really condemned the destruction of the pre-British economic structure, except nostalgically....Even the first generation nationalist writers rejected the classical economics or laissez faire approach not because it was relentless in its modernity, promoting disintegration of the old order, but because its application to India tended to perpetuate the old legacies."[3] It might be pointed out that these nationalist writers were not hostile to capitalism itself; and in some cases not even to foreign capital. They were too well brought up on liberal social theory for that; nor, for that matter, did their own class affiliations dictate otherwise. Chandra, in his major study of nationalist writing, points out that "A section of the Indian leadership...favoured the use of foreign capital in India" and justified it on a variety of grounds.[4] Thus in the nineteenth century, at any rate, Indian nationalist writing did not provide a fundamental challenge to the colonial social order, much less the capitalist social order. All that the nationalists were asking for at the time was a share within it for the rising new Indian bourgeoisie that had to begin to grow in the second half of the nineteenth century.

Contemporary Indian scholarship does not share the consensus among classical writers about a static, backward and unresponsive society and economy in pre-colonial India. On the contrary they recognise some indications of development and change in a society that, however, was still pre-capitalist. Given the changes that were already taking place in pre-colonial India, Irfan Habib takes up the question: why India failed to industrialise and develop a capitalist economy.[5] He shows how both in agricultural production and non-agricultural production, production for the market was extensive, that "in agriculture there existed khud kasht (lit. 'self-cultivation') based on hired labour, representing an advance in form towards capitalist farming. In handicrafts, merchant capital had developed considerably and had brought artisans under control through forms of the putting out system". But wage labour and a market economy are not, by themselves, sufficient conditions for a capitalist economy. He concludes that some necessary conditions for an advance towards "full blown capitalism" were still missing, though he does not specify them.[6] The burden of Habib's work, however, is to demonstrate that there were tendencies in pre-colonial India for a movement towards capitalism.

Much earlier, similar questions were raised by Ramkrishna Mukherjee in his work on the "Rise and Fall of the East India Company". He suggested that "because of forces attacking the institutions from outside and within, feudalism in India had begun to weaken from about the fourteenth century onwards".[7] Following a survey of the evidence, he continues:

> This situation in India in which new social, economic and ideological forces were emerging has been characterised by some writers as that: "A bourgeois revolution was thus maturing in Hindustan". Whether such a characterisation is entirely true or not and whether it is not a fact that because of the tremendous tenacity of Indian feudalism (as explained before) as well as because of the inability of the Indian merchants to undertake by themselves long-distance trade on a large scale (as explained in the following pages) the new forces while emerging in Indian society had not yet been able to turn the scale against the previous forces, the available evidence surely indicates that the nature of developments in India in those days was in all essentials similar to those in Europe in that period of transition as has been briefly summarised in Chapter 1 of this study.[8]

Thus, again, the situation in India was favourably appraised, with reference to prospects of transition to capitalism.

India, however, was still a pre-capitalist social formation when the British conquest came about; the Northern Indian society could in fact be characterised, structurally, as a feudal society. How far the structure of Northern Indian society did in fact correspond to that of a Marxist conception of a "feudal mode of production" and in what way that structure was altered by the colonial impact is what we propose to examine here. It is the last question that is the essential object of this chapter namely the structure of Indian society that resulted from the colonial transformation. This would not essentially be altered by a demonstration that elsewhere in India there was not a 'feudal' but an 'Asiatic' mode of production.

Modes of Production and Social Structure

I will begin with a conception of the feudal mode of production (FMP) as a concept of the structure of a society, having the following attributes combined and constituted as a complex unity. In identifying these structural properties of FMP I will also contrast them with the corresponding properties of the capitalist mode of production (CMP), so that later on we may proceed to consider in that light the precise significance of the structural changes that were brought about in the course of the colonial transformation.

Thus I would list the components or properties of FMP as follows:-

(i)   Unfree labour rendered not necessarily in the
        form of labour services but taking a variety of
        possible forms. That would be contrasted with
        free labour in CMP, in a double sense (a) in that
        it has been separated from (or 'freed') from
        possession of means of production (land) and (b)
        that it is free from feudal obligations to serve
        a lord; the direct producer is now free to sell
        his labour power - or starve!

(ii)   Extra-economic coercion in the extraction of the
        surplus from the direct producer, as against
        economic coercion as the basis of exploitation in
        CMP.

(iii)   A fusion of economic and political power at the
        point of production and a localised structure of
        power, as against separation of economic (class)
        power and political (state) power within the
        framework of a bourgeois state in CMP. The power
        of the exploiting class, the bourgeoisie over the
        exploited class is then exercised indirectly,
        through the state apparatus and subject to the
        rule of (bourgeois) law, and not arbitrarily and
        directly as in FMP.

(iv)   Self-sufficient ('subsistence') economy of the
        village (or the manor), commodity production
        being secondary for the direct producer; subject
        to the condition that he produces also a surplus
        that is appropriated by the exploiting class of
        which a significant proportion may enter into
        circulation as commodities. That contrasts with
        generalised commodity production in CMP where (a)
        production is primarily of commodities i.e. to be
        sold for the value to be realised on the market
        and (b) labour power itself is a commodity.

(v)   Simple reproduction where the surplus is largely
        consumed by the exploiting class which acquires
        it, instead of being accumulated, so that the
        economy and society merely reproduce themselves
        on the existing level of productive resources and
        technology, whereas in CMP we have expanded
        reproduction of capital, where the surplus is
        primarily deployed towards capital accumulation
        (though not without supporting rising consumption
        levels of the exploiting classes) and consequent
        expansion of the forces of production and
        technological advance.

The concept outlined above is a Marxist concept of
"structure". In defining the feudal mode of production as a
particular type of social structure, in terms of which we may
look at medieval Northern Indian society, it is not suggested
that it was identical to feudal societies of Europe. Indeed

we find particular differences not only between Indian medieval societies and those of European feudalism but also quite wide differences between different European feudal societies themselves. For example the differences between feudal society in England and those of Eastern Europe and Russia were no less than those between it and Indian feudalism. But such differences do not, as such, exclude structural homology.

In setting out the concepts of the "feudal mode of production" and "the capitalist mode of production" as above, I am guided by Marx's analysis of the capitalist mode of production, which he examined systematically in Capital and by his relatively brief references to characteristics of the feudal mode of production. The difficulty, however, that we do have in this respect is that nowhere does Marx offer a concise and precise definition of the concept of "mode of production". As a scientific concept that underlies his whole theoretical system, it has to be made explicit from his writings. Contemporary Marxists have turned to this problem. But their interpretations vary with their particular reading or translation of Marxism. The Althusserian school, for example, have restored this concept to the centre of Marxist analysis and Balibar's work on the concept of mode of production is well known. However, I find that the Althusserian interpretation of Marxism is a metaphysical translation of it and I do not follow that school of thought - an issue that we cannot debate in the present context. Likewise I would reject also the conception of mode of production, and its place in Marxist analysis of society, as put forward by Hindess and Hirst.[9] I have had therefore to reconstruct the concept as I understand it, from my own reading of Capital, and Marxist works which have informed my own understanding of Marxism - too numerous of acknowledgment here. The interpretation is therefore not entirely original and readers of this will find many echoes in it. What I have attempted to do, however, is to systematise the statement of the concept and I hope that it will go some way towards clarifying it. I have discussed the relevant theoretical questions more fully elsewhere.[10]

A failure to grasp the concept of 'mode of production' as a complex unity was very well illustrated by a 4,000 words long, rather virulent, attack on my earlier paper on "India and the Colonial Mode of Production"[11] by an Indian Marxist.[12] In that article too I had spelt out the various levels of determination of the feudal mode of production, as I have done above. Banajee, in his critique, singles out each of these separately and pronounces my reference to each of them, seriatim, as 'banal'. In doing so he displays his inability to grasp the fact that these are levels of determination of a theoretical concept, to be taken as a unity, and not simple descriptions of separate aspects of European feudalism, which is the sense in which he has understood my listing of them as simple categories that describe European feudalism rather than levels of structural determination that are aspects of a unified whole.

A similar failure to grasp the concept of mode of production as a theoretical concept that entails determination at several levels simultaneously, seems to lie also at the root of some of the difficulties in the famous debate on Transition from Feudalism to Capitalism[13] arising out of Paul Sweezy's review of Maurice Dobb's Studies in the Development of Capitalism.[14] Here each of them, while recognising the various 'features' of feudal societies, at the level of description, fasten on particular aspects of it that they, respectively, consider to be the defining characteristic. Dobb emphasises the "obligation laid on the producer by force and independently of his own volition to fulfil certain economic demands of the overlord."[15] This Dobb says is "virtually identical with what we generally mean by serfdom" - but he does not by that token limit the definition of feudalism to serfdom and the provision of labour services, as he is sometimes misinterpreted as having said. Dobb's definition thus embraces the first three points of the definition outlined by me above. Sweezy, on the other hand, emphasises production for use and the self-sufficiency of manorial production under feudalism as against commodity production for the market. Sweezy thus singles out point (iv) of the above list. The issues of the debate would be better illuminated if we reconsider them by recognising that the concept of structure of social formations is a holist conception and we must take the various levels of determination together rather than singling out one or the other as the primary or the only criterion.

The Structure of Indian Feudalism

The search after the 'owner of the soil' in India before the British conquest has exercised the ingenuity of many modern writers. No little influence on this debate has been commanded by evidence of the European travellers of the period, who declare without a single voice of dissent, that the proprietorship of land vested with the king alone. This conception has found favour with authoritative exponents of agrarian history, but now seems no longer to be part of the official doctrine as it once was.[16]

But this issue, itself, is a red herring. As in other feudal societies, we find in medieval northern India too a hierarchy of 'rights' won or realised, in the final analysis, by the exercise of force. The essence of the feudal relationship lay in the capacity to deploy power, at various levels, mediated only to some extent by customary law which after all was itself interpreted and applied by the powerful. While

31

custom did provide some restraint on them, an excessive preoccupation with legal prescriptions that tends to preoccupy scholars in this field perhaps obscures rather than clarifies the social reality. Moreover, rights existed not so much in land, though expressed as such, but in the shares of the surplus that was extracted from it by the peasant who laboured on it. We are then concerned with the actual organisation of the feudal society and the mechanisms by which that surplus was extracted and appropriated by those who occupied various positions in the hierarchy of power and authority rather than in purely the formal prescriptions.

The Mughal ruling class, it has been said, consisted of the Emperor himself and about 8,000 mansabdars, in 1647,[17] or nobles, who were under obligation to maintain military contingents available at the service of the Emperor. Military obligations to superiors was a feature of the system at all levels, including the zamindar, the local lord, the primary locus of power in holding down the peasantry, the linchpin of the whole system. Habib quotes a Mughal official census of 1595 according to which the zamindars maintained within the Mughal Empire (Northern India) nearly 4.7 million retainers, (4.3 million 'infantry', and 0.3 million horsemen), a formidable total indeed. Although these are officially recorded figures, they might nevertheless be an overestimate. They do, however, point to a very considerable aggregation of force at the base of the system, the fusion of economic and political power at the point of production, which is the distinguishing characteristic of the feudal mode of production as contrasted both with the concept of the 'Asiatic' mode of production as well as the structure of capitalist state power.

Mansabdars were either paid salaries in cash or more often were given jagirs or assignments of land revenue over a territory and, accordingly were known as jagirdars. Land which was not given out in jagirs but from which the land revenue accrued directly to the Emperor, was known as the khalisa. The extent of the khalisa fluctuated over time, depending upon the policy of the Emperor in granting jagirs but is estimated to have ranged from one-fourth to one-fifth of the total. A rather special feature of the Mughal system was that "... jagirs were constantly transferred, after a short period, so that a particular assignment was seldom held by the same person for more than three or four years", the exceptions, it might be added, being in the case of watan jagirs which were held by virtually autonomous chiefs.[18] The temporary tenure of jagirdars, held at the pleasure of the Emperor, distinguishes them from the baronial aristocracy of feudal Europe. Raychaudhuri suggests that the jagirdars may be considered to be officials rather than feudal lords. Reviewing Habib's general findings he writes that "The impression left by this restatement of known facts is that this system of revenue assignment in lieu of cash salary was

32

simply a convenient arrangement for maintaining a bureaucracy."[19] Referring to unpublished work of Noman A Siddiqi, Raychaudhuri, however, speaks of a mutation in the character of the jagirdars, with the virtual dissolution of the Mughal Empire in the eighteenth century, when they tended to become permanent and hereditary and virtually independent chiefs. With that change Raychaudhuri associates the emergence of a less oppressive and more peaceful era of "virtually independent provincial kingdoms."[20]

Mughal society was founded, of course, on the sweat and blood of the peasant in the village held down by the (village) zamindar. Evidence about the nature of village organisation is conflicting. In the main one would accept Habib's judgement that

> No evidence exists for communal ownership of land .... The peasant's right to his land, as we have seen, was always his individual right. What is suggested here (with reference to the village community constituted on the basis of biraderis or lineages) is that there were some spheres outside production where the peasants of a village , usually belonging to the same fraternity, often acted collectively.[21]

The account of the 'Economic Organisation of the Village' in Gupta's study also bears this out.[22]

The medieval village community did have a corporate character in some respects, as far as certain common affairs of the village are concerned, such as management of common lands and common services. The most important aspect of the village community, as is well known, was of course both its self-sufficiency and the fact that there existed in the village members of various occupational castes who provided specialised services needed by the community. They were not however remunerated out of a common fund. Each peasant was required by custom to pay to each of the 'village servants' a customary prescribed fraction of his harvested crop. Thus although they are designated as 'village servants' they were neither the employees of nor remunerated by a corporate entity.

Villages were of two broad categories, zamindari villages and raiyati villages. In zamindari villages the zamindar was the local lord and master, subject to his obligation to the state to collect and turn over to it land revenue. His crucial functional role in the structure of Indian feudalism was analogous (though by no means identical) to that of the manorial lord in England. This aspect of his role has not been brought out sharply enough in descriptive Indian historiography, the conceptual identity of his role being refracted by descriptive complexities of overlapping rights and functions and semantic plurality. The term zamindar, it has been pointed out, has been used to designate

33

alike, lords of different degrees of power and status, from the small lord of the village to the 'master of a large kingdom'. Habib's classic work provides a very detailed and elaborate account of these. Nurul Hasan offers a simplified classification of zamindars in the Mughal empire, into three broad categories thus: (1) autonomous chieftains, (2) intermediary zamindar and (3) primary zamindars. He adds the caveat that in any attempt to distinguish them by rights and functions we will find that these categories are by no means mutually exclusive in the sense that individual zamindars may bear rights and functions appropriate to more than one of these categories.[23]

These essential distinctions which enable us to identify the structure of the feudal mode of production are lost in Habib's analysis which is not directed at that theoretical concept of structure but, rather at an identification of groups which shared in the appropriation of the surplus taken from the peasant. He writes:

> The use of the same term for chiefs and ordinary zamindars...has one important virtue...in its stressing the fact that from the point of view of the Mughal government there was a chain of local despotisms, covering the whole empire, here semi-independent, there fairly subdued, here represented by chiefs, there by ordinary zamindars. In various contexts the two categories could appear as forming a single class.[24]

This vertical conflation of the feudal hierarchy obscures rather than clarifies the essential structural features of that society, especially the crucial role of the zamindar in the village who directly controlled the peasant, a control which was the key to the whole system. Thus, while I rely heavily on Habib's definitive study, justly celebrated for the evidence about Mughal society, my analysis differs from his.

The zamindar at the village level, the primary zamindar as Nurul Hasan designates him, was the kingpin of the system. It was he who in the first instance, and directly, controlled the extraction of the surplus from the peasant. Without him performing that indispensable role, the whole system is unthinkable; he was the necessary basis for the whole feudal structure. He controlled the peasant and exercised direct jurisdiction over him, the direct coercive force that is a necessary condition of the feudal mode of production. Included in their wide jurisdiction over the peasants was the crucial power by virtue of which, as Nurul Hasan points out, "The zamindars enjoyed the right to restrain the tenants from leaving their lands and to compel them to cultivate all arable land held by them".[25] Habib, points out, further that "a right was assumed to lie with the authorities to bring back fugitive peasants by force". That was an important reason for a primary zamindar to seek the patronage of a powerful chief, who would help him retrieve the fugitives; thus the higher level zamindars fulfilled a necessary function in maintaining the feudal structure.

In raiyati villages, the dispensation was slightly different, for there the peasant community, in theory, enjoyed a relative degree of autonomy from the zamindar or the taalluqdar. However, in such villages there existed the office of muqaddam who was responsible for collecting land revenue and enjoyed wide powers. It was a hereditary office but, as Habib points out, "He was never, properly speaking, a government servant". He adds "In accordance with the process of development of his office and powers...once the office came into the hands of richer peasants it became an instrument for establishing their domination over the rest of their brethren".[26] He writes: "The distance that grew up between the headman (muqaddam) and the ordinary peasant and the considerable power that he wielded over the village, seems sometimes to have led to his claiming or acquiring certain rights identical to those of the zamindar".[27] Thus in such circumstances the muqaddam was virtually a surrogate for the zamindar, performing a necessary function at the crucial level of the structure of the FMP of holding down the peasants and extracting the surplus.

Thus the zamindar or his surrogate the muqaddam had a pivotal role in the system, a role that needs to be more clearly identified and understood. In a footnote to his article from which we have quoted some passages here, Nurul Hasan writes: "This article is intended to focus the attention of historians on the urgent need for a detailed study of the working of the zamindari system during the Mughal period"; and rightly so. Given the well established tradition of detailed and careful examination of historical evidence by Indian historians, however, one would emphasise that what is needed no less is a theoretical clarification of the structures of economic and social relationships and the dynamics of Indian society of the time.

A conception that seems to be the most elusive in this context is that of a localised structure of power, defined earlier as a necessary condition of a feudal mode of production, given the overall framework of the 'absolutist state' of the Mughal empire. How far does the Mughal system meet that condition? We have already considered the fact that the zamindar exercised direct dominion over the peasant in the village and his function was to hold the peasant under his control and to make him undertake the maximum amount of work that he could make him do. The prosperity of the whole system rested on that. But, furthermore, there was a necessary tension (as well as complementarity) between the localised power of the zamindar and that of the structures of power above him, a tension that manifested itself at all levels and underlined the perpetual fragility of the

'absolutist state'. Nurul Hasan has grasped this tension very well and it is worth quoting him at some length.
He writes:

> The zamindar class played a vital role in the political, economic and cultural life of medieval India...The power exercised by the zamindar class over the economic life of the country - over agricultural production, handicrafts and trade - was tremendous. In spite of the constant struggle between the imperial government and the zamindars to secure a greater share of the produce, the latter became partners of the former in the process of economic exploitation. Politically, there was a clash of interests between the Mughal government and the zamindars and yet, simultaneously, the zamindars as a class became the mainstay of the empire. Most of the difficulties which the Mughal emperor had to face were the result of the activities of zamindars; but, at the same time, the administration had to lean heavily on the support of the latter. In the cultural sphere the close links of the zamindars with the Imperial court contributed in no small measure to the process of cultural synthesis between the distinctive traditions of various communities and different regions, as also urban and rural cultures. However, separatist, 'localist' and parochial trends received powerful patronage from the zamindar class."[28]

Thus the absolutist state did not obliterate the localised power of the village zamindar which (paradoxically) was a necessary condition for its own existence.

Here we find that all the necessary conditions, by which we define a structure of the feudal mode of production, were realised in what we have examined of the structure of rural society in medieval northern India. The term 'feudal' or 'semi-feudal' is used even today to describe the contemporary structure of Indian rural society. This is a misconception derived from a descriptive rendering of the situation rather than a theoretical analysis of it. The structure of the contemporary Indian society has been shaped by 200 years of the colonial experience and cannot be grasped without fully understanding the nature of the colonial transformation.

In the exposition so far, I have referred primarily to peasants who were subjects of lords, the feudal zamindars. There was, however, a substantial class of independent peasant proprietors, although the nature and degree of their 'independence' would be problematic and would be contingent on the constellation of power within which they were located. These would presumably be in raiyati villages where communal organisation was strong and the muqaddam had not usurped a position of power that made him, virtually, a surrogate of the zamindar. There was, however, also another set of class relations, which, to Habib, seems to be an incipient form of rural capitalism. That is the category of substantial landholders who engaged hired labour. This was termed khud kasht (or 'self-cultivation'). Such landholders, it is stated in a reliable account,

> employ labourers as their servants and put them to the tasks of agriculture; and making them plough, sow and reap and draw water out of the well; they pay them their fixed wages, whether in cash or grain, while appropriating to themselves the gross produce of cultivation.[29]

Habib also speaks of the presence of

> a very large class of landless labourers, who could be called upon to work in the fields in return for the provision of their barest needs of subsistence....The landless belonged to menial castes, compelled to serve the interests alike of peasants and of superior cultivators and forming therefore a vast rural semi-proletariat, maintained entirely by non-economic compulsions.[30]

The classes that carried on khud kasht says Habib, were principally the zamindars and village headmen (muqaddams). But it seems that this practice was confined to the cultivation of specialised crops. Furthermore, as Habib points out, the authorities imposed "official bans upon the conversion of peasant-cultivation (raiyat kasht) into khud kasht, by revenue guarantees and revenue officials."[31] Thus, it is arguable that within the dominant feudal mode of production in medieval India, tendencies towards capitalist agriculture were beginning to appear. Wage-labour, however, is not a sufficient condition for capitalism and we have yet to see evidence of processes that might have separated the producer from the means of production and the domination of the lord and thus created a class of free labour.

Profound changes were however brought about in the character of the Indian rural society, following the imposition of British rule, and the structure of relationship between the cultivator and the exploiting classes, the social relations of production, were fundamentally altered. This, however, is an area of much fruitless and often pedantic debate that tends to obscure rather than clarify issues. For our discussion it is convenient to begin with Embree's view of the impact of "British institution(s) introduced into India in the nineteenth century(which) had some effects on landholding". He singles out three as being the most significant in this respect. The first of these was the institution of property "as understood in Britain" introduced in the late eighteenth and early nineteenth century - Embree adds that "The time span is emphasised because the crucial impact was made by the 1850s". The second institution was "that of efficient government" and the third "The legal system, the establishment of which was intimately connected with questions of ownership of property."[32]

The idea that the colonial regime "introduced" the institution of property in land is contested by some who point out that it existed already in the Mughal period when zamindari rights etc. could be bought and sold. The 'property' in land during the Mughal period was, as we have seen, a right to share in the surplus that was extracted from the peasant, who was himself in possession of the land. And, such rights had to be enforced in fact by the exercise of power by the claimant, without which they could be elusive. Moreover, land, in the Mughal period, was in itself worth little; for those who shared in power, there was plenty of arable land that was available, more than could at the time be brought under cultivation . Real appropriation of land was in fact contingent on appropriation of the labour that would make it yield its fruits. What was precious was not the land but the peasant who cultivated it. The zamindar was far more concerned about the possible flight of peasants away from his land than he was about any who might make his land yield more. But the new concept of property in land that was introduced by the colonial regime was premised on dispossession of the peasant. The "British concept" of ownership that Embree refers to, therefore, cannot be grasped if we limit ourselves to the notion of property in land alone without referring to the status of the peasant and the concomitant changes in the social relations of production and the structure of political power that corresponded to them, the institution of "efficient government" and the "legal system" that Embree associates with it.

The main impact of the change brought about by the colonial dispensation was the elimination of petty sovereignties of chieftains and zamindars who ruled the land, as much as they owned it. Thus the "fusion of economic and political power at the point of production", that we identified as a structural condition of feudalism, the power of the landlord over the peasant, was dissolved and was reconstituted in the form of bourgeois landed property, under the authority of the colonial state which marked a separation of economic and political power. The most important turning point in the evolution of new system of landownership brought about by the colonial regime was the "Permanent Settlement" in Bengal (of land revenue obligations) of 1793 which was instituted in conjunction with fundamental changes in the rural social and economic structure. The peasant was dispossessed of the land which now became the 'property' of the zamindar. Concomitantly the direct coercive powers of the zamindar (and his private armies) were abolished and as one historian puts it: "Cornwallis took away from the

38

zamindars their judicial and police duties".[33] The word 'duties' here is but a euphemism for authority and power. The idea was stated more plainly by Thomas Law, a colonial official, who wrote: "Formerly the Lairds in Scotland and Barons in England ... exercised power of imposing fines and held Courts of Justice; but these injurious rights have been taken away, and the proprietary rights remain. The same has been done in Asia".[34] The landlord became landowner.

Land was now 'bourgeois landed property' in the sense that Marx used the term, in his critique of Guizot, when he wrote:

> Unlike the French feudal landowners of 1789, this [i.e. English] class of big landed proprietors, which had allied itself with the bourgeoisie and which incidentally, had arisen already under Henry VIII, was not antagonistic to but rather in complete accord with the conditions of life of the bourgeoisie. In actual fact their landed estates were not feudal but bourgeois property.[35]

At that early stage of the bourgeois revolution in England we are yet a long way from major transformation of the "labour process" on the land, for great improvements in techniques of cultivation and huge investments in the form of new kinds of equipment had yet to come. But what were being then transformed were the social relations of production. This is also what was being brought about in India; the relations of production were transformed and bourgeois landed property created. The actual process of change in India was spread over a long period of time, as colonial rule extended itself over different regions which had different pre-existing patterns of relationships in the countryside. The complex patterns that emerged cannot easily be summarised here. But what was common to the whole process was the fact that access of the exploiting classes to the surplus produced by the peasant depended no longer on the exercise and organisation of direct coercive force but on the institution of property rights by the colonial regime and the concomitant dispossession of the peasant, so that in place of direct physical coercion he was now subjected to the economic coercion experienced by the dispossessed who had to turn to the landlord for access to their means of livelihood and to whom therefore they sold their labour power.

There was no need any longer for the landowner to hold the cultivator in bondage by direct coercive force, nor could he pursue him as a fugitive if he left him. Nor was that any longer necessary. The peasant was no longer subject to feudal obligations. He was 'free' - free, indeed to work for a landowner, his only means of access to land, or to starve. The land that was not given over for private appropriation was made Crown land to which there was no more free access.

Thus the peasant was trapped by the fact of his dispossession and he was now subject to economic coercion. Indeed one can see why the situation of the 'free' peasant was much worse than that of the unfree subject of the zamindar in the feudal system.

In the old feudal system the main concern of the zamindar was to keep the peasant on his land, which set a limit on the degree of coercion and exploitation that a feudal landlord could inflict on his peasants without the risk of driving them away to a more tolerant master. When there was too much oppression peasants did run away, if only to another zamindar who would welcome them as additions to his labour force. A zamindar who could attract peasants away from others stood to gain a great deal more from the labour of the extra hands than he could possibly benefit from the little extra that he might extract by intensification of coercion. Thus, in the feudal system, despite the concept of 'coercive extraction of surplus', there were good reasons for landlords to adopt a paternalistic attitude towards the peasants under them; and their bonds were reinforced by ideological ties of mutuality such as those of the jajmani system. But under the new colonial dispensation, given the economic coercion of the dispossessed peasant who had now to beg the landlord to be given a piece of land for cultivation (who feared eviction, pointless in the feudal system) there were now no limits to the oppression that the landowner might exercise over him. There were several factors that intensified the dependence of the peasant on the landowner, of which the landowner's monopoly of the possession of land was only one. There were also the pauperisation of the artisan class (about which more later), urban depopulation and demographic growth, which made the plight of the share-cropper and the rural labourer much worse than ever before. It is common for writers, in emotively charged accounts of the conditions of the peasantry, to describe such contemporary oppression as 'feudal'. But it is ironic that such terrible oppression was made possible precisely by the dissolution of the feudal basis of the relationship between landlord and peasant and it was the fate of the 'free' peasant in the post-feudal society to be subjected to oppression that reached unprecedented levels.

In the above discussion, to simplify the exposition and to make the central arguments sharply, I have proceeded as if there were only two classes for us to contend with namely the non-cultivating landowner and, subordinated to him, the actual cultivator, either a share-cropper or farm labourer. The actual picture was a little more complex, and varied regionally, in part due to differences in the basis of Settlements namely Zamindari Settlements vs Ryotwari Settlements. In Bengal, for example, the Permanent Settlement conferred ownership rights on holders of large tracts of land who employed intermediaries through whom their relationships with peasants were operated. The fact that the revenue settlement was fixed in perpetuity and, especially, because it was no longer necessary for the landowner to exercise direct coercive rule over his peasants, there was much incentive for the landowners to enter into arrangements with tenants who paid them a fixed cash rent, enough to cover their land revenue obligations and to leave a substantial profit besides. The landowners then established themselves in cities, like Calcutta where their sons could be educated, in due course, to become the members of the 'new petty bourgeoisie'; who were in time to make demands for a measure of self-government and in so doing draw the full wrath of the British Indian bureaucracy both against the 'absentee landlords', a term that now became emotively charged, as well as the much despised Westernised Oriental Gentlemen or wogs.

In fact it was not the absentee landlord who was the worst oppressor of the peasant from day to day, as the smaller resident landlord or the tenant of the absentee landlord (or even a resident one) who had taken over the land, who made demands on the peasants directly and oppressed them mercilessly. The "tenants" in due course, acquired 'occupancy' rights that were heritable and transferable, thus acquiring permanent leasehold ownership of the land. The occupancy tenants became de facto landowners. The landowner himself in effect became a rentier, who visited the village on feast days, which coincided with harvests, to collect his share of the rent and then disappeared. His proportional share of the surplus fell progressively; as Romesh Dutt points out, the real burden of land revenue (to which the rents were related) fell from 90% of the surplus to 28% in a hundred years. On the other hand, a new class of de facto owners, the occupancy tenants, emerged in Bengal, known variously as jotedars etc. who were now to be favoured by the colonial regime as against the old zamindars. Thus we find that instead of a single class of landowners standing over the peasants, there were several layers in the pattern of rural stratification. But, again, the crucial layer was that of the occupancy tenant, the de facto land owner, who was the direct employer of peasant labour.

In other areas, whereas ownership rights were vested in zamindars who were not such great landlords as in Bengal, superior rights of strata which had lorded over them in the past were recognised, as in Uttar Pradesh. In Madras Presidency and elsewhere, where ryotwari settlement was introduced, ownership rights were vested, it was argued, in the actual cultivator; but that was by no means the case, for many of the so-called ryots were substantial landowners. Both by virtue of the variety of original Settlements and also by virtue of 'tenancy' legislation that recognised occupancy rights, a bewildering hierarchy of rights in land emerged in the course of the 19th century, which awaited land reforms after independence to simplify (though the land

41

reforms have by no means eliminated inequality in landownership; far from it). The point that is germane in the present context, however, is that all these various interests and rights now rested on a new basis, on a contractual basis between landlord and tenant, which was given a new substance by legislation, or on rights vested by the colonial state in particular categories of people on the land. They did not rest any longer on a 'feudal' basis and the local power of zamindars who had lorded it over the peasantry.

The structural condition of the fusion of economic and political power at the point of production that distinguished the feudal mode of production was now dissolved and there was a separation of the economic power of the landowner and the political power that vested in the colonial state. The landowners did come to play an important part in the articulation of power in the colonial state, but their place in the new structure of state power was different in kind from that of the zamindar in the Mughal state.

The Burden of Land Revenue

Devastating changes of a different kind were brought about as a consequence of the land revenue policy of the colonial regime. One aspect of the change was the extra-ordinary rise in the revenue burden. As before, under the Mughals, land revenue was the principal source of taxation. But under the colonial regime of the East India Company it was collected with a rapacity and ruthlessness that India had not experienced before. The other aspect of the new situation was that the revenue now accrued to a regime which remitted a large part of it outside the country instead of disbursing it within, a fact of very considerable significance in a number of respects.

Until 1765 Bengal, where British rule in India began, was still nominally under an Indian ruler, a protege of the East India Company after its victory at the Battle of Plassey in 1757. About those early years Romesh Dutt writes:

> Every occasion for setting up a new Nawab was considered a suitable opportunity for shaking the proverbial pagoda-tree of the East. When Mir Jafar was first made Nawab after the battle of Plassey in 1757, the British officers and troops had received a bonus of £1,238,575, out of which Clive himself had taken £31,500 besides a rich jagir in Bengal. When Mir Kasim was made Nawab in 1760, the presents to the British officers came to £200,296, out of which Vansittart had taken £58,33. When Mir Jafar was made Nawab a second time in 1763, the presents amounted to £500,165. And when Najim-ud-Daula was set up in 1765, further presents came in to the extent of £230,356. Besides these sums received in

42

presents, amounting within eight years to £2,169,665, further sums were claimed and obtained as restitution within this period amounting to £3,770,833.[36]

These data are quoted by Dutt from the House of Commons Committee's Third Report of 1773.

After 1765, when the East India Company itself acquired (appropriated) the feudal domain, the <u>Diwani</u>, of Bengal (under the Mughal Emperor in Delhi), the land revenue impositions began to escalate.

> In the last year of administration of the last Indian ruler of Bengal, in 1764-5, the land revenue realised was £817,000. In the first year of the Company's administration in 1765-6, the land revenue realised in Bengal was £1,470,000. By 1771-2 it was £2,341,000 and by 1775-6 it was £2,818,000. When Lord Cornwallis fixed the Permanent Settlement in 1793, he fixed it at £3,400,000.[37]

It was a crushing burden.

Romesh Dutt, in his classic work, made two points that entail different questions about the consequences of these developments. Firstly he pointed out the combined effects of the excessively heavy burden of the enhanced land revenue and its rigorous collection, contrasted with the customary flexibility of the feudal dispensation. Under such a heavy burden agriculture declined.[38] As for the consequence of the inflexibility in the collection of land revenue (given the erratic nature of agricultural production subject to vagaries of the weather) he referred, in particular, to the Company's disregard for the conditions of the people at the time of the great Bengal famine of 1770. He wrote:

> Early in 1769 high prices gave an indication of an approaching famine, but the land tax was more rigorously collected than ever . . . (In their letter of November 1769) the Court of Directors . . . specified no relief measures to be undertaken. But on 9th May, 1770 they had to acknowledge that: 'The famine which had ensued, the mortality, the beggary, exceed all description. Above one third of the inhabitants have perished in the once plentiful province of Purneah, and in other parts the misery is equal.'...It is painful to read of this rigorous collection of the land tax during years of human sufferings and deaths perhaps unexampled in the history of mankind.[39]

It was not for another half a century that the burden of land tax was to be eased, relatively, when commercial cash cropping of raw materials required for the metropolitan economy got under way.

The second main point that emerges from Dutt's account is that land revenue now accrued to a regime which <u>transferred</u> the bulk of it abroad instead of disbursing it within the country as in the case of earlier indigenous regimes.

> Every country reasonably expects that the proceeds of taxes raised in the country should be mainly spent in the country . . . But a change came over India under the rule of the East India Company. They considered India as a vast estate or plantation, the profits of which were to be withdrawn from India and deposited in Europe.[40]

He added

> They reserved all the high appointments in India for their own nominees seeking a lucrative career in the East. They bought their merchandise out of the revenues of India and sold it in Europe for their own profit. They vigorously extracted from India a high interest for their stock-in-trade. In one shape or another all that could be raised in India by an excessive taxation flowed to Europe, after paying for a starved administration.[41]

The consequences of this transfer of resources will be examined below, not only with reference to 'primitive accumulation' for the rise of industrial capitalism in Britain but, especially, also with regard to the disintegration of the Indian economy and society.

III

The Medieval Urban Society

Contrary to the stereotype of the medieval Indian society, usually pictured as an overwhelmingly rural one, we find evidence of quite a high degree of urbanisation, much of it parasitic in character but combined with a comparatively well developed market economy and a flourishing textile industry based on domestic production both urban and rural catering for local consumption and, especially, a rapidly growing export trade. These aspects have received relatively little attention in the literature.

In his study of the <u>Agrarian System of Mughal India</u>, Irfan Habib offers a picture that militates against the old stereotypes. As far as the urban society is concerned he writes: "It is impossible to read the sources of the period without gaining the impression that there was a very large urban population; the multitudes of artisans, peons and servants found in the towns provide a frequent topic of comment to foreign observers." In a footnote to that passage in his book he quotes from <u>Baburnama</u>, (early sixteenth century) that "Another good thing in Hindustan is that it has unnumbered and endless workmen of every sort." Habib continues:

> In Akbar's empire [second half of the sixteenth century] we are told there were 120 big cities and 3,200 townships . . . The largest city in the 17th century was Agra with a population estimated at 500,000 - 600,000. In 1583-6 Agra and Fatehpur Sikri were each judged to be larger than London. Delhi (when the court was shifted to it) was now held to be as populous as Paris, then the biggest city in Europe, Patna had an estimated population of 200,000 and Ahmadabad in the early years of the 17th century was stated to be as big as London with its suburbs...[42]

In a paper in which Habib has attempted to evaluate the "Potentialities of Capitalistic Development in the Economy of India", he made an attempt to extrapolate the likely size of the total urban population from a variety of data, in particular the size and commodity composition of the surplus that was extracted from the rural economy. He arrives at the conclusion that "We should therefore expect to have had an urban population of a considerable size, but probably amounting to less than a fifth of the total population."[43] This conclusion he adds,

> is largely corroborated by our information about the size of Indian towns. Towards the beginning of the seventeenth century, the largest towns of Mughal India appear to have been much larger in population than the largest European towns; but during the course of that century, as the urban population in Europe grew, the largest towns in both seemed to be equal in size to contemporary European visitors. . . . We may conclude then that based on the collection of enormous revenues from the agricultural sector and their concentration in the hands of a small ruling class, the Indian economy had achieved a considerable expansion of its urban sector during the height of the Mughal period from 16th to 18th Century. Not only was a high proportion of the urban population employed in industrial crafts, but it would appear that in actual volume of output per head the period could invite comparison with the early decades of this century.[44]

- for, in the intervening years there had been a decline of Indian urban society, in the course of the colonial impact. The mainstay of the urban population was the nobility and the functionaries of the state through whom the surplus extracted from the peasantry was funnelled into the urban economy and society although, it should be added that the vast expansion of foreign trade in manufactures added not inconsiderably to the resources sustaining urban growth. These latter catered both for the various categories of urban classes serving the apparatuses of state power as well as trade; production itself was primarily in the form of petty production by artisans some of whom employed apprentices (nikari) and journeymen (kareegar). Both the nobles and the military were liable to transfers and it was the latter classes who were the backbone of established and growing towns and cities. As Naqvi put it "it was the craftsmen and the professionals who, unlike the fleeting nobility or fluid soldiery, constituted a permanent urban population."[45] The craftsmen were organised in powerful guilds which, as in England just before the Industrial Revolution, were a constraining factor by virtue of their regulations. But we have little knowledge of the ways in which these guilds actually functioned and the effects of their restrictions. What might be pointed out is that the evidence points against the widespread notions about the obstructing role of caste in development, for the guilds embraced craftsmen of different castes and religions; and Hindu weaver (kori or koli) as well as the Muslim weaver (julaha). The guild rather than the caste regulated their activities.[46] The towns and cities were, according to Naqvi, divided into craftwise arrangement of wards. Apart from craftsmen, nobles and the soldiery, there were large numbers of functionaries, clerks and accountkeepers, traders and merchants, entertainers and ecclesiasts who together constituted a substantial body of local 'consumers' of manufactured products as well as food from villages. Habib grossly underestimates the size and economic significance of these middle income groups, and therefore the importance of the domestic market in supporting the local manufacturing production.[47]

The available evidence points not only to a relatively high degree of urbanisation but also a developed market economy. Land revenue, for example, was collected in cash - it is said that this was so, in the central regions at least, from as early as the 13th century,[48] although crop-sharing, and collection in kind, existed too. The fact that assessment and collection of land revenue in cash was practised widely, and preferred by the Mughal administration, betokens a fairly well developed market economy - as well as circumstances in which the rural merchant and money lender flourished. But, as far as the peasant was concerned, his relationship with the market and the towns was a one way relationship. The object of his involvement in the market was no more than to raise the cash required to pay his land revenue. Otherwise the village economy remained self-sufficient and impervious to the lures of the market; but possibly not altogether so though we do not have enough available evidence for this. Mukherjee, for example, speculates about how far "the penetration of commodity circulation in the village on a large scale", as he takes it to be, and the role of usurers, "indicated how the subsistence character of the village communities was undergoing a change in this period."[49] But he does not go beyond raising that question nor does he put forward evidence that might indicate the actual process of such a transformation if it was in being. Thus, on the whole, the available evidence suggests that the traffic in goods between the peasant villages and the towns was essentially one way and the towns had nothing to offer to the peasants in return.

Manufacture in Pre-Colonial India

Insofar as the village economy itself remained impervious to commodity production (as far as its internal organisation was concerned, the surplus alone being marketed), the base for manufacturing industry was geared primarily to the luxury consumption of the aristocracy which Habib emphasises exclusively and, as we have noted above, also to the more modest needs to the urban population in general. There were karkhanas or manufactories, run by the Emperor and the nobles, where the workers and craftsmen were brought under one roof to work with tools and raw materials which were provided, to cater to their own special needs. These were not capitalist enterprises engaged in commodity production, for they produced goods exclusively for the private use of their employers.

But a manufacturing industry, and a very substantial one, did develop, especially in the case of the cotton textile industry, catering for the urban middle classes and lower middle classes and, above all, for export. The rapid growth of this industry in the seventeenth and eighteenth centuries especially, is quite remarkable. By all accounts the manufacturing industry consisted of independent artisans working in their own homes, although one does come across occasional references to master craftsmen employing assistants. Raychaudhuri thinks that this was not widespread. But there are also indications that this was not inconsiderable. It is generally also suggested that the artisans were predominantly village-based although recent urban studies point to the contrary. Since the 17th century boom there was a "wide growth of cities and towns as centres of cotton manufacture [which] may be taken as adequate [justification for] characterisation of the industry as primarily urban."[50]

The idea that manufacturing industry was predominantly village based is particularly difficult to accept in respect of those industries that catered primarily for the export trade, especially cotton textiles. There were of course weavers based on the villages who catered for the needs of the villagers and probably of people in nearby towns, for we know that the limitation that applied in the case of the

47

other village servants did not apply to weavers. There was some logic in this, of course, for the weavers provided employment for women in the village who spun the yarn and expansion in their business profited the village as a whole. But it is by no means clear that the highly skilled weavers who produced cloth of exquisite quality, not commodities that would be consumed by peasant households, were all village based. Factors favouring location in the village would be (1) that village women did the spinning at extremely low cost - but we do not know whether there were not women in towns and cities doing that too, and (2) that cotton is a bulky item to transport, as compared to the finished product - but there is no reason to suppose that yarn is any more difficult to transport than finished cloth. The factor that would favour location in towns or in peri-urban villages was not merely the advantages of being near the buyer who dictated what he needed but also, and especially, a system that developed of cash advances that were given to the weavers by merchants who bought their cloth, for whom it must obviously have been a considerable advantage to have their debtors and suppliers near at hand. These considerations fortify Naqvi's conclusions, based on her study of northern Indian cities, that the cotton textile industry was primarily urban, though that does not, by that token rule out the possibility that some of it was rural based.

We do not know how old is the system of cash advances given to weavers by merchants. The logic of the situation would suggest that it must have grown considerably, if not originated, in the seventeenth and eighteenth centuries against the background of a rapid export-led growth of the industry that was brought about entirely by new weavers entering the trade rather than by changes in technology. Prospective new entrants would need working capital, as well as capital with which to buy the necessary equipment for which the meagre accretions of savings of their families, if any, are hardly likely to have grown as rapidly as their need for more capital.

This system of cash advances, one would suggest, pre-empted two possible alternatives of a movement towards capitalist production and may well be regarded therefore as one of the important reasons militating against the development of indigenous capitalism, - though one of these two alternatives modes was by no means necessarily ruled out. One of these was that of development of capitalism 'from below', that is by artisans accumulating savings, acquiring more equipment and deploying more working capital so that they could employ assistants, or hired labour, thus themselves turning into capitalists. The other alternative was that of the development of capitalism 'from above', through a mutation of the putting-out system, the merchant capitalist becoming more and more involved in the production process itself.

48

The system of cash advances has been described by a number of authors as a 'putting-out system'.[51] But that would be quite misleading, for the logic of the relationship between the creditor and the weaver inherent in the Indian system is quite distinct from that of the putting-out system that developed in England where the merchant was directly involved in the purchase and provision of materials and even equipment (that he often hired) to weavers. Given that, in the English case, he would see advantages for himself in organising provision of these raw materials on a large scale, say, acquiring a warehouse, or even getting involved in the production of the raw material itself, yarn, and perceiving also advantages of geographical proximity of his weavers, possibly having them under one roof and so on. With the system of cash advances there was no such involvement by the merchant in the organisation of production and provision of materials and equipment and the first alternative was thus ruled out. All that was demanded in this case was that the weaver, to whom money was advanced to procure for himself the raw materials that were required, was bound to deliver the finished goods to the person who had furnished him the advance. The weaver was left to his own devices. Given the fact that the advances bound him down and imposed on him the monopsony of the creditor, in general he was reduced to a bare subsistence income and the full surplus was extracted from him, leaving him with little possibility of lifting himself up into the role of a prospective capitalist. This second possibility, therefore, was contingent on the degree of exploitation of the weaver. In earlier years this was perhaps less harsh and we do come across reports of artisans with substantial means employing others (even if they were relatively few, as Raychaudhuri argues). They do indicate that this road to capitalist development was open and some did take it, and in time more might do so. The view that their number was by no means inconsiderable is reinforced by the fact that Section XV of the Additional Supplement to the Regulations for Weavers of 30th September 1789 relates specifically to "weavers possessed of more than one loom and entertaining one or more workmen". The fact that they merited such special legislation suggests that the numbers of such master weavers were, after all, not insignificant.

The East India Company, operating through its agents, enforced the regime of cash advances in a manner that was designed to subordinate the weaver totally to the agents of the company. A practice developed of forcing advances on unwilling weavers. The object was to pre-empt his services, at low prices, as against other competitors, including other European operators who were thus elbowed out. Thus : "The conditions of the weavers in the days of Alivardi Khan was very different. They used to manufacture their goods freely and without oppression, restrictions, limitations and prohibitions. There was no attempt to restrict their goods to the one market of the East India Company".[52] Sinha continues: "The harassment of the goomastas [agents of the East India Company] commenced in 1753 when the dadni merchants were displaced, but the goomastas had not yet the backing of political power....It was after the revolution [sic!] of 1757 [i.e. the beginning of British conquest] that they were unrestrained." The dadni merchants were independent moneylenders who were now being pushed out by the East India Company so that it could have direct control over the weavers.

In these circumstances the decline of manufacture was inevitable because the weavers were obliged to work, as Bolts, a contemporary, put it, "against their will at whatever prices are arbitrarily imposed upon them". Given widespread desertions of weavers a practice of direct physical coercion was introduced. Thus Romesh Dutt writes: "The Company's servants assembled the principal weavers and placed guard over them until they entered into engagements to supply the Company only. When once a weaver accepted an advance, he seldom got out of his liability. A peon was placed over him to quicken his deliveries". This last point refers to the practice that was introduced of having a man with a cane who would watch over the weaver and beat him "to quicken his deliveries". Detailed Regulations were promulgated (and additions made to them from time to time) under which the oppression of the weavers was given a legal basis and was enforced under the authority of the colonial state. That is a far cry indeed from laissez faire, believed to have been the guiding principle of colonial policy. But here we are anticipating other developments. First we must consider the role of foreign trade in the expansion of the indigenous industrial production in medieval India.

Export of Indian Manufactures to Europe

It seems that the prosperity of the seventeenth and eighteenth century India was closely associated with the boom in exports, especially cotton and silk textiles. India was, for several centuries at the centre of a network of world trade, principally as a supplier of fine cotton textiles, most of all to the Middle East, Africa and the Far East. In his classic work on the cotton textile industry, Baines remarks that it was a curious fact that despite the ingenuity of the Chinese people in the arts of manufacture, and the fact that cotton could easily be grown in China, that country "should have remained without cotton manufacture until the end of the thirteenth century, when it had flourished among their Indian neighbours for probably three thousand years."

It was the discovery of the sea route from Europe to India at the end of the fifteenth century that inaugurated a new era for India's trade in cotton textiles, for bulky goods could now be carried to Europe in large quantities and

50

cheaply, thus catering not merely for the luxury needs of a tiny aristocracy but for much wider sections of the people. It was not, however, until the beginning of the seventeenth century that we find the trade booming; and led by that export boom, the seventeenth and the eighteenth centuries were periods of exceptional prosperity for India, although the return for these exports in the form of bullion sterilised wealth. The European maritime powers were engaged in fierce rivalry for control of that trade. Following the Portuguese and the Dutch, the English too joined the race for supremacy. The East India Company that received its Royal Charter in 1600, was eventually to secure monopoly control over that trade on the strength of British naval supremacy and its territorial conquest of India.

The expansion of the overseas trade was fully matched by expansion of Indian manufacturing production. Far from being stagnant and inert, as the pre-colonial Indian economy is so often pictured, it was very responsive indeed to the new stimulus. Raychaudhuri, thus, found that on the Coromandel coast "Industrial production . . . could respond to an increased demand, which offered means of livelihood to a larger number of handicraftsmen. . . . . A concentration of industrial producers around the centres of export definitely appears to have taken place around this time."[53] The three chief sources of supply of Indian textiles for exports were Gujarat, Coromandel and Bengal, though there were several other lesser centres too, quite apart from the fact that production of cotton textiles was universal throughout India. But export production was specialised - and there was a regional specialisation too. "Bengal is celebrated for the production of the finest muslins, the Coromandel coast for the best chintzes and calicoes and Surat [Gujarat] for strong and inferior goods of every kind."[54]

The Iberian conquest of Latin America and the flow of precious metals into countries of Europe that followed it must be recognised as an essential ingredient of the new 'world-economy' that was being constituted. But in that 'world economy' it was India that fulfilled the role of supplier of manufactured productions, on the basis of a domestic manufacturing industry that did show some potentiality for movement towards a capitalist mode of production, which existed within the pre-capitalist social formation in an embryonic form. Europe's role in that 'world ecoomy' was to exchange precious metals seized from Latin America for the Indian manufactured goods. That raises questions about the concept of 'world economy' and the designation of Western Europe as the 'core' of a 'modern-world-system' independently of its relationship with India in the seventeenth and eighteenth centuries, as a market for India's manufactures, and the forcible method of reversal of that relationship. In the seventeenth and eighteenth centuries India had not yet been reduced to a colonial status; though it must be acknowledged that although India had a flourishing mercantile shipping industry, it lacked naval power, for which it had seen no necessity until the sudden and full impact on her of the more highly developed naval power of the maritime nations of Europe. In a sense it might even be said that India's reduction to a colonial status began on the high seas, when her merchant ships had to obtain 'passes' from the Portuguese and then the Dutch and English and, often all of them together, to be able to go about their business at all.

The import of precious metals into India, as an exclusive form for payment for Indian goods, must be put into perspective. Knowles wrote: "The whole difficulty of trading with the East lay in the fact that Europe had so little to send out that the East wanted . . . . Therefore it was mainly silver that was taken out."[55] This was certainly so in the case of early Portuguese trade at the beginning of the seventeenth century for which Krishna provides detailed information. "It appears that the provisions were for the use of Portuguese settled in the East, the imported money was invested in buying Indian goods at various centres, while Jewels were carried to the Court, Agra and Brahmpur and the proceeds were employed in indigo and cloths."[56] As for the size of the trade, Krishna estimates that annually (in the early years) "150,000 crowns were sent out of Portugal on each ship".[57] But from his detailed study we find that the figures multiply from decade to decade and escalate further when the Dutch and the English come to occupy, successively, a predominant position in the trade. The profits were high too. "We know that imported goods were expected to produce in England three to four times their original cost at least"[58] – the 'terms of trade' were loaded against India.

But the trade was not exclusively financed by the export of bullion to India, although this was predominently the case; and soon this was to be decisively changed after the British colonial conquest, with devastating consequences. During the period 1708 to 1760, i.e. the period just before the conquest, of the total "exports" from England to India, amounting in all to £36.8 million, for the whole period, bullion amounted to £27.5 million or 75%. The rest comprised a variety of merchandise of which the largest single item, by far, was "woollen goods" valued at £5.4 million; the other main items being copper valued at £1.1 million, lead at £0.5 million, and iron at £0.3 million.[59]

Already towards the end of this period, however, another factor was entering into the financing of this trade, a change that was to transform its character entirely. This was the acquisition of funds in India by the British in a variety of ways, which were used to purchase goods for export from India, thus obviating the need to bring goods or bullion from England for the purpose of financing that trade. It led to a large unrequited flow of resources from India to England, the "Economic Drain", as it has been referred to, which will be discussed below.

Finally, a word about the relative importance of the India trade for the British economy. During the 40 year period from 1663 to 1703, we are told, the export of coin and bullion from England to India amounted to £24,000,000. This is compared with similar exports to France amounting to £10,000,000 and to Denmark and Sweden of £2,000,000.[60] Before any conclusions are derived from these figures, consideration must be given to the balance of trade in other goods in order to arrive at an overall picture. Nevertheless the figures do suggest that the India trade loomed quite large in Britain's commerce at the time. It is particularly interesting to note that this trade was permitted and encouraged, although financed largely by the export of bullion, despite the prevailing hostility of Mercantilist ideas to the export of precious metals. Moreover, the size of the trade cannot be judged in terms of bilateral trade between Britain in India. The British purchased Indian textiles for re-sale in the Far East (as well as on the Continent of Europe) where they fetched a profit of three times their price in India, the proceeds being used to purchase other commodities there. The overall size of the trade was therefore very much larger than the exports to England and to Europe.

Destruction of Indian Industry and the Industrial Revolution

It is generally believed that it was the autogenous rise of the Industrial Revolution in England and the consequent cheapness of English textiles, with which the Indian textile industry, based on primitive techniques, could not compete that finally destroyed it, because of a relentless pursuit of laissez faire policy by the colonial regime. Facts point to quite the contrary. We can see that the prior destruction of the Indian textile industry was a pre-condition for the rise of British industry and that it was done by determined colonial state intervention against the Indian industry and not by laissez faire. The Industrial Revolution itself was thus, an early example of an import substitution strategy for industrial development. But this aspect of the dynamics of the Industrial Revolution does not figure in discussions of its "causes": although, as we shall see, this was at the core of it, we find no reference to it in standard works on the subject.

What is involved is the conflict between Indian and English cotton textile interests. After all it was the development of the English cotton textile industry that provided the main thrust that led to the broad based growth that followed. As Landes pointed out the "threshold" of the Industrial Revolution in England "was crossed first in the

cotton manufacture".[61]   In fact Landes himself comes close
to a recognition of the import substitution strategy when he
remarks briefly and in passing that "The closing of England
to East-Indian cottons simply encouraged the domestic
producers, whose fustians and linen-cottons (they were not
yet able to turn out pure cottons) did not come under the
interdiction", i.e. prohibitions against the use of fabrics
competing with wool.   But this line of analysis is not
followed up by him or, to my knowledge, any others.

Cotton manufacture became established in Manchester by
about the middle of the seventeenth century - introduced, it
is suggested, by Flemish Protestant immigrants.   But the
development of cotton manufacture in England was slow.
"Owing to the rudeness of the spinning machinery fine yarn
could not be spun and, of course, fine goods could not be
woven."[62]   In the latter part of the seventeenth and the
beginning of the eighteenth century there was vehement
opposition to the large scale imports of cotton goods from
India and this resulted in the imposition of several
protective measures.   But at that time "The jealousy felt in
England was not, however, on behalf of our cotton
manufacturers but of our woollen and silk manufacturers which
sufficiently proves that no cotton goods were then made in
England of the fine and light qualities of those in
India."[63]   There was, likewise, opposition to imports of
silk manufactured goods from India.

The East India Company itself, however, had a major
vested interest in the preservation and expansion of that
trade.   It is true that it was through the Company, in charge
of government in India, that British colonial policy in India
was made and implemented - and the Company was constantly
under pressure, through Parliament, to undertake particular
courses of action that suited the various British interests,
not least the rising industrial interests.   But it would be a
mistake to identify the making of British colonial policy in
India wholly with the interests and activities of the East
India Company.   It was, first and foremost, a commercial
corporation, concerned primarily with its trading profits and
exaction of wealth from its political control over India.
Its interests conflicted with those of the rising industrial
bourgeoisie in England.   The fate and the future of British
industry was by no means its foremost concern.   There was
pressure in England therefore to reorient its policies and
curtail its activities.   Thus, its trading monopoly was ended
in 1813 and it was required to stop its commercial operations
in 1833, thus eventually becoming exclusively an organ of
colonial government.

Because of its monopoly over East Indian trade as well
as the fact that it was the channel for importation of large
quantities of manufactured commodities from India, the East
India Company was under fierce atack, especially in the
eighteenth and nineteenth centuries.   It did, under the

54

circumstances, yield to some of the demands that were being put forward on behalf of British industrial interests. A notorious example is quoted by Romesh Dutt when in March 1769 the Directors of the East India Company sent a letter to Bengal instructing, inter alia, that the manufacture and export of raw silk should be encouraged and that of manufactured silk be discouraged. Dutt quotes the remarks of the Ninth Report of the House of Commons Select Committee concerning that letter.

> This letter contains a perfect plan of policy, both of compulsion and encouragement which must in considerable degree operate destructively to the manufacturing of Bengal. Its effects must be (so far as it could operate without being eluded) to change the whole face of that industrial country, in order to render it a field for the produce of crude materials subservient to the manufactures of Great Britain.[64]

But, in general, the Company resisted measures to restrict imports from India and, as in 1681, when Parliament threw out a petition to restrict import and use of Indian silken goods, it even had an occasional success. More protection was, however, being demanded by British textile industries, including the budding cotton textile industry. "A battle royal raged between the parties, for and against protection" in the following decades.[65] Protective duties cut deeply into the Company's profits on goods that it bought in India as a virtual monopolist. But it was unable to resist the powerful pressures for their imposition.

Against the background of considerable agitation for protective measures, in 1685 a 10% customs duty was imposed on "all calicoes and all other Indian linen imported from the East Indies and on all wrought silks..." etc. In 1690 that duty was doubled. More restrictions, of various kinds were demanded and introduced. In 1619, for example when a demand was made, and later granted, for a ban on "the wear and use of Indian silks, and calicoes, painted, stained or dyed in India", the East India Company protested that it

> had carried on the East India trade much to the advantage of the nation and the woollen manufactures thereof', that the proposed measures would cut off a large branch of their trade...would weaken their settlements in India, would render the English contemptible in the eyes of the Indian princes and encourage other European nations to attempt the gradual engrossing of trade and power of India, that the British revenues would suffer.[66]

But it was steadily losing ground to the demands of industrial capital.

By the time the Company began its conquest of India, the duty on Indian cotton goods imported into Britain by the company had already gone up to 50%. That was on the eve of the Industrial Revolution. At the time "Up to the year 1760, the machines used in cotton manufacture in England were nearly as simple as those of India".[67] The inventions of Arkwright and Kay and Hargreaves did not yet make it possible for the British textile industry to stand in competition with the Indian goods because of their fine quality that was as yet unmatched. It was only after the invention of Crompton's mule, and its general use in the 1780s, that it was possible for the first time to manufacture fine muslin from English yarn. But despite the advances in the technology of production, the English industry still demanded more protection and was given it, for the Indian goods were still more competitive. The rate of import duty was progressively raised, until by 1813 half a century after the Industrial Revolution had got underway it was no less than 85%. This evidence shows up as fallacious the line of reasoning that represents the English cotton textile industry and technology to have grown up entirely independently, to be explained solely in terms of endogenous factors and which attributes the destruction of the Indian textile industry, simply to the greater competitive power of machine made British textiles, ignoring the actual sequence of development. It was the wall of protection that made possible the survival and growth of British cotton textile industry in the face of Indian competition and facilitated large capital investments in the industry. Without it the English industry would have found it impossible to get a foothold in the home market, let alone abroad, and would not have got off the ground.

Despite the ruling free trade orthodoxy of the time, there was evidently no compunction about the resort to heavy protective measures. The evidence of John Ranking before House of Commons Committee is quoted as not untypical, where no pretence was made about purposes other than restriction of trade, when he said that he looked upon these prohibitive duties "as a protecting duty to encourage our own manufactures". H.H. Wilson, the historian of India wrote:

> Had not such prohibitory duties and decrees existed, the mills of Paisley and Manchester would have stopped in their outset and could scarcely have been again set into motion even by the power of steam. They were created by the sacrifice of Indian manufacture. Had India been independent, she could have retaliated, would have imposed prohibitive duties on British goods and thus have preserved her own productive industry from annihilation. This act of self-defence was not permitted her.[68]

A substantial part of the East Indian Company's trade in

cotton textiles imported into England was for re-export to Europe. In 1789, when the issue of the large scale imports of Indian textiles by the Company was, once again, raised, the Company explained, that "17/20ths of the whole of the calicoes imported were re-exported and that 12/20ths of the whole of the muslins were re-exported."[69] Continental Europe was a major market for Indian textiles even though the East India Company carried the bulk of it. This trade was dealt a decisive blow with the closure of the continental ports during the Napoleonic wars; after the war it was the British textile industry that inherited that market. Thus Indian exports collapsed all round and at the same. The country which was for centuries supplier of cotton textile for the whole world, was itself soon reduced to importing textiles from Britain. But it took a long time to kill the Indian industry. During the decade 1741-50 the total value of the exports of Indian calicoes alone, to Britain, averaged £1.2 million annually. In 1815 the total value of all cotton goods exported from India to Britain amounted to £1.3 million in value. By 1832 it fell to £100,000. On the other hand, in 1815, several decades after the Industrial Revolution had got under way, the value of British cotton textiles imported into India was a mere £26,000. By 1832 it had gone up to £400,000 and by 1850 India was the market for one quarter of the total British textile exports.[70]

It was not the destruction of the export trade alone that finally destroyed the Indian cotton textile industry. Its basic weakness lay in its exclusive dependence upon exports, on the one hand, and the relatively small class of the Indian urban consumer on the other. The village economy and society, the vast bulk of the Indian population, remained impervious to it. A decisive factor in the destruction of the industry was the destruction of its local urban base. Urbanisation in India, which as I pointed out earlier was relatively high, was parasitic on the land revenue that was extracted from the peasantry. But it did constitute a source of demands for the products of local industry. When the East India Company appropriated the land revenue, the economic basis of that urban society (and industry) collapsed. This is an aspect of the picture which is too easily ignored; in fact it is not discussed at all. Habib, one of the few who poses the question at all dismisses too easily the importance of the urban factor.[71]

After the colonial conquest the bulk of the revenues raised were transferred out of India, via unrequited exports. Of the part that was spend in India itself much was spend on military operations - in fact India was made to pay for its own conquest, as well as that of much of the British Empire in the East. During the decade 1771 to 1779 "military charges" absorbed between half and one-third of the revenue whereas "civil charges" were between one-seventh and one-fifteenth of it, the balance being used for the purchase of goods for export to England. A large share of the civil expenditure was taken up by salaries of British employees of the Company which too were in fact substantially remitted out of the country along with similar proportions of salaries of military officers. Amounts averaging £1.3 million a year were "invested" by the Company in the purchase of Indian goods for export to England.

After the colonial conquest very little of the Revenue, therefore, found its way into the hands of the members of the Indian urban society whom this money had supported in the past. The result was a devastating and dramatic decline in the urban population, not least of the old manufacturing towns. According to Sir Charles Trevelyan, (quoted by Dutt) the population of Dacca, the 'Manchester of India' dropped from 150,000 to 30,000.[72] It was not only the weavers who were driven out or perished. The various categories of the urban population, who had bought their products in the past, were gone also.

It was not until much later, in the nineteenth century that a new process of urbanisation, catering to the needs of the new colonial economy, got under way. But the new middle classes were products of the culture of colonialism.

> The demand from this class did not amount to even as much as the demand from the Europeans. (Who demanded ornamental knick-knacks, souvenirs, etc., as cheap as possible). Indeed with a few exceptions they entirely turned their backs on the indigenous arts. One of the most harmful effects of a foreign rule is the imposition on the conquered peoples of the ideals of the conquerors; and the newly created Indian 'bourgeoisie' showed itself ready to accept European standards and to pour scorn on everything Indian.[73]

The Indian cotton weaving industry did survive, though it was much diminished. But in the nineteenth century it was subsumed under the domination of small merchant capital and also, it depended for its survival on the import of yarn from Manchester. It was put on a new basis. In due course, with the rise of large scale textile industry in India, beginning from the second half of the 19th century, the old cotton weaving industry was finally marginalised, although it survived to some degree on the basis of imported yarn.

The "Economic Drain" - India's "Aid" to Britain!

It seems to me that the destruction of the Indian textile industry and thereby an "import-substitution strategy" was decisive in getting the Industrial Revolution off the ground. That strategy, it might be said, however, was fundamentally different from that which is contemplated by the ideology of developmentalism for dependent capitalist development of the Third World. In England's case the growth of an indigeneous textile industry generated demand for machinery, chemicals etc., thus triggering off expansion in all departments of an integrated economy i.e. in the production of capital goods as well as consumption goods. By contrast, in the contemporary Third World, within the framework of a world capitalist system, this is just not possible because the "feedback" by way of demand for capital goods is immediately transferred to the metropolitan economies, in generating a demand for the products of high technology industries in the metropolis. There were no such integrated development in colonial India. The argument being implied here is not necessarily for a philosophy of autarchic development, but rather a question of the constraints of one-sided dependent development with a hierarchically structured world capitalist system. Therefore the dynamics of import substitution in England in the eighteenth century and the Third World today are, respectively, quite different.

A suggestion was made by Eric Williams that the triangular trade between Britain, Africa and the West Indies was a major factor in providing both resources and the stimulus for Britain's industrial development - Britain exported manufactured goods to Africa which were exchanged for slaves and the human cargo, in turn, was exchanged for colonial merchandise. He wrote: "The first stimulus to the growth of Cottonopolis came from the African and West Indian markets."[74] But the scale of the trade was too small for it to have played the decisive role that Williams attributes to it, as compared to what we have just considered with regard to the Indian trade and unilateral exactions; it was small also in comparison to the magnitudes that were involved in the capital formation in Britain during the Industrial Revolution. In fact Crouzet dismisses Williams' argument in a derisory way.[75] As Williams points out, the export trade was £14,000 in 1739 and by 1759 it had increased to £303,000. These are indeed insignificant figures if we consider that during the first half of the eighteenth century Britain's export of bullion and goods, alone to India, to finance her purchases there, mainly of cotton textiles, had averaged over £700,000 a year. That is not a derisory figure; and Crouzet is unwise in dismissing the more general argument about the role of the colonies by reference to Williams' statement of it alone.

But there is one sense in which Williams' argument may have some weight. Until the mid-1780s the British cotton textile industry just could not produce fine textiles, equivalent to Indian calicoes and muslins. It produced a coarse fabric, not an easily marketable product. That may well have figured in the equation that Williams has put before us, namely a strong stimulus to the budding and inefficient British cotton textile industry, which exported on average £18,000 worth of cotton textiles annually during the first half of the eighteenth century; much of which was probably disposed off on the coast of Africa and in the Caribbean, captive markets that no doubt gave some boost to that industry at a critical stage. A. Gunder Frank has examined this process on a wider canvas in a recent work.[76]

India's role in providing resources on quite a large scale to Britain at that time, could not but have made an important contribution to the process of capital formation during the Industrial Revolution. The argument merits a closer examination, to make an assessment of the order of the magnitude of the transfer of resources in relation to the actual size of capital formation in Britain. The question of unilateral, unrequited flow of resources from India to England has been much discussed, the so-called "Economic Drain", but entirely with reference to causes of Indian poverty. The phenomenon can be considered also in the context of its contribution to British development.

The issue of the "Economic Drain" from India occupied quite a central place in discussions of the problems of India, during the early days of the Indian nationalist movement in the second half of the nineteenth century. But the concept itself, as the reality that it expresses, is much older. As early as 1783 attention was drawn to it in proceedings in the British Parliament - it was mentioned by Edmund Burke in his speech on Fox's East India Bills, and by others. The House of Commons' Select Committee's Ninth Report on India refers to the "greatness of these drains." But it was, understandably, in the late nineteenth century, when the Indian nationalist movement got under way, that the issue came into prominence. Dadabhai Naoroji, one of its leading lights, is credited with the origin of the theory; he was certainly amongst the first to make a systematic attempt to compute its magnitude. So was William Digby in his sarcastically entitled work "Prosperous British India".[77] But these calculations cover the period after 1835, a much later period than that with which we are concerned here. For the earlier period we find illustrations in the literature rather than systematic calculations. For the moment therefore we have only rough and ready figures to work with which we can carefully consider to give us an order of magnitude of the amounts involved though not a precise figure.

In the literature, particularly about the earlier period we notice some confusion between three distinct aspects of the problem of outflow of resources, namely: (1) sources of the funds that were transferred, (2) the financial mechanisms through which transfers were made, and (3) the corresponding mode of transfer of real resources. There is a further problem that arises in the present context, though not when the "Economic Drain" is discussed with reference to its burden on India. This further problem arises from the fact that the resources that were extracted from India were

not only transferred to England by way of unrequited exports
but also much of them were expended on Imperial military
enterprises not only in the Middle East and East Asia but,
above all, in India itself - India had to pay for its own
conquest. Also considerable resources, especially those
obtained by the Company's officials and business men,
remained in India where they were invested in colonial
enterprises, to generate a future flow of resources to
England. For our present purposes, we must leave these
leakages out of account and try and assess the broad order of
magnitude of resources that were transferred to England
recognising therefore that the actual total is larger. A
further point of clarification: it is sometimes argued, in
the case of private fortunes that were made by English men in
India and transferred to England, that not the whole of such
amounts went into investment into industry in England, for
substantial amounts were invested in other forms. Such
private fortunes comprised a quarter or a fifth of the total
outflow of resources from India. Irrespective of the actual
use made of such resources by particular individuals
transferring the wealth, the fact remains that, in the
process, the British economy as a whole, was acquiring real
resources from abroad underpinning its capacity to sustain
large investment efforts. The sources of the resource
transfer that we are concerned with were, principally, the
revenues and profits of the East India Company (less local
disbursements), the very large earnings and exactions of its
civilian and military employees which were substantially
saved and remitted to England and, finally, the earnings of
private businessmen operating in India which were likewise
remitted.

An attempt has been made recently to compute the
earnings and exactions of the British community in Bengal,
the main base of its operations at the time. (To get the
whole picture we would have to consider also those in other
regions in India.) According to that cautious calculation:
"It seems probable that some £3,000,000 was sent home before
1757 and about £15,000,000 between 1757 and 1784. An average
of rather more than £500,000 a year."[78] The dates are
rather convenient from our point of view for they cover the
crucial period when the Industrial Revolution got under way.
Marshall confuses the issue a little in respect to the points
that I made at the beginning of the preceding paragraph, for
he writes:

> only a minute part of private remittances produced a
> physical transfer of specie out of Bengal and only a
> relatively small part directly involved the shipment of
> goods. The great bulk of remittances were made by bill
> of exchange for money advanced in Bengal to the British
> East India Company or to foreign companies who used it
> to defray the costs of their Bengal establishments and

to purchase cargoes for export.[79]

One must not confuse financial mechanisms and the movements of real resources that are related to them. These financial transactions represented the fact that the exports from India were no longer financed by imports of bullion. The now unilateral flow of trade was based on purchases of the goods in India from funds raised in India in various ways as above, the remittances being paid out at the other end from sale proceeds, that far exceeded their original cost, leaving a huge profit. This alerts us to the fact, however, that if we were to base our computations on trade figures, we must take that trade also into account; indeed not only their trade with Europe but also with the Far East and elsewhere, for here too we find an example of a "triangular trade" in the process of transfer of resources. But that would be a major undertaking to try and compute. Likewise, in the case of cash remitted by way of bills drawn on the East India Company in London, the funds so received by the Company would have to be added to its other receipts when assessing the net surplus generated by the excess of its receipts over its disbursements in India. Thus we can take it that in one form or the other, these funds added to the resources that were, in real terms, i.e. in the form of commodities, taken out of India to augment Britain's resources at a crucial period in the rise of industrial capitalism there.

The bulk of the resources that were available for transfer, of course, were the revenues and the various exactions obtained by the East India Company. The bulk of the revenues were from land revenue. We find that during the three years 1792-93 to 1794-95 the surplus of gross revenue over gross expenditure amounted to £1.5 million, after which time the surplus diminished for a few years because of large scale military operations under Wellesley, to be restored to a much higher level again, when between 1810 and 1814 it ranged between £2 million and £4 million. Furthermore, interest on the Indian Debt, paid in England which, for our purposes we must therefore add to the transferable resources from the Company along with the current revenue surplus.

These figures of the amounts available from the two main sources are broadly in keeping with the annual figures of 'Investments' of the Company, which was the term used to indicate the funds employed in purchase of Indian goods exported by the Company. That suggests that we are not far wrong in assessing the order of magnitude of the resources being unilaterally transferred. For the ten years from 1793-4 to 1802-3 they averaged £1.5 million annually. If we recall that a substantial part of the transfer or real resources was also taking place through transfer of goods by private individuals and businessmen and partly through other european trading companies, as referred to above, we may estimate that broadly funds of the order of about £2 million a year were being transferred. This estimate rests on the rule of the thumb, as is only too evident. But I hope that it is not too wild a guess, hopefully a carefully enough reasoned approximation that we can go on with, until we have more accurate calculations at our disposal.

We may consider this figure of the subsidy for Britain from India to the tune of £2 million annually, in relation to the magnitude of capital formation in Britain at the time. Phyllis Deane estimates that after mid-eighteenth century investments absorbed, as a long term average, 5% to 6% of the national income as against a long term average figure of 3% in the preceding period. Pollard, quoted by Crouzet, suggests much higher figures - 6.5% around 1770 reaching "9% in the exceptional boom years from 1790 to 1793".[80] One may parethetically add that it is precisely in such 'boom years' that the availability of resources from outside could prove to be critical, making possible the extra investment effort. From Pollard's (higher) estimates Crouzet arrives at estimates of Gross Capital Formation in the British economy of a grand total of £9.4 million in 1770 and £16 million in 1790-93. Of that grand total, investment in machinery was £0.8 million in 1770 and £2 million in 1790-93 and additional investment in stocks £1.5 million and £2 million respectively.[81] If we consider the annual resource flow from India of about £2 million, it is not quite so insignificant a magnitude after all. It is difficult to avoid the conclusion therefore that the "Economic Drain" from India has not only been a major factor in India's impoverishment, as it has been argued for two hundred years, but that it has also been a very significant factor in the Industrial Revolution in Britain.

The Structure of Colonial Capitalism

The picture of the economy of pre-colonial India diverged a little from our theoretical conception of the feudal mode of production in two respects. Firstly we recognised some tendencies, though as yet only in their infancy, towards the development of indigenous capitalist production both in agriculture and in industry. It would appear to be idle to speculate whether India would have made a transition to capitalism in the circumstances but for the colonial impact; though the conditions for that were not entirely unfavourable. The second point is that we have identified as a condition of the feudal mode of production that production is mainly for use, whereas there was a very substantial element of petty commodity production, especially for export and, not least in cotton textile manufacture. However, these are both elements that may be found in late feudalism in Europe.

At this point it might be useful to recall the distinction between the concept of 'social formation', that refers to a particular, actual society, and the concept of 'mode of production' which is a theoretical concept of structure that does not denote societies in all their particularities but rather connotes structural properties of societies or social formations. In the course of historical development of societies, a particular mode of production would be the dominant mode of production in that society but, at the same time, elements of another mode would be found already to be forming within it. With their development, and the rise of the new mode of production, the forces representing the new mode, and their new requirements at the economic, political and social levels, would generate conflicts and struggles, the fundamental contradictions between modes of production that, within a Marxist conception of the process of societal development, constitute the hinge of history. Such contradictions and the emergence of capitalist relations, were as yet in their embryonic form in India, when the colonial impact made itself felt. It was a society in which the process of transition was abruptly intercepted not just by the operation of external forces at the economic level but, indeed, by the application of force; as we have seen the destruction of Indian industry was achieved by state intervention. That fact brings into question purely economistic conceptions of the colonial expansion and the establishment of a "modern world system" or Imperialism. Those who translate Marxism into a narrow economism might do well to reflect on Marx's words in this context: "These methods depend in part on brute force, for instance the colonial system."[82]

The colonial regime, as we have seen, instituted changes that dissolved feudal structures, at least in respect of the first three conditions of the feudal mode of production that we identified earlier, in particular the separation of the producer from the means of production, land. We have yet to consider the last two conditions namely (i) generalised commodity production and (ii) extended reproduction, that differentiate the structure of capitalism from that of feudalism, before we can arrive at a conclusion about the structure of colonial India. To anticipate the argument that follows, I would argue that both of these conditions are also realised, but in their case in a form that is distinctive, and which differentiates the character of generalised commodity production and extended reproduction of capital in colonial social formations from the structure of metropolitan capitalism. What we have in colonised India therefore is a capitalist mode of production, but a capitalist mode of production that has a specifically colonial structure. One thing is clear. The feudal mode of production was dissolved and there is no basis on which we can justify designation of relations of production in agriculture, that resulted from the colonial transformation, any more as feudal. The resulting social relations of production in agriculture were

64

founded on a "formal subsumption" of production under capital although not yet a "real subsumption" under capital.[83] This will be examined below. But let us first consider in what manner are the two conditions, referred to above, realised in colonised societies.

In medieval India we found self-sufficiency of the village economy combined with a not inconsiderable development of petty commodity production, comparable perhaps to that which we find in late feudalism in Europe. The 'destructive' impact of colonialism resulted not only in the destruction of the petty commodity production, not least in cotton textile production which I singled out for discussion above, which was the largest but by no means the only industry of any importance. There was also a progressive dissolution of village self-sufficiency. That occurred in two ways. On the one hand village domestic manufactures declined, and peasants devoted themselves exclusively to agriculture which was now drawn more and more into the national and indeed the international market. Previously too, it was pointed out, there was a 'market' for agricultural commodities, a fact that was inferred from the payment of land revenue in cash. But that was a limited relationship - in fact a one way relationship, for the towns had nothing to offer to the peasant in return. The peasant economy itself was based on self-sufficiency both with regard to non-agricultural goods as well as agricultural produce that the peasant needed to support himself and his family.

This was progressively changed. One by one village 'manufactures' gave way to purchase of factory made goods, that were imported into India and, later, with the development of indigenous capitalist industrial production, those which were locally produced. To purchase these goods, which the peasant community now no longer made locally, the peasants had to produce agricultural commodities for the (colonial) market to raise cash for the purpose; he was subject now to "unequal exchange". He produced cash crops - and now not only for payment of land revenue. Secondly, there was a concomitant specialisation in the production of agricultural crops also. Some regions, which were specially suited for the purpose, turned to an increased proportion of production of non-food cash crops whereas other regions began to produce increased amounts of food crops for sale in these other regions and not merely for the peasants' own consumption. Thus, overall, there was a progressive movement towards generalised commodity production in the rural economy. We may look upon this process as one of internal disarticulation and external integration of the rural economy. This process was, of course, greatly accelerated after the mid-nineteenth century and the railway age. By contrast the first half of the nineteenth century was a period of stagnation, starvation and frequent famines when the burden of the colonial regime was heavy by way of land revenue, the burden of which gradually eased as the century progressed. In the late eighteenth century and early nineteenth century it was a parasitic regime entirely. But as the nineteenth century progressed, instead of relying mainly on direct extraction of surplus, by way of land revenue, there was progressively greater capitalist extraction of surplus value, by the subordination of the peasant economy to capital. Here we may consider also the economy of the small, 'independent' peasantry which we have not discussed above, for lack of space. It too was also brought progressively under the rule of capital, both as a producer for the capitalist market, an ancillary to metropolitan capitalist production, and likewise as a consumer of products turned out by the metropolitan industry. I will return to some theoretical issues that arise in connection with the subsumption of peasant production under capital presently.

From the above we conclude that condition (iv) that we listed as one of the defining characteristics of a capitalist mode of production was also realised in the colonial economy. But it was realised in a special and distinctive way that differentiates the structure of metropolitan capitalism from the structure that was created in the colony. In the metropolitan economy capitalist development had brought about a complementary development in various sectors of the economy; though by no means an autarchic development. There was, however, a balanced development between agriculture and industry and between different branches of industry, in particular, between industries producing consumer goods and those producing capital goods. It was an integrated development in these terms.. By contrast in the colonies the pattern of production was progressively lop-sided, geared to the requirements of the metropolitan economy, (i.e. exports) and also providing a market for the products of metropolitan industry (i.e. imports). Thus the circuit of generalised commodity production was not completed within an integrated and internally balanced economy but only by way of the linkage with the metropolitan economy, through dependence on exports and imports. It was a disarticulated generalised commodity production, characteristic of colonial economy and not an integrated generalised commodity production characteristic of the metropolitan economy. Although the condition of generalised commodity production was, thus, realised, it was realised in a specifically colonial structural form that distinguishes the structure of colonial mode of production, from that of metropolitan capitalism.

Likewise the last of our conditions, condition (v), namely extended reproduction of capital. In this case also, as in the case of generalised commodity production, there is a mutation in the manner in which extended reproduction of capital was realised in the colonised economy. Extended reproduction of capital refers to the realisation of surplus value and its accumulation in the process of capitalist production and reproduction. That leads to 'a rise in organic composition of capital' or rise in capital intensity, or a higher degree of mechanisation. In the colony, although surplus value is realised, it is not accumulated locally within the colonial economy. By virtue of colonial exploitation it is drained out of the colony and leads to capital accumulation and rise in the organic composition of capital not in the colony but in the imperialist metropolis. This, again is a colonial structure, in which the essential condition of the capitalist mode of production is realised but in a distinctive colonial form, which, thus, differentiates the colonial structure or the colonial mode of production from the structure of metropolitan capitalism.

Thus we find that all five of the conditions that were specified at the beginning of this paper for a transition from feudalism to capitalism are realised in the colonised society, a process of transformation that spanned much of the nineteenth century in India. But two of these conditions, namely generalised commodity production and extended reproduction of capital, are realised in a specifically colonial form. For that reason, while recognising that the colonial transformation and the domination of imperialist capital brought about a capitalist transformation in India, it was a capitalist transformation of a special kind, that is specific to colonial societies. This specific form poses a problem of conceptualisation. The internal disarticulation and the external integration of the colonised economy and the fact that both generalised commodity production and extended reproduction of capital are realised only through the imperial metropolis, means that we cannot grasp the structure of colonial capitalism if we look exclusively within the colonial social formation without locating it in its global integument. When I developed this argument in a previous article, several of my colleagues, even sympathetic ones, found this difficult to accomodate within their own perceptions of the meanings of the terms "social formation" and "modes of production". For example Harry Cleaver, by this stage of the argument, concluded that my analysis "of the colonial mode of production is in a state of chaos" and, further he suggests that we must accept "the impossibility of answering the questions of the relations between agrarian structures and the world capitalist system in terms of a mode of production analysis".[83]

Only in terms of a concept of a mode of production, which is basic to a Marxist view of structure of societies, I would argue, can we analyse societies, their class formation and class alignments. Only on that basis can we proceed at all. The answer to the difficulty lies not in abandonment of the concept of mode of production but in clarifying it and acknowledging the fact that whereas the founding fathers of

Marxism did not discuss the structures of colonial social
formations, we have to. For contemporary Marxists Lenin's
analysis of Development of Capitalism in Russia provides a
basic theoretical framework for analysis of social formations
and, within them, of modes of production. In the Russian
social formation the feudal mode of production was dominant
but the capitalist mode of production (and the class forces
embedded in it) were growing rapidly and challenging the
feudal structures, the dominant feudal classes – the
resolution of the contradiction inherent in the existence of
two modes of production in that social formation would,
necessarily, be brought about through a destruction of old
and, with the inevitable development of capitalism, the
triumph of the new. Given this framework, there is a
tendency to view the 'mode of production' as something that
is internal to a social formation, descriptive of a part of
it. In fact while the concept of social formation is a
descriptive concept, that refers to particular societies, the
concept of mode of production is a concept of an entirely
different conceptual level and cannot therefore be thought of
in the manner referred to above. Mode of production is a
concept that connotes various conditions of structure,
whereas social formation is a concept that denotes particular
societal entities. In the case of Lenin's Russia the
concepts of the two modes of production could be comprehended
within a discussion of that social formation as if they were
'internal' to it in some sense, unlike colonial societies
whose structures necessarily transcend the societal
(national) entities and their juridical boundaries. Russia
was not a colonised society. India is. We cannot
contemplate the structure of colonial social formations in
isolation from their imperialist integument. They are
subordinate to the metropolis. Subordination is a relation;
as such we will not find its full significance, structurally,
if we try to locate the relation of subordination exclusively
within the narrowed context of the subordinated colonised
social formation itself. The structure of the colonised
social formation, the colonial mode of production, in that
sense transcends the geographical and societal boundaries of
the colonised country, and necessarily so.

   Finally, I must clarify a major theoretical problem,
even if, for reasons of space, rather briefly. This relates
to the subsumption of both the small 'independent' peasant
proprietor as well as the rural economy based on production
by share-croppers and wage-labourers under the landowners
under the new, colonial, dispensation. Especially with
regard to the latter the question has been raised if we can
really appropriately designate the relationship of
share-cropping for non-cultivating landowners, as
'capitalist'. In fact the accepted convention amongst
Marxists in India is to equate sharecropping with 'feudalism'
and 'wage labour' with capitalism, in what I could consider

68

to be an empiricist interpretation of the concept of 'relations of production', that looks at the appearance and the form of that relationship, ignoring the underlying structural bases on which they rest. I would refer in this context to a debate on the mode of production in Indian agriculture which was not in effect a debate at all about the concept itself for it proceeded on the basis of the empiricist definition, except for one or two clarificatory or challenging interventions. Given these definitions the main argument was really about how far Indian agriculture had moved towards a capitalist basis. A bibliography will be found in my article "India and the Colonial Mode of Production", and I would refer in particular to the work of Utsa Patnaik, which represents the best of the writing expressing the point of view that I dissent from.[85] The question put to me whether I would not in fact recognise any difference in Indian agriculture as at the end of the eighteenth century and that in recent decades, is a fair one. And my answer is that I do recognise a very large difference. But that is not on the basis of supposedly different 'relations of production', as interpreted in terms of an empiricist interpretation of the term (I do not use the term 'empiricist' at all pejoratively) equating sharecropping with feudalism, but rather on the basis of conditions of reinvestment of the surplus and thus a transitiion from 'formal' subsumption' of production under capital to a 'real subsumption'. I must explain the theoretical basis of my argument.

As we have seen the structural basis of sharecropping before and after the colonial transformation was altered by virtue of the separation of the direct producer, the sharecropper, from the conditions of production, land. The 'feudal' basis of his relationship with the landowner was decisively ended. This formal subsumption of production under capital followed by real subsumption under capital, needs theoretical clarification. But first, before we proceed to the theoretical issues, which I will briefly explain below, I would point out some facts about the manner of disposal of the surplus that was extracted. As I have said, in the colonial mode of production the surplus is drained out of the colonial economy and transferred to the metropolis. In the early years of the colonial regime, say until the mid-nineteenth century, a very large proportion of the surplus from the land was thus expatriated and, as I have suggested, it led to an expanded reproduction of capital via the metropolis and, as I have tried to show above, it contributed very substantially to the rise of industrial capitalism in England. In later years that burden eased progressively, as the basis of the colonial exploitation shifted. However, for a time, much of the surplus that was left with landowners was reinvested not in agriculture but in urban property and other such avenues which were ancillary to the development of the new colonial economy and society. Nevertheless investment in agriculture was not insignificant in the latter half of the nineteenth century, in the course of expansion of production for the colonial market. New land was reclaimed and prepared for cultivation, wells were dug, the persian wheel replaced the old leather bucket method of lifting water (charas), new varieties of crops were experimented with and grown and so on. The process of investment in agriculture was continuous, with occasional periods of depression - especially the long depression of the Thirties. During World War II, the rich peasants and landowners made windfall profits and by the end of the war they had large liquid resources which they could not yet invest because the relevant input goods were not available until post-war shortages were overcome. But the pressure to invest was there and we find that large investments in Indian agriculture already got under way in the 1950s. Sulekh Gupta, in his article in Seminar of 1963 was already able to point out a category of "capitalist farmers", using data for 1956.[85] Thus by 1956 the 'capitalist farmers' in the sense they are understood in contemporary debates, were already a significant and identifiable group. Utsa Patnaik's work follows on and confirms Gupta's analysis - but she and others regard this phenomenon as entirely one of the very recent years; in doing so they underestimate the continuous movement towards real subsumption of agriculture under capital. It has been under way for a long time. It would not be very accurate to assert that until recently no investments were taking place in Indian agriculture.

Thus to return to the question of subsumption of agricultural production under capital, we need to clarify and consider Marx's conceptual distinction between 'formal subsumption of labour under capital' and the 'real subsumption of labour under capital' which I have referred to above. The formal subsumption of labour under capital must not be confused with Marx's references to antediluvian forms of capital, such as merchant capital, usury capital, etc., for this category refers to subsumption of production under capital. As Marx puts it, formal subsumption of labour under capital is "the general form of every capitalist process of production". The real subsumption of labour under capital entails the formal subsumption; but not necessarily the other way around.

The formal subsumption of labour under capital entails separation of the producer from the means of production and creation of free labour. It "does not itself imply a fundamental modification in the real nature of labour process, the actual process of production. On the contrary capital subsumes the labour process as it finds it, that is to say it takes over an existing labour process."[86] By contrast the real subsumption of labour under capital entails a rise in 'organic composition of capital', or an increase in capital intensity, and thus a rapid expansion in productivity that comes with capital accumulation and extended reproduction of capital. In conditions only of a form all subsumption of labour under capital, the limits of exploitation are marked by the limits of 'absolute surplus value'. With real subsumption of production under capital, the rate of surplus value rises rapidly with increase in relative surplus value.

Thus in India what followed the transformation of the medieval feudal economy by metropolitan capital was at first, as Marx outlines the process, a formal subsumption of labour under capital. The basis of the relationship between the landowner and the cultivator, the share-cropper was now a capitalist one. But there was not yet a major transformation of the production process itself - the progress towards real subsumption of labour under capital was slow to come. The nature of the colonial structure of extended reproduction, which entailed draining of resources to the metropolis, and the heavy reliance of the early colonial regime on land revenue, were major factors in the slowness of that process of transformation of Indian agriculture - though change was not wholly absent as I have indicated above. In recent years the changes have proceeded with great rapidity, a marked change that has come about representing a decisive acceleration in the movement from formal to real subsumption of labour under capital on a new scale. The answer to our problem thus lies not in representing 'sharecropping' as 'feudal', but in recognising the true nature of the changes that were brought about as a consequence of the colonial transformation and the subsequent shift in conditions of capital accumulation in agriculture.

My main object in this chapter was to identify the nature of the structural transformation of the Indian economy and society, that was brought about by virtue of the colonial impact. What follows from the analysis is that the colonial impact brought about a specific, colonial, type of 'bourgeois revolution' in the colonies, establishing a structure of specifically colonial capitalism. Given that structure, various internal developments follow in the process of the creation of a colonial economy. Certain sectors of the economy are destroyed and others developed, as part of the development of a colonial economy. Given the establishment of the necessary conditions for capitalist development, various institutions and above all a bourgeois (colonial) state and bourgeois law, indigenous capitalist development does get under way, inspite of resistence from the colonial regime to begin with and, especially from about the latter part of World War II and in the post-colonial period, in collaboration with metropolitan capital. But although the patterns of generalised commodity production and expanded reproduction of capital are modified as a consequence of such industrialisation, to some degree, the structure is not fundamentally altered after independence. In my 1975 paper I was wrong therefore to speak of a 'post-colonial mode of production'.[87] The structure of the colonial mode of production will not be transcended within the framework of peripheral capitalism and world imperialism for it is itself an aspect of the global capitalism of our times. But it is neither a universalised world of undifferentiated capitalism, as some tend to suggest, but a hierarchically ordered, colonial, capitalism which can be superceded not by national independence within the framework of world capitalism (with a 'dependent' relationship) but by a decisive structural break with it.

NOTES

1.   I. Wallerstein, "Three Paths of National Development in the Sixteenth Century Europe", Studies in Comparative International Development, No. 7 (1972). "Rise and Future Demise of the World Capitalist System: Concepts for Comparative Analysis", Comparative Studies in Society and History, Vol. 16, No. 4 (September, 1974).

2.   K. Marx, On Colonialism (Foreign Languages Publishing House, Moscow, 1960), p. 77.

3.   B. Chandra, "Reinterpretation of the Nineteenth Century Indian Economic History", Indian Economic and Social History Review, Vol. V, No. 1 (March, 1968), p. 41.

4.   B. Chandra, The Rise and Growth of Economic Nationalism in India (Peoples Publishing House, New Delhi, 1966), p. 94 ff.

5.   I. Habib, "Potentialities of Capitalistic Development in Mughal India", Journal of Economic History, Vol. XXIX, No. 1 (March 1969), pp. 32-78.

6.   ibid., p. 77.

7.   R. Mukherjee, The Rise and Fall of the East India Company (Veb Deutscher Verlag Der Wissenschaften, Berlin, 1958), p. 174.

8.   ibid., p. 212.

9.   B. Hindess and P. Hirst, Pre-Capitalist Modes of Production (Routledge and Keegan Paul, London, 1975).

10.   H. Alavi, "The Structure of Colonial Social Formations", unpublished, 1979.

11.   H. Alavi, "India and the Colonial Mode of Production", Socialist Register, 1975. (Also in Economic and Political Weekly, Special Number, August 1975).

12.   J. Banajee, "India and the Colonial Mode of Production", Economic and Political Weekly (6 December, 1975).

13.   R. Hilton (ed.), The Transition from Feudalism to Capitalism (New Left Books, London, 1976).

14.   ibid., pp. 33-56.

15.   M. Dobb, Studies in the Development of Capitalism (International Publishers, New York, 1975. First published

1946.), p. 35.

16.   I. Habib, The Agrarian System of Mughal India, 1556-1707 (Asia Publishing House, London, 1963), p. 110.

17.   Habib, "Potentialities...", p. 54.

18.   Habib, The Agrarian System..., p. 260.

19.   T. Raychaudhuri, "A Reinterpretation of Nineteenth Century Indian Economic History?" Indian Economic and Social History Review, Vol. V, No. 1 (March, 1968), p. 102.

20.   ibid., pp. 103-4.

21.   Habib, The Agrarian System..., pp. 123-4.

22.   S.C. Gupta, Agrarian Relations and Early British Rule in India: A Case Study of Ceded and Conquered Provinces, Uttar Pradesh, 1801-1833 (Asia Publishing House, London, 1963), p. 33 ff.

23.   N. Hassan, "The Position of the Zamindars in the Mughal Empire", Indian Economic and Social Review, Vol. 1, No. 4 (1964). Reprinted in R.E. Frykenberg (ed.), Land Control and Social Structure in Indian History (University of Wisconsin Press, Madison, 1969), p. 108 ff.

24.   Habib, The Agrarian System..., pp. 183-4.

25.   Hassan, p. 117.

26.   Habib, The Agrarian System..., pp. 129-30.

27.   ibid., p. 133.

28.   Hassan, p. 107.

29.   Habib, "Potentialities...", p. 47.

30.   ibid., p. 48.

31.   ibid., p. 36.

32.   A. Embree, "Landholdings in India and British Institutions" in R.E. Frykenberg (ed.).

33.   N.K. Sinha, The Economic History of Bengal, Vol. 1 (Firma K.L. Mukhopadhyay, Calcutta, 1961), p. 153.

34.   Quoted in R. Guha, A Rule of Property for Bengal: An Essay on the Idea of Permanent Settlement (Mouton, Paris, 1963), p. 177.

35.   K. Marx, On Britain (Foreign Languages Publishing House, Moscow, 1955).

36.   R.C. Dutt, The Economic History of India (Paul, Trench, Trubner, London, 1901), Vol. 1, p. 32-3.

37.   R. Palme Dutt, India Today (Victor Gollancz, London, 1940), p. 114.

38.   R.C. Dutt, Economic History ... p. 43.

39.   ibid., p. 51-2.

40.   ibid., p. xii.

41.   loc. cit.

42.   Habib, The Agrarian System..., pp. 75-6.

43.   Habib, "Potentialities...", p. 60.

44.   ibid., p. 61.

45.   H.K. Naqvi, Urban Centres and Industries in Upper India: 1556-1803 (Asia Publishing House, London, 1968), p. 85.

46.   C.M. Birdwood, The Industrial Arts of India

(Chapman Hall, London, 1880), p. 139.

47.   Habib, "Potentialities...".
48.   Habib, The Agrarian System..., p. 236.
49.   Mukherjee, p. 181.
50.   Naqvi, p. 142.
51.   Habib, "Potentialities...", pp. 67-8.
52.   Sinha, Vol. 1, p. 159.
53.   T. Raychaudhuri, Jan Company in Coromandel, 1605-1690 (Nijhoff's, Gravenhage, 1962), p. 141.
54.   E. Baines, History of the Cotton Manufacture in Great Britain (Originally published 1835, Republished as a second edition by Frank Cass, London, 1966), p. 75.
55.   I.C.A. Knowles, Economic Development of the British Overseas Empire (Routledge, London, 1924-36), p. 44.
56.   B. Krishna, Commercial Relations Between India and England, 1601 to 1757 (Routledge, London, 1924), p. 44.
57.   loc. cit.
58.   ibid., p. 64.
59.   ibid., p. 318.
60.   ibid., p. 126.
61.   D. Landes, The Unbound Prometheus: technological Change and Industrial Development in Western Europe from 1750 to the Present (Cambridge University Press, Cambridge, 1977), p. 82.
62.   Baines, Cotton Manufacture ..., p. 102.
63.   ibid., p. 106.
64.   R.C. Dutt, Economic History ..., p. 45.
65.   Krishna, Commercial Relations ..., p. 259.
66.   ibid., p. 263.
67.   Baines, Cotton Manufacture ..., p. 115.
68.   H.H. Wilson, The History of British India, 1805-1835, Vol. 1 (James Madden, London, 1848), p. 539.
69.   Baines, Cotton Manufacture ..., p. 330.
70.   R. Palme Dutt, India Today, p. 126.
71.   Habib, "Potentialities...".
72.   R. Palme Dutt, India Today, p. 127.
73.   D.R. Gadgil, The Industrial Evolution of India in Recent Times, 1860-1939 (Oxford University Press, Delhi, 1973), p. 41.
74.   E. Williams, Capitalism and Slavery (Russell and Russell, New York, 1961), Chs. 3 & 5 for the argument.
75.   F. Crouzet, Capital Formation in the Industrial Revolution (Methuen, London, 1972), pp. 7-8.
76.   A.G. Frank, World Accumulation: 1492-1789 (Macmillan, London, 1978).
77.   B. Chandra, The Rise and Growth ...
78.   P.J. Marshall, East India Fortunes: The British in Bengal in the Eighteenth Century (Clarendon Press, Oxford, 1976), p. 256.
79.   ibid., p. 262-3.
80.   Crouzet, Capital Formation ..., p. 23.
81.   ibid., p. 33.

82.   K.   Marx,   Capital,   Vol.   1   (Penguin   Books,
Harmondsworth, 1976), p. 1019.

83.   H. Cleaver, "The Internationalisation of Capital
and   Mode   of   Production   in   Agriculture",   Economic   and
Political Weekly, Review of Agriculture (March, 1976), p. A8.

84.   H.   Alavi,   "India   and   the   Colonial   Mode   of
Production";   Utsa   Patnaik,   "Capitalist   Development   in
Agriculture - A Note", Economic and Political Weekly, Review
of Agriculture, (25 September, 1971) and "Development of
Capitalism in Agriculture", Social Scientist, Vol. 1, No. 2
(September, 1972) and Vol. 1, No. 3 (October, 1979).

85.   S.C. Gupta, "New Trends of Growth", Seminar, No.
38 (October, 1962), pp. 15-29.

86.   K. Marx, Capital, Vol. 1, pp. 1019-21.

87.   H.   Alavi,   "India   and   the   Colonial   Mode   of
Production", pp. 192-3.

Chapter 3

SOUTH INDIA, NORTH INDIA: THE CAPITALIST TRANSFORMATION OF
TWO PROVINCIAL DISTRICTS

Peter Mayer

Introduction

One might be excused, given the extensiveness and consistency
of the existing literature on this point, for thinking that
questions regarding the pre-colonial forms of production in
Indian agriculture, the effects upon them of British colonial
penetration, and the nature of post-colonial social relations
in agriculture were ones for which the answers were
established beyond reasonable doubt.[1] Reduced to its
essence, the prevailing analysis of Indian agrarian relations
rests upon four fundamental propositions, some, or less
commonly all, of which are affirmed by the authors under
consideration here. The first of these is that pre-colonial
India was dominated by productive relations essentially
equivalent to those of European feudalism. The second, which
invariably is assumed as a tacit corollary of the first, is
that this feudalism was the only dominant or important
pre-colonial form of production. The third proposition is
that the pre-colonial relations of production and structure
of classes were not significantly altered by colonial
capitalism. And fourth, that capitalist relations of
production are still far from dominant in the rural sector
and either co-exist with feudalism or are to be found in a
mixed form of 'semi-feudalism'. Concurrence with these
propositions is so general, even among authors who agree on
little else, that some temerity is required of anyone who
would seek to challenge them. Nevertheless, that is what I
seek to undertake here, for I am firmly of the view that the
present consensus stands in the way of our establishing an
accurate understanding of pre-colonial India and of the
effects of colonialism on the evolution of classes in Indian
society. Let me begin the justification of my position by
tracing these propositions as we find them in the existing
literature.

Proposition 1: Indian Feudalism.

As Daniel Thorner has pointed out, one of the earliest uses of the concept of feudalism in the Indian context was James Tod's "Sketch of the Feudal System in Rajasthan" in his Annuals and Antiquities of Rajasthan.[2] Tod's analysis, which focused upon the appurtenances of power and the juridical expression of hierarchy, was sharply criticized by his contemporaries and consequently played little further part in the development of the idea of Indian feudalism.

The origins of the modern consensus are to be found in Stalin's 1938 essay on "Dialectical and Historical Materialism" which appeared as part of the widely circulated textbook History of the Communist Party of the Soviet Union.[3] In particular, it is here that we find the enunciation of Stalin's dictum that "Five main types of relations of production are known to history: primitive communal, slave, feudal, capitalist and Socialist".[4]

S.A. Dange's India from Primitive Communism to Slavery which appeared in 1949 was perhaps the earliest work to interpret Indian history within the terms of the new orthodoxy.[5] Although Dange did not carry his analysis beyond the first two stages, his frame of reference is made clear in the text:

> Human history has seen five stages of social organisation, all rising or vanishing according to the changes in the productive forces. These stages are known as primitive communal, slave, feudal, capitalist and socialist.[6]

One of the earliest, and still one of the most important, attempts to interpret the broad sweep of Indian history in Marxist terms was D.D. Kosambi's An Introduction to the Study of Indian History.[7] Kosambi argued that India has seen two periods of feudalism, the first of 'feudalism from above' in the millenium which preceded the Mughal Empire, and the second of 'feudalism from below' which characterized Mughal rule itself.

> Feudalism from above means a state wherein an emperor or powerful king levied tribute from subordinates who still ruled in their own right and did what they liked within their own territories...By feudalism from below is meant the next stage...where a class of land-owners developed within the village, between the state and the peasantry, gradually to wield armed power over the local population.[8]

Drawing upon the work of Gibbs, Kosambi takes the defining characteristics of feudalism, at least in its European form, as: 1) a low level of technique; 2) production for consumption, not for a market; 3) demense-farming; 4)

78

political decentralization; 5) land held on service tenures; 6) exercise by the lord of judicial functions.[9]

In considering the application of these criteria to the medieval period, Kosambi argues that there was a low level of technique, and that production was largely for consumption with but minor commodity production. While there was political decentralization in India, there was decidedly no demesne farming. He notes as well the conditional tenures, especially of the jagirdars and suggests the existence of a long tradition of judicial functions exercised by Indian lords. Indian feudalism was distinguished from its European form above all by caste which replaced both guilds and church and by the existence at certain periods of slavery.

Not only are there serious difficulties which arise when one seeks to apply these criteria to India, but their very idiosyncrasy sets Kosambi's work somewhat outside the mainstream of the work I am considering here. A more representative example can be found in Bhowani Sen's Evolution of Agrarian Relations in India.[10] Sen draws his definition from the brief section of Marx's third volume of Capital.[11] The defining characteristics of feudalism in Sen's analysis are:

Firstly, feudalism consists in the extraction of surplus labour or surplus product by extra economic measures. Secondly, the producer is in direct possession of the means of production. Thirdly, the direct producer is independent of the nominal lord of the soil. Fourthly, he is not a free-agent, though this lack of freedom may take a variety of forms, from the overt to the covert.[12]

Sen then proceeds to enumerate the specific forms of feudalism in land relations:

(1) Land is the private property of those who are not the tillers of the soil...(2) The means of production, required for agriculture, (other than land, of course) belong to the tillers, and not to the landowners...(3) The tiller of the soil, i.e. the peasant, is not a free labourer, but is tied to land...(4) Landownership is not free.[13]

When Sen comes to confront Mughal society, however, these formal criteria of feudalism vanish from sight and in their place we are offered the following characteristics of the Mughal system:

Firstly, land belonged to the peasant, in the sense that he enjoyed hereditary occupancy right if he was a resident of the village....Secondly, land could neither be purchased nor sold. Thirdly, the Zamindars whose tributes to the ruler were fixed were themselves petty

rulers and had to fulfil the traditional duties of a
ruler for the betterment of agricultural operations.[14]

The internal inconsistencies are sufficiently obvious, even
in this summary, as to require no further comment.
    A more recent account of Indian feudalism has been
offered by Prabhat Patnaik who suggests an underlying
similarity in pre-colonial India and Tokugawa Japan.[15]
Patnaik points to the following specific features of Indian
feudalism: i) the agricultural basis of economic life; ii)
appropriation of surplus through political-legal compulsion
by the landlord class; iii) the existence of a state acting
in the interest of landlords. He points as well to the
development of commodity production, to the emergence of
peasant rebellions and suggests that free from external
intrusion, India might have followed a developmental path
comparable to that of Japan.
    Undoubtedly the most systematic and successful attempt to
describe Mughal India in terms of a feudal mode of production
is that of Hamza Alavi.[16] Alavi makes an important
contribution to the debate by seeking to draw a synthesis
from the debates between Dobb and Sweezy. In particular he
seeks to include both Dobb's emphasis on coercion and
Sweezy's emphasis on decentralization. The criteria which
Alavi proposes to apply to Mughal India are these:

> (i)   Unfree labour...(ii) Extra-economic coercion in the
> extraction of the surplus...(iii) A fusion of economic
> and political power at the point of production and a
> localised structure of power...(iv) Self-sufficient
> ('subsistence') economy of the village (or the manor)
> commodity production being secondary for the direct
> producer...(v) simple reproduction...[17]

Proposition 2: Feudalism was the Only Significant
Pre-colonial Form of Production in India.   The validity of
this proposition cannot be demonstrated by direct quotation
from the literature. Like the 'curious incident of the dog
in the night-time' in Conan Doyle's Silver Blaze, whose
significance, as Holmes pointed out, lay in that he did
nothing, the validity of this proposition is necessarily to
be found in the absence of the discussion of any other
pre-colonial forms. Even the Asiatic Mode of Production, of
which I shall have more to say shortly, receives almost no
mention. And we must thus necessarily infer that feudalism,
and it alone, is generally understood to have characterized
pre-colonial productive relations in India.

Proposition 3: The Pre-Colonial Structure of Classes and the
Relations of Production were not Significantly Altered by
Colonial Capitalism.

Proposition 4: Capitalist Relations of Production are Still
far from Dominant in the Rural Sector. These two
propositions may be conveniently treated jointly. Taken
together they represent the orthodox position in what we may
term the 'mode of production in Indian agriculture' debate.
Since this debate has been discussed with admirable lucidity
by Doug McEachern, I will only summarize its essence and then
consider at somewhat greater length the notion of
'semi-feudalism' in Indian agriculture.[18]

The core of the debate revolves around the degree to
which capitalist farming can be said to have emerged in
contemporary Indian agriculture. It received its initial
focus in Ashok Rudra's conclusion, drawn from a study of
large farms in the Punjab, that none of the farms met his
proposed criteria of a capitalist farm.[19] In her criticism
of Rudra, Utsa Patnaik urged that his criteria themselves
were faulty, and that, in particular, neither production for
the market nor the use of hired labour could be taken as
indicators of the penetration of capitalism into the sphere
of agriculture.[20] Despite this, her fundamental
conclusions were not strikingly different from those of
Rudra. Like him she argued that capitalism has only recently
began to penetrate into the agricultural sector. In a
subsequent restatement of her position she enlarged on this
point, arguing that merchant and money-lending capital grew
with the rapid growth in commodity production "...to the
exclusion of capitalist penetration into agricultural
production itself."[21] In her view, "accumulation and
reinvestment" are necessary parts of capitalist
agriculture.[22]

Paresh Chattopadhyay in his turn criticized Utsa
Patnaik's formulations, particularly her insistence upon the
necessity of expanded agricultural production.[23] In
essence he urged that the essential indicator of capitalist
relations in agriculture was the existence of generalized
commodity production; the higher levels of productive ability
to which Patnaik pointed indicate "...only the higher level
of capitalist development, not the capitalist development
itself".[24] In analyzing Indian agriculture, though,
Chattopadhyay, like Rudra and Patnaik, accepted the general
proposition that capitalism has made only minor inroads into
earlier modes of production.[25]

In his analysis of the debate, Doug McEachern considered
not only the contributions of those scholars we have just
considered, but also the ill-fated attempt by Alavi, Banaji
and Barbalet to describe a 'colonial mode of
production'.[26] McEachern rejected the implication found in
the work of Patnaik, Chattopadhyay and in the notion of a
'colonial mode', that India is characterized by two modes of
production, one capitalist the other a feudalism changed
little or not at all by colonial capitalism. He also
underscored Chattopadhyay's point that the existence of

tenancy and share-cropping in themselves "...cannot be used to prove that agricultural relations were feudal or semi-feudal in character".[27] Instead he urged that the only satisfactory indication of capitalist relations of production is the existence of generalized commodity production which "...indicates that these various attributes are combined in the manner of a capitalist mode of production. This means that the emergence of generalized commodity production constitutes the demarcation point between the previous mode of production and the capitalist one".[28]

Implicit in the position of Rudra, Patnaik and Banaji, though decidedly not in that of Alavi, is the argument that colonial capitalism did not destroy the 'feudalism' which it found in India and that it either left it largely untouched or transformed it only marginally.[29] In one form or another, sometimes merely as an unexamined premise, revealed in passing, at other times examined explicitly, this position characterizes the majority of the analyses of the political-economy of contemporary India.[30]

From the late 1940s, the postulation of a class of 'feudal' landlords has been an essential element in the class analyses made by parties on the left and in the strategies pursued by them. The existence of an unfinished 'anti-feudal' struggle has usually been taken as an indication that there is an objectively progressive role to be played by the bourgeoisie and the Congress Party. E.M.S. Namboodripad, for example, writing in 1952, criticised the line adopted by the Communist Party of India four years earlier when it opposed the capitalist nature of Congress land reforms and refused to admit rich peasants into the kisan movement.[31] This was partially rectified in 1950, he argued, with the rejection of "...the slogan of 'rich peasant, the main enemy in the villages' and [the restoration of] the concept of anti-feudal struggle as the key task."[32] By 1952, with the identification of the struggle as one of two stages, the first being directed against feudalism and imperialism, Namboodripad urged the application of

> ...the lessons of the Chinese Revolution which through its agrarian reforms is carrying out a policy of deliberately building a rich peasant economy which means nothing but promoting capitalism in agriculture....[Following such a policy] It has thus become possible for us to work out a policy inside the organised kisan movement which, while it relies mainly on the proletarian and semi-proletarian elements in the countryside, will firmly unite them with the middle-peasantry and rally all the anti-feudal elements including the rich peasant.[33]

In more recent writing, the dominant trend has been to analyze Indian agriculture in terms of the persistence of 'semi-feudalism'. Perhaps the most influential formulation of this concept has been that offered by Charles Bettelheim in India Independent.[34] Bettelheim argued there that

> Whatever may have been the original nature of production relations in India, their result has enough of the characteristics of the declining feudal system to be called semi-feudal. Typical of the situation is the absence of a labour market in a large part of the rural sector; the personal subservience of the immediate producer to the landowner; the excessive importance of land rent; the underdeveloped marketing system resulting in little social division of labour, a low rate of accumulation, and the use of produce mainly to satisfy immediate needs.[35]

Bettelheim's formulations have been directly utilized by Paresh Chattopadhyay, who states that,

> On the whole, one must not be left with an exaggerated idea about the dissolution of the old mode of production - basically semi-feudal - and the development of the capitalist mode in Indian agriculture.[36]

And comparable points have been raised by Meghnad Desai:

> The Indian economy is by no means fully capitalist. Nearly 75 percent of the population is engaged in agriculture, which remains predominantly pre-capitalist in character, stamped by feudal and customary relations...There is little division of labour on a truly national scale. Except for engineering and heavy industrial goods, most commodities are traded only locally. There is as yet no national market in food-grains.[37]

Debt bondage, though not discussed by Bettelheim, is taken as a central aspect of 'semi-feudalism' by a number of authors. One influential formulation along these lines is that of Amit Bhaduri. Bhaduri suggests that Indian semi-feudalism has four principal characteristics: "(a) sharecropping, (b) perpetual indebtedness of the small tenants, (c) concentration of two modes of exploitation, namely usury and landownership, in the hands of the same economic class and (d) lack of accessibility for the small tenant to the market."[38] Indebtedness, Bhaduri argued, forces tenants to take consumption loans from their land lords and forces them to give most of the harvest to the landlord either as rent or interest.

Nirmal K. Chandra suggests that a crucial fifth factor in this syndrome of exploitation is the existence of "...massive underemployment in our countryside...[which]...helps to explain the stability of the semi-feudal relations..."[39]

A similar point regarding indebtedness is made by Pradhan H. Prasad:

The characteristic feature of this set-up which we may call semi-feudal, is that an indissoluble bond between the semi-proletariat and his overlord is maintained by resort to usury. It is precisely because of this that the landless agricultural labourers have been characterised here as semi-proletariat. The proletariat as a class is found in a capitalist set-up where it is free to sell its labour power. On the one hand, in a semi-feudal set-up de facto it is not free to sell its labour power. Only in a very narrow legal sense of the term can it be said that its involvement in the labour market is voluntary.[40]

One common theme, as we have seen, in all these approaches has been the question of the relationship between those parts of the economy which are clearly capitalist and those which seem to the writers to be something else. Premen Addy and Ibne Azad wrestle with the question in this way:

Throughout India the social relations of production combined a capitalist market on the one hand with pre-capitalist forms of exploitation on the other. Outside the towns, capitalism had scarcely penetrated the underlying process of production, yet at the same time it had introduced a qualitatively stronger market framework than had existed hitherto.[41]

Upon occasion the attempt to discriminate between what appears capitalist and what does not reaches rather ludicrous dimensions as in this account by Richard Nations of Pakistani agriculture:

The vast rural expanse of West Pakistan is dominated by large landlords, who form a traditional aristocracy and gentry, owning over 30 percent of the privately cultivated land. For although rapidly transforming the rural economy of large parts of Pakistan - particularly the intensively irrigated region of the Canal Colony in Punjab - capitalism has not developed through an antagonism between the class of kulak farmers and the old feudal orders. Capitalist and feudal modes of exploitation often coexist and complement one another on the same estate, and under the regime of the same landlord. These landlords extract both feudal rents and capitalist profits from their estates, which are tilled by combinations of dependent peasants and wage-labourers. The emergence of capitalism has thus fused into a social formation which reinforces rather than weakens the social power of the previously dominant classes.[42]

When the argument has reached this point, it should be clear that there is something very seriously amiss indeed; if a landowner can be both a feudalist and a capitalist, then a peasant may be a serf in the morning and a 'free' wage labourer in the afternoon. To understand why I maintain that the formulations which I have summarized above are seriously and fundamentally in error, it is necessary to retrace our steps and consider some concrete instances.

Pre-Colonial Forms of Production

<u>Mirasi Production.</u>   Let us begin this reconsideration by escaping from the 'north Indian chauvinism' which permeates so much of the literature on Indian political economy and turn our attention to the Carnatic plain on the eve of European penetration. Until very recently the presumption of an Indian feudalism has been applied equally to South India. The earliest such description I have found is Lionel Place's 1799 report from Chingleput to the Madras Board of Revenue in which he suggested that the political economy he found there bore "...so strong an analogy to feudal tenure that mankind when formed into societies seems to have been intuitively directed to it."[43] More recently, Levkovsky has suggested that the areas of South India which were brought under <u>ryotwari</u> settlement retained a "feudalized upper layer of the community" which was invested with certain land rights, with the state remaining as "... a kind of supreme landowner."[44]

In her earlier writings on Tanjore, Kathleen Gough also employed the term in a relatively loose way, suggesting for example that "Today, Kumbapettai has moved halfway in the transition from this relatively feudal subsistence economy to a much more wide-scale, expanding economy"[45].

Within the last decade there has been a revival of interest in Marx's notion of an Asiatic Mode of Production.[46] One of the first to seek to describe pre-colonial South India in terms of something like the Asiatic Mode was Hisashi Nakamura in his study of a village in northern Tiruchirapalli District.[47] Nakamura does not present a systematic account of pre-colonial productive relations, nor does he refer to specific Modes, but the social relations he outlines - production for use, the absence of private property in land, extensive irrigation and drainage works and village autonomy - point unmistakably to the Asiatic Mode.[48]

The most explicit identification of the political economy of the Carnatic as being fundamentally that of the Asiatic

Mode is to be found in Kathleen Gough's article devoted to "Modes of Production in Southern India"[49]. Though I shall wish to criticize this identification shortly as well as the misleading account of colonialism to which it gives rise, let me emphasize here the importance of this article in at least one major respect: it points, if only indirectly, to the need to acknowledge the clear historical evidence of widely differing forms of production in pre-colonial India. In Gough's view, the defining characteristics of Chola society were the absence of private property in land and the consequent equivalence of tax and rent[50], and a centralized state with a developed bureaucracy a major part of whose duties was the organization and control of irrigation. At the village level, Chola society was typified by joint possession of village lands by kinship communities of peasants who cultivated either the entire village collectively or shares of the village which were periodically exchanged. In addition to artisans, village specialists, servants and priests were state-owned slaves who were allocated to villages. It should be noted that Kathleen Gough neither describes these groups as classes nor elucidates her ideas about what the relations of production in Chola Society were. In the light of her insistence that the Chola Raja was the sole proprietor of the means of production we are perhaps justified in assuming that she is describing a society formally free of classes, even if it is "contaminated" by the existence of castes and slavery.[51]

In the succeeding periods of Vijayanagar and Maratha dominance Gough describes a progressive 'feudalization' of the political structure, marked by the emergence of military governors, enlarged temple estates, the emergence of managers of village estates, and a general increase in the amount of surplus taken by the state. Saving a breakdown in the customary redistribution of land shares, Gough argues that the joint village community remained intact up to the eve of European conquest.[52].

In what follows I shall show, using material from a single south Indian district, why I reject both the conventional use of feudalism and the more recent use of the Asiatic Mode of Production to characterize relations of production in this region. The district in question, Tiruchirapalli, lies athwart the broad channel of the Kaveri, from its descent into the plains to the point that it fans out to form the rich and lush Thanjavur delta. In the eighteenth century, as now, the lands along the Kaveri supported a density of cultivation and population which set them apart from those drier but more sparsely settled tracts which form the greater portion of the district and it is to those wet lands that I shall chiefly refer in what follows.

Land constituted the principal means of production in pre-colonial Tiruchi. What is striking, and in part definitive, is that this land was private, alienable property in a sense very much approaching the modern western one. In Tamil, this property was termed kaaNiyaaTchi and those who possessed it were kaaNiyaaTchikaarars.[53] By what appears to be an accident of history, it was not the Tamil but a Persian term, miraas, applied originally by the officers of the Nawab of Arcot during their occupancy of Tanjore in 1774, which was brought into English usage by Mr. Harris, the Company's first collector at Tanjore. This kaaNiyaaTchi, or mirasi property as we shall term it henceforward, could be bought, sold, mortgaged, lent and bequeathed without reference to or permission from the state, whose only concern was to see that taxes were paid.[54] The form of ownership, however, was often different. In its most characteristic form we find collective ownership of the village lands known either by the Tamil pasung-karei or the Sanskrit samadayam, in which a group of mirasidars (holders of miras) each held a fixed number of shares or parts of shares in the whole.[55] At periodic intervals the actual pieces of land which an owner cultivated were redistributed in a karei edu or lottery.[56] In short, ownership of the means of production did not refer to a specific piece of land but to a share in the land, much as a capitalist owns a share in a corporation.

As this collective utilization of the means of production implies, the organization of production was often collective. One can form some idea of the nature of the process from this brief description given by Mr. Hepburn, the Collector of the neighbouring district of Tanjore, in 1819:

One part of the proprietors attend the Tahsildar or Collector, and conduct the business of the Village there, another portion of them are agents with the grain Merchants, and disposing of the produce, and for that purpose resorting to the sea ports and large towns, another number is gone to the neighbouring districts to supply the wear and tear of cultivating cattle and the remaining stay at home to manage the cultivation and other interior concerns of the Village.[57]

Cultivation itself, especially in those villages for which we have the most precise information, the agraharam villages dominated by Brahmin mirasidars, was carried out by two principal non-owning classes. The first, parakudis, were hereditary tenants who cultivated under a variety of crop-sharing arrangements. These tenants were of two kinds, uuLakuuDii who were traditional village residents possessing hereditary rights of tenancy, and puurakkuuDii who were outsiders whose status was that of tenants at will. The second class consisted of agricultural labourers, drawn mainly from the Harijan Paraiya caste and untouchable agricultural slaves drawn principally from the Pallar caste, who belonged either to the village collective or to individual mirasidars.[58]

These slaves could in principle be brought, sold and mortgaged by the mirasidars. In general, only men could be sold with their families and slaves were usually sold with the land they cultivated. The economic surplus in Mirasi Production was extracted directly from the producers, in kind, at the harvest. The state received something between 45 and 50 percent of the paddy, the cultivating share-cropper/ parakudi (or alternatively the wages of the pallars, village artisans, village servants, and other costs of production if borne by the mirasidar himself) between 25 and 30 percent and the mirasidar between 20 and 25 percent.[59] Some villages were assigned to temples for their maintenance, and in such cases the government share went directly to the temple.[60]

These shares are those which the British found, following their displacement of the newly established Muslim states in Tiruchirapalli. It was the opinion of those British who comment upon it that the share of the surplus which went to the Raja of Tanjore was considerably less. T. Clark, for example, put the share of the state at between 10% and 12%; the cost of production at 27% and the profit to the mirasidars at 61%.[61]

The role of the traditional state, itself in retreat when the British arrived, has been a matter of some comment. In a recent article Burton Stein has argued that there is no evidence to support the commonly held view that the Tamil state exercised any managerial role.[62] Stein himself, however, offers no opinion as to how the role of the state should be understood. There are indications in his work and elsewhere, though, which point, however unclearly, to more plausible state functions. One of these was the coordination and organization of external defence.[63] A second function was that of preserving the private property basis of production.[64] A third state function may perhaps be found in the remark of George F. Travers who noted in 1811 that previously state officials had been employed to make hereditary slaves "... and other labourers exert themselves to the utmost to carry on the cultivation to the greatest extent. The case is now wid[e]ly altered..."[65]

Seen schematically, Mirasi Production rested upon the private property ownership of land by a ruling class which both directly organized production using the labour of slaves or free agricultural servants and received rent in kind from cultivating tenants. While the surplus received was in kind, land itself was unambiguously a commodity protected by a specialized part of the state. None of the producing classes, whether tenants, agricultural labourers or slaves, were owners of the means of production. We may see that this model of Mirasi Production thus differs at every point from those of European feudalism and the Asiatic Mode of Production.[66]

Mughal Production. The second example I wish to consider, Jabalpur District in the present day state of Madhya Pradesh, poses some useful difficulties. Located on the north bank of the Narmada, it was at the periphery of the Mughal Empire. As such, some of the features of productive organization which appear to be at variance with those associated with the more canonical forms of the Gangetic plain might initially suggest its inappropriateness for study. I shall wish to argue, on the contrary, that it is this very awkwardness which is most likely to force our reconsideration of the shibboleths of northern 'feudalism'.

In the early years of the Mughal dynasty, Jabalpur was ruled by tribal chiefs, the Raj Gonds, who remitted revenue to the central treasury. In the period immediately prior to British dominance, however, it came under the control of the outwardly expanding power of the Marathas. The ruling Raj Gond families were reduced to the status of large zamindars and the Maratha revenue administration was controlled by a group of Brahmin 'pundits' who settled in Garha, a small village on the southwest edge of the present city.[67] These 'Saugor Pundits' were assigned the revenue from numbers of villages in the district in lieu of pay.

The central class in the organization of the process of production were the malguzars [literally, payers of revenue] who served as village head-men or patels. Though they were formally responsible for the payment of revenue from the village and for the organization of production, it is quite clear from all the documents I have consulted that this essential position in the process of production conveyed no right of ownership over the means of production. C.A. Molony, the first British collector in the district, wrote in 1818:

> They [the malguzars] are not recognized as having any right whatever in the Land, but are held liable to removal at pleasure on suspicion of mismanagement, or on a higher offer being made. Of course their office [is] neither saleable or hereditary. In theory, the Potel appears to have partly the character of Agent, and partly that of a contractor...In practice, however, I apprehend that the engagement was entirely a contract...[68]

There are two points to be underscored here. The first is that the ownership of the means of production was clearly and unmistakably claimed and exercised by the state. As Molony adds further in his letter:

> Under the Mahratta Government I believe that the Potels had been very frequently changed, and when I arrived, the dispossessed Potels (whose Petitions the Provincial Government had got rid of by rather rash assurance that their claim would be investigated on the establishment of

a Civil Court) crowded upon me, with the hope of setting up a right in the land.[69]

The malguzar's role in the organization of production is perhaps most succinctly stated by Sir Richard Temple:

> The country had long been the theatre of war and invasion. Revolutions sweeping in succession over the land, had beaten down and destroyed the villages. On the restoration of peace, people returned to their farms in twos and threes. Men of rank, wealth and influence undertook to restore ruined villages, to re-settle husbandmen on deserted fields.[70]

A third essential feature of the process of production in pre-colonial Jabalpur was the collection by the state of its revenues in the form of cash payments. The contrast with south India, where as we noted, revenue was collected in kind, is sharp. The collection of revenue in cash implies necessarily the existence of commodity production on a limited scale, markets for those commodities, and a class of merchants dealing in the sale and transportation of those commodities.

What was arguably unique about the system which Molony encountered in Jabalpur was the extraordinarily central position played by the merchant class as a consequence of the way in which the Maratha state obtained its share of the surplus.

> The manner in which the Government secured its revenue was always by levying it in advance through the Sahookars and Mahajans [i.e. money-lenders and merchants] whose charge of interest formed of course, a heavy additional demand on the land. This system, has, at the same time, brought much of the land directly into the hands of the Soucars, who have frequently a number of villages in farm....under the Mahratta system, by far the greatest part of the Revenue was payable before...[the ravi] harvest. This...formed the security of the Government for the realization of the Revenue, and of course distraint or imprisonment were unnecessary. The Potels were necessarily kept by the plan entirely in the hands of the Mahajans and Soucars, who exacted enormous interest, and secured themselves by always attaching the Crops.[71]

Comparable interest was charged on the grain which the bankers lent as takavi to enable the planting and cultivation of the next season's crop to proceed.

The earliest accounts have little or nothing to say about the direct producers save that they, like the malguzars, had no property rights in land. Molony noted that tax assessed on a village limited the amount which the malguzar could demand from his cultivating tenants. For his role in organizing their cultivation and in assuming responsibility for the payment of the revenue, the malguzar was given 1/5th of the land of his village free from assessment. Nowhere have I found an estimate of how much of the gross produce was left with the direct producers.

How are we to understand what we find in Jabalpur, with a state monopoly of land ownership (relinquished, as we shall see shortly, only in 1863), a rapid circulation of village head-men and possibly of cultivators and an important if limited role for commodity production? What I shall be arguing here is that the process of production in Jabalpur is best understood as a local variety of a general form of production which I shall call Mughal Production.

When we come to look at the elements of Mughal Production, we find a somewhat paradoxical situation: although the overall form of Mughal agrarian relations is well known, our most authoritative sources do not agree on the interpretation of some of the most fundamental features. In these circumstances we must proceed from what is certain and move to what is less so.

At the apex of all, we have of course the Emperor himself, and surrounding him a class of nobles who between them received the bulk of the surplus production of the land.[72] The nobles were not a landed aristocracy but were rather the commanders of contingents of cavalry. These mansabdars were minutely ranked and graded according to the number of horsemen under their command and were assigned for short periods to areas or jagirs whose revenues were considered sufficient to support them. As Habib notes,

There was, therefore, an intimate connexion between the military power of the Mughals and the jagirdari or assignment system. It was the great merit of the latter that it made the mansabdars completely dependent upon the will of the Emperor, so that the imperial government was able to assemble and despatch them with their contingents to any point at any time, where and when the need arose.[73]

Habib has reported elsewhere evidence which indicates how enormous was the concentration of the agrarian surplus. Some 68 princes and nobles in 1647 received 37% of the total revenue of the Empire and are presumed to have had as their assignments one-third of its territory in their jagirs. Some 445 mansabdars in all were considered important enough to be tabulated separately in the records, and they received collectively 62% of the total revenue; of the remaining 38%, Habib estimates that between 25 and 30 per cent went to 7,555 small mansabdars who comprised the petty nobility.[74]

While we consider the surplus received by this class, we must note as well the form in which it was received. From as early as the end of the 12th century, peasants in the core region of the Empire were paying their land tax in cash.[75] By the time of the Mughals, the revenue demand in most of the Empire was stated in terms of cash. Though the existence of taxation in cash is by now one of the commonplaces of the Mughal agrarian system, its theoretical importance has not received sufficient emphasis in the literature.[76] In my opinion it is one of the central and defining features of Mughal Production. The origins of cash taxes is an area for speculation, though their advantages if not necessity for a highly mobile class of nobility seem clear enough. There can be no doubt about its consequences. The conversion of the agrarian surplus into money implies, first, widespread commodity production, markets for the sale of these commodities, and a mercantile class to effect the conversion and transportation of the grain. The fact that the merchant class was an integral and essential part of Mughal Production serves among other things to explain why this class did not develop the antagonistic role toward the existing form of production that their counterparts in Western Europe did.

When we turn to the villages and the direct producers, we find that we are less well served by our sources and many central aspects of Mughal Production are unclear. Let us begin with the 'awkward class' of pre-colonial India, the zamindars. Zamindar is an elusive term applied indifferently to the hereditary rulers of major territories, to important officials in the land revenue administration and to a very widespread and numerous class holding heritable rights over some portion of the surplus a number of villages, a single village, or even some specified parts of one village.[77] The latter were very much the most numerous, and it is with regard to them that the most important theoretical questions arise. While there is general agreement that zamindars of this sort - what Nurul Hasan terms primary zamindars - were hereditary, there is no clear agreement as to what the substance of that heritage was. Nurul Hasan states fairly categorically that,

> The primary zamindars were for all practical purposes the holders of proprietary rights over agricultural as well as habitational lands. In this class may be included not only the peasant-proprietors who carried on cultivation themselves, or with the help of hired labor, but also the proprietors of one of several villages. All agricultural lands in the empire belonged to one or the other type of primary zamindars. The rights held by the primary zamindars were hereditary and alienable.[78]

Irfan Habib is rather more circumspect. He points in the first place to the unquestioned existence of private property in urban land, as well as to claims to the ownership of villages or parts of villages.[79] He points as well to the undoubted fact of the sale of _zamindari_ rights.[80] But unlike Nurul Hasan he does not accept that a _zamindar_ had a proprietary right over land. "The possessors of _zamindari_ rights were not possessors of a visible article of property, like any other, but of a title to a constant share in the product of society."[81] In Habib's view, ordinary cultivating peasants had a title to 'permanent and hereditary occupancy' of their lands.[82] But this right did not imply, as Hasan suggests, the right of alienation.

> ...there was no question of really free alienation - the right to abandon or dispose of the land as its holder might choose - which is an essential feature of modern proprietary right. If in one sense the land belonged to the peasant, in another the peasant belonged to the land. He could not (unless, perhaps, he found a successor) leave it or refuse to cultivate it.[83]

On the face of it we would seem to be faced with an irresoluble conflict as to the nature of property in the Mughal system. Before I turn to ways of resolving the question, consider the following:

> An early settlement officer in a district of Oudh asked cultivators if they had an occupancy right to the land they tilled. They replied that they definitely did have an hereditary right of occupancy. The officer pursued his inquiries, asking if it were possible for the zamindar to evict a cultivator. The cultivators immediately replied that, of course, it was possible for a zaminar to evict cultivators: "The man in power can do anything".[84]

We have here, I think, the key to some of our difficulties. These Oudh peasants, like those Habib describes, have a right to the land they cultivate, one which is heritable but hardly alienable. If, on the other hand, the holder of such a right can be turned out of it by the _zamindar_ of his village, one can see the logic in Nurul Hasan's argument that "for all practical purposes" it was the _zamindars_ who should be seen as the proprietors. Indeed, one has only to extend the process upward to find a plausible explanation why European travellers of the time should have reported with such unanimity that the emperor was the owner of all the land in the empire.[85] I find great merit in Walter Neale's argument that in pre-colonial north India, the idea of land as something to be owned, if it was not entirely irrelevant, was very certainly subsidiary to the idea that land is an area over which authority is exercised.[86] Though I dislike Neale's chosen term for this, 'land is to rule', the recognition that local political domination was a prerequisite for zamindars is essential if we are to make sense of Mughal Production.

Irfan Habib recognizes this point with especial clarity when he traces the relationship between caste and zamindari.

> ...traditions describing the origins of local zamindari rights usually reveal a long process according to a set pattern: There is, first, a settlement by members of a caste or clan, perhaps dominating over peasants settled earlier, or, perhaps, peasants themselves. Then another clan appears, drives them out or establishes its dominion over them; and then still another. At some stage, if not from the beginning, the dominion of the victorious caste crystallizes into zamindari right, held by various leading members of it over different portions of the subjugated territory...we find that the one great instrument by which every caste established its possession of zamindari was the armed force it could command. Indeed, armed force appears as the first historical pre-requisite for the establishment, as well as the retention, of zamindari right.[87]

Habib goes on to note that every zamindar maintained armed retainers and most had small fortresses. At the core of the zamindar's armed power was the ulus which Habib plausibly suggests would have been drawn primarily from the zamindar's own caste.[88] If these loyal caste-fellows were in all probability mounted soldiers, Habib suggests, it was equally likely "...that the foot troopers of the zamindars consisted largely of peasants or villagers, impressed to serve their zamindars in times of need".[89] Lastly, let us note that this armed power was there not merely to be of service to the emperor should he require it, but at least in part to defend the zamindar from the innumerable challenges to his position made by rival members of his class.[90]

When we ask what zamindars did to justify the share, minor though it might be, of the surplus which they received, the answers we receive are less satisfactory. We are told that they were malguzars, that is, those who were responsible for paying the land revenue collected from the peasants to the state. In addition to their role as tax collectors, they were expected to maintain order if not law, within their territories. And of course, if necessary, they would have to supply troops for the imperial armies. Impressive as these obligations may appear, they fail to account for what is most material for our present enquiry: the role of the zamindar in the process of production.

Since this role is not discussed by those who have consulted the primary documents of the Mughal period, I shall rely here upon the Jabalpur materials to which I referred previously and to some complementary observations made by

94

Walter Neale. The situation in Jabalpur on the eve of British penetration, like that in much of the southern periphery of the empire was somewhat unusual. Decades of turbulence, incursions by rival armies, sporadic rapine and pillage by freebooters like the Pindaris had all combined to make fixed agriculture almost impossible; those peasants who survived had necessarily been forced to flee to areas of greater safety. When conditions of peace were restored what appears to have occurred is somewhat surprising, and thereby instructive. The 'natural community' did not spontaneously regenerate itself. On the contrary, it was necessary for malguzars (zamindars in all but their hereditary claim) to be recognized by the state for the organization of cultivation to occur. I would submit, though the present evidence for it is admittedly slight, that it is this managerial and organizational function which alone can explain why successive emperors found it necessary to tolerate and accomodate such a perennially dangerous and fractious class as the zamindars, of which undoubtedly they would have been only too glad to rid themselves.

Walter Neale suggests with great insight that for the zamindars the organization of production was not an end in itself, but that it grew out of and was inseparable from the political basis of their class position.

> Faction and village were the unit ideas of primary relevance. Security, fame, and respect resulted from effective management of people grouped in families and castes. To manage a village meant to manage people by manipulating the rules of their hierarchy. The farming of land was certainly necessary for the control of people because followers had to be fed or provision made to assure that they could feed themselves. A crucial difference between [English] estate management and [pre-British Indian] village management was that the estate manager maximized the net produce of his lands while the village manager maximized the number of mouths he fed...The improving estate manager employed land, labour, and capital to increase wealth; the village manager employed land, and did not employ capital, to increase the size and unity of his faction. Labour was an input for his farming operations; but his farming operations were also supposed to produce loyal people as an output. The association of estate were productivity, profit, efficiency; an estate was land viewed as an element in economic activity. The associations of mahal were faction, village, power, clientele; a mahal was land viewed as an element in village politics.[91]

Having come thus far, we stand at the point where we might figuratively breathe life into the model whose elements we have now delineated. But to appreciate it properly it is essential first to make a detour, however cursory and shallow into the literature critical of Marx's Asiatic Mode of Production.

As we saw before, the prevailing analysis of north Indian political economy from writers on the Left has been in terms of 'feudalism' or 'semi-feudalism'. Despite the remarkable revival in recent years of interest in Marx's own attempt to analyse pre-colonial India, there has been no serious attempt to apply the concept of the Asiatic Mode of Production to north India in the light of our present understanding of Mughal India; on the contrary, that knowledge has been used in several powerful essays to attack the fundamental basis of Marx's formulation. On my own reading of the matter, the prime object of Marx's interest in the subject was to explain what he understood to be the unchanging character of Indian society over long periods of time, the "...undignified, stagnatory, and vegetative life..." which was inherent in a society essentially outside of, or antecedent to, history, one locked into a "...never changing natural destiny...".[92] In the course of his writings Marx located the source of this immutability in the absence of private property in land, itself a consequence of climatically imposed, despotically managed, irrigation works, and in the self-sufficient nature of the village community.[93] The cellular nature of the village isolated it both from its neighbours and from the fortunes of the state. The state, both landlord and king, presided over the 'classless' "general slavery of the Orient".[94]

Marx's formulations on the Asiatic Mode of Production have been subjected recently to profound, and indeed unanswerable, criticisms. It is necessary to consider them here, not to recite Marx's errors, but because, in a paradoxical way, the criticisms point the way to a more satisfactory account of Mughal Production than those we now have. Of those who have undertaken a rigorous analysis of the empirical basis of Marx's account, undoubtedly the most important and influential has been Daniel Thorner.[95] Thorner demonstrated easily that the village community of Marx's description was not that characteristic of most of north India, and in particular that north Indian peasants did not hold or cultivate their land in common.[96] Thorner was equally forceful in his dismissal of Marx's analysis of the state.

> In point of fact, Marx's central thesis that the self-sufficient nature of the villages together with the need for large-scale centrally administered waterworks provided a basis for Asiatic despotism does not find much support in what we know today of Indian history. In India strong central governments have been rare and have not lasted long. Before the coming of the British there were only three great empires, the Mauryan, the Gupta and

the Mughal. None of these was powerful for more than 150
years.
    Agriculture in India has, of course, benefitted from
irrigation canals, but canal networks have never been the
outstanding feature of Indian crop production. Rather,
Indian agriculture as a whole has always turned on
rainfall and the local wells or ponds of the villages.[97]

    Perry Anderson in his consideration of the Asiatic Mode
of Production raises the additional questions of caste
inequality and the logical inconsistency of postulating
self-sufficient villages and a centralized 'hydraulic'
state. "...[public irrigation works of the despotic state]
precisely [involve] the direct intervention of the central
state in the local productive cycle of the villages - the
most extreme antithesis of their economic isolation and
independence".[98]
    The most sustained, though by no means the most
accessible, criticism of the Asiatic Mode, on purely formal
grounds, is to be found in the now repudiated Pre-Capitalist
Modes of Production of Barry Hindess and Paul Q. Hirst.[99]
To summarise their argument drastically, Hindess and Hirst
ask whether the mode of production described by Marx is
possible. Production they note was conducted entirely at the
village level, quite independently of the state. The state,
as both ruler and landlord, extracted revenue which though it
may be termed rent, is in fact indistinguishable from any
other form of taxation. Since production proceeds
independently of the state, Hindess and Hirst (ignoring
curiously Marx's early emphasis on the essential role of the
state as a provider of irrigation) conclude that the state
cannot be a part of the mode of production.

    In essence, the constitution of the tax/rent couple as an
    exploitative mode of appropriation of the surplus-product
    is possible only if the state is superimposed on forms of
    production which do not suppose exploitation or classes.
    The state has no necessity in this case, it appears
    suspended over society as a given without conditions of
    existence in society.[100]

Brief though this recapitulation is, it will, I hope, serve
for the purposes of the subsequent discussion.
    We have now in hand the elements which are necessary to
understand the structure and dynamics of Mughal Production.
Perhaps the clearest way to approach it is to examine what
Irfan Habib has called the 'agrarian crisis' of the Mughal
empire. Habib suggests that there was a tendency inherent in
the very nature of the assignment system which led jagirdars
to demand an ever-increasing portion of the agrarian surplus,
to the point that it deprived the peasants of their means of
subsistence.[101]   The   peasants   responded   to   this

encroachment on survival by defiance, banditry, flights to religion, sheer physical flight, and armed rebellion.[102] It is hardly surprising that this enhancement of the state's share of the surplus should have placed the zamindars in an intolerable position. The necessity of maintaining political support from their peasants placed very real limits upon the extent to which they could simply extract the enhanced revenue demand from villagers. Their possession of independent armed power made it natural that they should have been the leaders of armed resistance to the exactions of the state. This tendency to resistance could have only been enhanced by the perception of individual zamindars that the state, pace the suggestion of Hindess and Hirst, seemed to contribute little or nothing to the process of production, but merely took the lion's share of the surplus.

In other words, far from being immune to change there was a logical tendency within Mughal Production for the system to disintegrate. As disorder became widespread, the need to keep larger and larger armies in the field could only intensify yet again the pressures exerted by the state - and its opponents - for more money. Few have expressed the dynamics of the Mughal system in decline from the point of view of a minor participant better than Stewart Gordon who describes the career of a hypothetical adventurer in central India.

> He is presented at court...through the influence of a patron. Proof of ability leads to increasing numbers of troops under his control. The individual ruler he serves decides that an area, either unconquered or in a state of rebellion should be invaded. Our ambitious parvenu is given just enough money to raise troops, rather little since mercenaries furnished their own horses and equipment, and a "symbolic sanction", for example a sanad to collect chouth in the area, or the "right" to quarter his troops on the conquered lands. Invasion and plunder follow, with extortion of towns or villages which pay not to be plundered.
>
> He then comes to terms with local powers. This is meant quite literally. For example, the invading Marathas offered lower land revenues than the prevailing Muslim administration. The Rajputs switched allegiance quite readily. The invader needed to use them to collect revenue. The aid of these lower-level powers might be active, on the side of the invader, or passive, merely withholding aid from the formerly dominant power.
>
> The next stage - and it is a crucial one - is finding a banker to advance cash against future revenues. Until some banker considers the invader's claims legitimate enough and his prospects for collecting regular revenue bright enough, he is forced to plunder somewhere every few months to pay his troops, especially

if his "initial sponsor" makes no payments beyond the first one.[103]

At every stage in the process which Gordon describes, the adventurer is forced by the shortage of land revenue to attempt to increase the area under his control and the regularity of his administration or face the necessity of plundering one of his neighbours, with the risks that entailed, simply to pay his troops.

I dwell on this process because it affected and embroiled all power holders in the Mughal system from the small zamindar to the great prince. It is this universal involvement which exposes as clearly as any other example the 'fallacy of composition' in the argument that Indian villages were self-sufficient. The experience of peripheral areas gives reason for us to suppose that there were ultimate limits to the extent to which the process of disintegration could proceed. At a certain point production ceased, for its preconditions no longer obtained; if everyone has been forced to abandon agriculture and turn freebooter there can be no surplus over which to struggle. And it is here, where perhaps we least expect it, that we find the mechanism for the reversal of the process of disintegration, and discern the essential part played by the central state in the process of production. The re-establishment of central dominance constituted the political prerequisite for the recommencement of agriculture operations. Once secured, commerce and long distance trade could resume, and so forth, until rising revenue demands at some future point restarted the cycle of disintegration again.[104]

The model I have presented of Mughal Production is admittedly schematic and overly mechanical, but it accounts for the known facts in a far more satisfactory fashion than does even the most loosely constructed typology of 'feudalism' or the beguiling impossibilities of the 'Asiatic Mode of Production'. If we place it alongside Mirasi Production it is palpably obvious that the two forms of production differ at every significant point. I have not proceeded far enough in my research to be certain that these two forms typify the process of production in other intensively cultivated areas of India on the eve of colonial penetration; production in remoter tribal areas provides a minor but by no means trivial example of an additional form or forms of which we must ultimately take cognizance. Taken together, though, they serve to make the point that there was no single form of production which applied to all of India prior to colonialism and hence no single pattern of class forces which confronted colonial capital. Equally, it is my unshaken contention that neither of these forms of production can in any meaningful or useful way be equated with or assimilated to a notion of feudalism that makes sense of the European experience. I would urge that attempts to persist

in that mis-identification be seen as the Procrustean
ideological acts they are.

The Penetration of Colonial Capitalism

Mirasi Production. In a monographic paper presented
elsewhere, I have traced in some detail the stages by which
colonial capitalism transformed Mirasi Production in
Tiruchirapalli; what follows is a summary of the conclusions
I presented there.[105]
    The East India Company assumed direct control of
Tiruchirapalli in 1801 following the overthrow of the Nawab
of Arcot for having entered into seditious correspondence
with Tippu Sultan in 1799. Tiruchirapalli had never been
more than a peripheral and tenuously held Muslim possession
and at the point of its direct administration by the Company
there had been little change in the structure of mirasi
relationships. The assumption of direct rule by the Company
can be usefully seen as the termination of a brief and
inconclusive period of Mughal imperialism and the
commencement of a second, and in some ways still unfinished,
period of outside domination.
    The first collector, Mr. J. Wallace, reported finding
that, for as far back as record or memory extended, the state
had exercised a monopoly over the acquisition and
distribution of rice.[106] As a monopsonist it 'commuted'
its share of the surplus, which it acquired in kind, at a
fixed rate and then resold the grain to those needing to
purchase it at a rate approximately 25% higher. Wallace's
first positive action was to permit a free market in grain,
with the predictable result that the price of grain fell
almost immediately.[107]
    Wallace had rather greater difficulty in implementing his
second objective: the substitution of a money tax for the tax
in kind. The existing tax, even with the distortions
introduced by the Nawab of Arcot, had considerable justice in
it; the state, being entitled to a fixed share of the gross
produce, shared with the proprietor the risks of agriculture,
and whatever else might befall him, the landowner was at
least certain that he would be able to pay his taxes. Unlike
the traditional government, the Company could not pay its
servants nor its shareholders in grain; a conversion to a
money tax was imperative, and despite the gravest of
objections from the landowners, Wallace imposed a money tax
by fixing the 'commutation price' at which the traditional
share of the state would be henceforth expected in cash.
    The deep concern of the mirasidars was that the actual
price ruling in the newly established open market might be
lower than that at which their grain was 'commuted' into
taxes, and that they would have to make up the shortfall as
best they could. After ten years' experience with Wallace's
settlement it had become unavoidably clear that these fears

100

had been amply justified.[108] Perhaps the clearest indication we have of the elevated rate at which surplus was being extracted is furnished by C.M. Lushington in 1816 who reported to the Board of Revenue that if the entire disposable production of the district had been sold at prevailing market prices, it would have fallen short of the fixed government assessment by Rs. 62,000.[109]

The initial phase of colonial penetration covered some twenty years. During that time the indigenous recipients of the surplus had been replaced by an alien mercantile company, a money tax had been imposed and with it the necessity on the part of cultivators to produce commodities for sale in a free market. The inability of mirasidars to pay the elevated demand for land revenue set the stage for the succeeding phase in which the collective organization of production was dismantled. The process by which this occurred was most succinctly stated by H. Dickinson in 1827:

> In the wet Talooks of the District a practice used universally to prevail of the inhabitants of each village at fixed periods to change the lands which they held between themselves.[110] The ceremony was denominated Curray Edoo and it was conducted on the principles of a lottery, the several portions of land being written on tickets, and they drawn by the inhabitants who until the time of the next Curray Edoo each enjoyed the land according to which he might draw a ticket. In some villages this practice still continues, but in others it has been abolished, and loud complaints are in consequence made of this infringement of custom.
>
> In the villages in which the Custom does not now prevail I find that at some period or other since the Country fell under the Company's Government portions of land have been sold, under the Regulations, on account of balances due by the inhabitants who held them, and that the persons who purchased them whenever it has been proposed that a general Curray Edoo should be performed have objected to it, alleging that when they purchased those lands they made no stipulation that they would ever resign them under the chance of obtaining land of an inferior quality for them...the discontinuance of the practice appears to me to be a cause of much discontentment among the old inhabitants of those villages.[111] (emphasis added)

Dickinson's evidence unambiguously shows that it was the creation of commodity production by colonial capitalism in Tiruchirapalli which led to the destruction of the collective management of production there. To locate this transformation, as Kathleen Gough does, in the pre-colonial period necessarily yields a seriously distorted account of the impact of colonialism.

The sale of collectively held village lands for failure to pay the revenue demand was followed by the introduction in 1827 of a ryotwari settlement in which individual mirasidars, rather than the village as a whole, were held responsible for the payment of revenue on the lands they then held. In 1833 the lands of individual revenue defaulters were first put up for sale. By the end of the 1830s the new settlement had completely undermined the traditional forms of land tenure and, in many cases, the traditional organization of production. By 1907 all vestiges of corporate tenure had disappeared save the joint ownership of dry lands in some riverine villages.[112]

The next aspect of Mirasi Production to be affected by colonial legislation was the dependence, especially of Brahmin mirasidars, upon the labour of hereditary slaves. In 1843 the Company formally outlawed slavery in India. The immediate effect of the law at the district level was, as one might expect, minimal. But over the succeeding decades the impact of the legislation was to force mirasidars to convert their hereditary ownership into a form of dominance based upon debt bondage, the padiyal indenture, which was enforceable in the Company's courts under the Breach of Contract Act.[113] If one searches for the material motives behind the Company's concern for the welfare of slaves, they are not far to seek. This third phase was one in which there was extraordinary growth both in commercial agriculture in the coffee, and later tea, plantations of south India and Ceylon and in the construction of numerous infrastructural public works, most notably the railways. Both of these were heavily dependent upon inputs of labour and both of them drew away large numbers of those who had been previously hereditary slaves or tenant farmers, to the extent that one finds complaints by landlords from the 1850s onward of the scarcity of labour.[114]

If we summarize the first sixty years of colonial rule in Tiruchirapalli, we can see the imposition of commodity production, the destruction of traditional forms of productive organization and the forcible freeing of hereditarily bound labour. Decisive as each of these changes was, indeed taken together we can hardly think of them as less than revolutionary, their visible effects upon social organization were paradoxically subtle. To understand why this was so we have to look at the way in which Mirasi Production was undermined and transformed. Commodity production, for example, had existed in a minor form, especially in the dry areas of the district under Mirasi Production; its extension and gradual generalization in the wet areas did not lead to the dominance of new classes but was rather adapted to by the existing mirasidars.[115] The prime reason for the success with which the existing class of mirasidars adapted to the changed relations of production lies undoubtedly in the fact that both Mirasi Production and

colonial capitalism rested upon a base of private property
ownership of land. Although many villages along the Kaveri
practised collective agriculture and held their lands
collectively, instances of separate tenure were certainly
known and denoted by indigenous terms. The ryotwari
settlement, while it destroyed the joint holding of village
lands and the collective process of production where it
existed, served to convert all land into a single, but known
and pre-existing, form. In a similar way, the legal freeing
of slaves and the absorption of many of them into public
works and plantation agriculture did not produce a revolution
in social relationships in the villages. As we have seen,
though hereditary bondage and the right to sell slaves was
abolished, capitalist laws and institutions were used to
regulate the labour force. One of the most important
benefits of this analysis is that it makes clear that the
existence of a large class of agricultural labourers and
tenants-at-will in the colonial period was one of the few
crimes which cannot be laid at Britain's feet.[116] As we
have seen, both of these classes existed in, indeed were
integral to, Mirasi Production; capitalism certainly 'freed'
them, but it did not create them.

In sum, though the composition of indigenous social
classes remained basically unchanged, the penetration of
capitalism in this period decisively transformed the nature
of their interrelationship. The retention of many
pre-existing forms of dominance and deference in the
relationships between castes represents the inevitable
continuation of pre-conquest forms of exploitation. But it
is a serious error to confuse the fact that the new society
bore many features of the pre-conquest form from which it was
forcibly created, with the continued persistence of the old
form itself. By 1860 one can no longer speak of Mirasi
Production in Tiruchirapalli, save in a historical sense, for
it no longer existed; what we have, albeit in its infancy, is
colonial capitalism.

Mughal Production.   It is difficult to trace the
penetration of capitalism in Jabalpur in great detail. Early
settlements were made for a number of years at a time and we
lack therefore the detail which emerges from annual reports.
In addition, a number of important revenue documents once
held in the Board of Revenue's Collections at the India
Office Library, were culled and destroyed by nineteenth
century archivists. Despite this, the broad outlines are
easily discerned.

The production of commodities, as we have seen, was an
integral part of Mughal Production. The first and most
obvious transformation which occurred under British rule was
the intensification of the existing level at which it
occurred. Whereas under the Marathas a certain portion of
the revenue had been collected by the troops of the army

directly in kind, now the entire revenue was demanded in cash. This increased requirement for specie was coupled with an overall decline in demand as a result of the massive reductions in armed forces which followed pax Britanica; the short-term result was an agrarian crisis, as a result of which many peasants and malguzars were impoverished. Among the first instructions Molony received from Calcutta was one directing him to undertake "...the removal of all artificial obstructions to the free transport or sale of agricultural produce, such as transit duties or the like."[117]

The surviving documents say little about the condition of agricultural labourers. It seems safe to say that their 'liberation' occurred with the collapse of central order in pre-colonial period. Contending armies forcibly dispersed villagers from the traditional ties which held them to the land. It was only after order had been reimposed following the triumph of the East India Company's armies that abandoned villages were resettled. Though we may date formal freeing of labour from the 1820s, there seems to have been little capitalist demand for labour from this region until the third quarter of the nineteenth century when railway construction, cotton mills and systematic recruitment to the Assamese tea plantations began.[118]

The overall transition to generalized commodity production occurred quite slowly in Jabalpur, and we can usefully distinguish two broad stages which spanned nearly 40 years. The principal change which occurred in the first period was the introduction of a capitalist legal structure, especially the law of contract. In other parts of north India, this introduction was specifically coupled with the creation of private landed property which undercut and destroyed the essentially political basis of land control. As Bernard Cohen has shown for the area around Benares, the conversion of land into a commodity produced a revolution in the rural class structure, with some 40% of land changing hands in the 50 years following the Permanent Settlement of 1795.[119]

In Jabalpur, rather unexpectedly, the colonial government retained the existing state monopoly in land ownership which it had inherited. As a consequence, malguzars were unable to offer land as a security for loans and instead had to put up their malguzari rights as security in case of default. Thus village management, rather than the means of production, was transformed into a commodity in this period. The result of this was this was that the names of an increasingly large number of merchants began to appear in the government registers as village lessees. Though the government disliked this change, it found itself unable to reverse it. R. Low, writing in 1834 to the Bengal Sudder Board of Revenue, noted that,

104

Such transfers however much they were to be regretted could hardly have been prevented and would certainly have occurred to much greater extent, under the more fixed unrelaxing system of Revenue Management in the Regulation Provinces. At the present I should propose to get rid of all such men when it can be done properly and with due attention to their rightful claims, but there are many cases in which it cannot be done without injustice, and in which their leases must be renewed.

The manner in which these Murwary [Marwari] Merchants chiefly oppress their Cultivators is, by the usurious interest of 24 per cent which they demand from them on all advances of money made for cultivation or other purposes, but in this respect I am sorry to say they are generally imitated by all the other Malguzars of the Country.[120]

For the merchant and money-lending class, the penetration of colonial capitalism represented an unprecedented liberation from the political bonds to which they had been subjected under Mughal Production. Like the rising bourgeoisie in Europe their interest in gaining the landed property hitherto closed to them went deeper than the profits to be made in money-lending. "One feature", Maurice Dobb observed of the English merchant class, "...that is at first as surprising as it is universal, is the readiness with which this class compromised with feudal society once its privileges had been won".[121] It finds its echo in H.R. Crosthwaite's report, submitted in 1912, in which he noted that for these "...men of business...[the] desire to acquire landed interests arose (as M. Joseph Chailly has so accurately observed) chiefly from the fact that rights in land give to their possessor special social prestige."[122]

The admixture of class interest and compromise is most clearly seen in the career of Seth Kusal Chand, an important Marwari merchant of the mid-nineteenth century. It is not known exactly when the family moved from Jaisalmer in Rajasthan to Jabalpur, but it was at some time before the town came under British control in 1817, by which time the family was already in possession of a number of villages in the district. The family's rise to social and economic dominance derives directly from the period of the 1857 'Mutiny', when colonial capitalism was assaulted by a proto-nationalist movement, led by the displaced dominant classes of Mughal Production.

In the darkest period of the Mutiny of 1857, when others held back, Seth Kusalchand...advanced a large sum of money for the purchase of cavalry horses to Major Erskine on his simple note of hand. He also furnished supplies for a column in the field in the height of the rains of 1857 when these could not otherwise have been obtained. In addition, he lent large sums of money to enable the authorities at Allahabad to find transport for the several columns advancing for the relief of Lucknow. His villagers also helped to capture and destroy bands of rebels.[123]

In the course of time, Seth Kusal Chand was rewarded by the British with the malguzari of a number of villages, some held free of rent, numerous rights and privileges. His son, Gokul Das, was rewarded for his numerous public benefactions with the personal title of 'Raja'. Despite his 'Rajput' title, a commanding palace erected in the centre of Jabalpur and the other marks of landowning gentility, commerce remained the primary source of his influence and power. In 1909, the District Gazetteer noted that,

> The family now possesses 158 villages in the Jubbulpore District... In addition they have valuable landed property in many other districts of the Province. The family is very influential on account of its vast banking business which is carried on by a net-work of shops scattered throughout the Province.[124]

The adoption of 'Rajput' titles and manners by other, less prominent, mercantile families could be easily illustrated if space permitted.

The final transition to capitalist relations of production began in 1863 when the colonial state abolished its monopoly in land ownership and bequeathed it as a private property right upon the existing malguzars.[125] The development of the railways in the 1870s connected the district directly with the world market and in the late nineteenth century 'wheat boom' large quantities of wheat were shipped annually to Britain and Italy.[126] The transition to generalized commodity production produced, inevitably, a further strengthening of the position of dominance of the merchant class over the countryside and involved them increasingly in direct production.[127] As Crosthwaite summarized in his 1912 report,

> The records of the district show that prior to 1834 villages seldom remained long in the same hands. [Between 1834 and 1863]...about 25 percent of the villages changed hands, the common reason being indebtedness. Between 1863 and 1893, 16 percent of the villages changed hands, and this percentage would have been much higher had it not been for the Court of Wards. Again, the general reason for transfer was indebtedness.[128]

Not only do we find an increasing separation of direct producers from the ownership of land, we also find that the concentration of capital in merchant hands provided the basis of industrial investment. This is well illustrated by Raja

106

Gokul Das. In 1885 he established the Gokuldas Ballabhadas Spinning Weaving Mills which employed some 700 men, women and children. In 1905 he founded the Perfect Pottery Co. Ltd. In addition to these he established many cotton ginning and pressing factories in the Central Provinces and in the adjoining United Provinces.[129]

Mode of Production and Class

We have, now, travelled widely in space and time: but to what end? I believe that we are now in a position to consider critically the propositions of the prevailing wisdom regarding Indian classes, with which we began. I have tried to indicate that rather than one single, all-embracing mode of production, India on the eve of colonialism was characterized by at least two major forms of production. Those I have described here, Mughal Production and Mirasi Production were utterly unlike in structure, antagonistic and incompatible in interaction. Taken together they demonstrate that the assumption of a single, pre-colonial form of production is not merely drastic, but fundamentally misleading. Prescriptively, the need for detailed regional descriptions of pre-colonial production is, at least to me, both clear and urgent.

My evidence has also indicated the grounds on which I reject the characterization of either of the forms I have described in terms of European feudalism. It is on that basis that I consider those analyses which take feudalism as their point of departure to be simply wrong and, by this catechresis, incapable of describing with either accuracy or insight the complex process by which the pre-colonial forms of production were transformed into the present constellations of class forces we find in contemporary India. The same, I am sure, applies to much of the rest of the Third World.

If there is no feudalism, in a narrow definitional sense there can be no feudal remnants and no semi-feudalism. But it will be now be evident that my argument is far broader than this. In the areas which I have studied, and, I am confident, in most of the rest of India as well, by the second half of the nineteenth century capitalism was not merely dominant, but it had irreversibly destroyed the basis of the pre-existing forms of production which it had conquered. From that period onward traditional ruling classes, where they survived, cannot be understood in terms of the old relations of production; mirasidar and malguzar alike are involved in capitalist relations of production. After that period there are no 'feudal' classes against whom an 'anti-feudal' struggle can be waged; after that period debt-bondage, imperfect access to the market whether as sellers of commodities or of labour, all of these make sense not in terms of 'semi-feudalism' but only in terms of the specific way in which capitalism developed in India.

Thus in central India the pivotal role of merchants and money-lenders in the pre-colonial mode of production largely explains how, within the limits of colonial hegemony, they were able to secure increasing domination over land and agricultural production. This is a development that, almost certainly, would not have occurred without colonial intervention. Equally, we can see the way, especially from the 1870s onward, labour becomes a commodity. The movement of labour to the Assamese plantations and into the newly established urban factories demonstrates that the demand for this commodity was 'continental' in scale and that the 'formal subsumption' of labour to capital was followed almost immediately by its employment in industrial production both rural and urban.

The contrasts with Tiruchirapalli are instructive. Though colonial capitalism in south India destroyed the collective basis of production, it did not create a new property-owning class. The principal reason for this was the basic compatibility between Mirasi Production and capitalism in terms of land ownership. The generalization of commodity production was thus more subtle in its visible effects. In Mirasi Production the village mirasidars themselves had undertaken the transportation and sale of grain to the state's granaries, and merchant capital played at best an insignificant part in production. This was but little altered by the capitalist transformation and merchant capital as a consequence did not come to dominate agricultural production as it did in central India. The steady overseas demand for labour from industrial agriculture in Ceylon, Malaya and elsewhere put pressure on land owners to tie labour down, and it was this which produced the 'debt bondage' which is so often interpreted, not as the modern form of labour relationship that it was, but as a form of traditional domination.

If we accept that 'feudalism is dead' what follows is that there was no single structure of classes which confronted colonial capitalism or which emerged under its patronage. Rather, each distinctive form of production interacted with colonial capitalism in a complex matrix formed by social relations on the one hand and the changing nature of capitalism on the other.

NOTES

1. The research reported here was conducted under study leave grants from the University of Adelaide. I wish to thank Doug McEachern for his comments on an earlier draft of this chapter.
2. See James Tod, Annuals and Antiquities of Rajast'han, or the Central and Western States of India (Routledge and Kegan Paul, London, 1972) and Daniel Thorner, "Feudalism in

India" in Rushton Coulborn (ed.), Feudalism in History (Princeton University Press, Princeton, 1956), Ch. VII. I am particularly interested here in those arguments which identify the period immediately preceding colonialism as feudal and am not, therefore, considering works such as R.S. Sharma's Indian Feudalism, 300-1200 (University of Calcutta, Calcutta, 1965), nor approaches such as Dipankar Gupta's interesting monograph "From Varna to Jati: The Indian Caste System from the Asiatic to the Feudal Modes of Production", (Centre for Developing Area Studies, McGill University, Montreal, July 1978) Working Paper Series, No. 22.

In this discussion I shall adopt the characterization of feudalism developed by Doug McEachern in Chapter 1. Specifically, I shall take the following to be the defining characteristics of European feudalism: i)proprietorship of the means of production divided between direct producers and the landed ruling class; ii)land not a commodity; iii)initiation and organization of production by the landed ruling class; iv)labour formally unfree but not a commodity owned by the ruling class (i.e. 'bond men' not slaves); v)an unspecialized state, with most aspects of state power, including that of the military, exercised by the local landed ruling class.

3. See for example Bruce Franklin (ed.), The Essential Stalin (Anchor Books, Garden City, N.Y., 1972), pp. 300-333. Irfan Habib suggests that the line emerged out of the 1931 Leningrad debates. See, Irfan Habib, "Problems of Marxist Historical Analysis", Enquiry (Delhi), N.S., Vol.III, No.2 (Monsoon, 1969), pp. 59-60. I am grateful to Tapan Raychaudhuri for calling this to my attention.

4. Ibid., p. 323. It is striking that as late as 1940, R. Palme Dutt in India Today (Victor Gollancz, London, 1940) proceeded from Marx's work on the Asiatic Mode of Production, which led him to ask, directly, "Why, then, did primitive communism in the East not develop to landed property and feudalism, as in the West?" (p. 94)

5. S.A. Dange, India from Primitive Communism to Slavery (People's Publishing House, Bombay, 1949).

6. Ibid., p. 15.

7. D.D. Kosambi, An Introduction to the Study of Indian History (Popular Book Depot, Bombay, 1956).

8. Ibid., p. 275.

9. Ibid., p. 326-9.

10. Bhowani Sen, Evolution of Agrarian Relations in India (People's Publishing House, Bombay, 1962).

11. Marx, Capital, Vol. III, Part VI, Ch. XLVII, "Genesis of Capitalist Ground-Rent".

12. B. Sen, Evolution..., p. 42.

13. Ibid., pp. 45-46.

14. Ibid., pp. 55-56.

15. Prabhat Patnaik, "On the Political Economy of Underdevelopment", Economic and Political Weekly, Vol. VIII, Nos. 4-6 (Annual Number, 1973), pp. 197-212.

16. Hamza Alavi, "The Colonial Transformation in India", Chapter 2 of this volume. See also Alavi's earlier discussion in "India and the Colonial Mode of Production", Economic and Political Weekly, Vol. X, Nos. 33-35 (Special Number, 1975), pp. 1235-1262.

17. Alavi, "Colonial Transformation...", p. 17. Harbans Mukhia's "Was There Feudalism in Indian History?", which rejects the applicability of European feudalism to India, appeared too late to be discussed in the body of this chapter. See, Journal of Peasant Studies, Vol. 8, No. 3 (April, 1981), pp. 273-210. I am grateful to Peter Burns for calling this to my attention. Ashok Rudra's "Against Feudalism", Economic and Political Weekly, Vol. XVI, No. 52 (December 26, 1981), pp. 2133-2146 appeared as this chapter was being set in type. I am indebted to Prof. S. Ambirajan who drew it to my notice.

18. Doug McEachern, "The Mode of Production in India", Journal of Contemporary Asia, Vol. 6, No. 4 (1976), pp. 444-457.

19. Ashok Rudra, A. Majid and B.D. Talib, "Big Farmers of the Punjab", Economic and Political Weekly, Vol. IV, No. 39, (September 27, 1969), pp. A-143--A-146; "Big Farmers of Punjab", Vol. IV, No. 52, (December 27, 1969), pp. A-213--A-219. "In Search of the Capitalist Farmer", Vol. V, No. 25 (June 20, 1970), pp. A-85--A-87.

20. Utsa Patnaik, "Capitalist Development in Agriculture: A Note", Economic and Political Weekly, Vol. VI, No. 39 (September 25, 1971), pp. A-123--A-130.

21. Utsa Patnaik, "On the Mode of Production in Indian Agriculture", Economic and Political Weekly, Vol. III, No. 40 (September 30, 1972), pp. A-145--A-151.

22. Ibid., p. A-148.

23. Paresh Chattopadyay, "On the Question of the Mode of Production in Indian Agriculture: A Preliminary Note", Economic and Political Weekly, Vol. VII, No. 13 (March 13, 1972), pp. A-39--A-46.

24. Ibid., p. A-45.

25. Ibid., p. A-44.

26. McEachern, "The Mode...", p. 451.

27. Ibid., p. 450.

28. Ibid., p. 452. Significantly, he adds that he has not sought to work out "...How to identify the point at which commodity production becomes generalized."

29. Alavi, "India and the Colonial Mode..." pp. 1257-8, explicitly rejects the a priori assumption of a persistence of feudalism in agriculture.

30. See for example "A Correspondent" who characterized Indira Gandhi's strategy during the Emergency as representing an attack on semi-feudalism, as a form of "...anti-feudalism without anti-imperialism...". "The Emergency in India", Bulletin of Concerned Asian Scholars, Vol. 7, No. 4 (Oct.-Dec., 1975), pp. 5-6. It need hardly be added that such

examples could easily be expanded by an order of magnitude.

31. E.M.S. Namboodripad, On the Agrarian Question in India (People's Publishing House Ltd., Bombay, 1952), p. 26.

32. Ibid.

33. Ibid., p. 27.

34. Charles Bettelheim, India Independent (Monthly Review Press, New York, 1968).

35. Ibid., p. 23.

36. Paresh Chattopadhyay, "Some Trends in India's Economic Development" in K. Gough and H.P. Sharma (eds.), Imperialsm and Revolution in South Asia (Monthly Review Press, New York, 1973), p. 113. Chattopadhyay urges there that the existence of wage labour is the best evidence of capitalist penetration in agriculture, p. 112.

37. Meghnad Desai, "India: Emerging Contradictions of Slow Capitalist Development" in Robin Blackburn (ed.), Explosion in a Subcontinent (Penguin Books, Harmondsworth, 1975), pp. 23-24.

38. Amit Bhaduri, "A Study in Agricultural Backwardness under Semi-feudalism", The Economic Journal, Vol. 38, No. 329 (March, 1973), pp. 120-121. See also A. Bhaduri, "An Analysis of Semi-Feudalism in East Indian Agriculture", Frontier, (September 29, 1973), pp. 11-15. The empirical validity of Bhaduri's analysis has been severely undercut by the work of Pranab Bhardan and Ashok Rudra who note that bonded labourers "...do not seem to be significant at all in West Bengal". "Types of Labour Attachment in Agriculture: Results of a Survey in West Bengal,1979", Economic and Political Weekly, Vol.XV, No.35 (August 30, 1980), p. 1478.

39. Nirmal K. Chandra, "Farm Efficiency under Semi-Feudalism: A Critique of Marginalist and some Marxist Formulations", Economic and Political Weekly, Vol. IX, Nos. 32-54 (Special Number, 1974), p. 1327.

40. Pradhan H. Prasad, "Reactionary Role of User's Capital in Rural India", Economic and Political Weekly, Vol. IX, Nos. 32-34, (Special Number, 1974), p. 1305.

41. Premen Addy and Ibne Azad, "Politics and Society in Bengal" in Robin Blackburn (ed.), Explosion ..., p. 127.

42. Richard Nations, "The Economic Structure of Pakistan and Bangladesh" in Robin Blackburn (ed.), Explosion ..., p. 253.

43. Lionel Place, "Final Report on the Jagire", 6th June, 1799. Reprinted in W.H. Bayley and W. Hudleston (eds.) Papers on Mirasi Right (Pharoah and Co., Athanaeum Press, Madras, 1862), pp. 38-70, esp. pp. 43, 46, 53-4.

44. A.I. Levkovsky, Capitalism in India: Basic Trends in its Development (People's Publishing House, Delhi, 1972), p. 15.

45. K. Gough, "The Structure of a Tanjore Village" in McKim Marriott (ed.), Village India (University of Chicago Press, Chicago, 1969), p. 42.

46. Marx's own writings are summarized in two bibliographic essays. Maurice Godelier, "Les Ecrits de Marx et d'Engels sur le Mode de Production Asiatique", La Pensee, No. 114 (Janvier-Fevrier, 1964), pp. 56-66; Anne M. Bailey and J.R. Llobera, "The Asiatic Mode of Production: An Annotated Bibliography", Critique of Anthropology, vol.2 (Autumn, 1974), pp. 95-103 and vols.4-5 (Autumn, 1975), pp. 165-176. Most of the major writings of Marx are brought together by Maurice Godelier in Sur les Societés Précapitalistes: Textes Choisis de Marx, Engels, Lenine (Editions Sociales, Paris, 1970). Among the most important secondary sources are: Lawrence Krader, The Asiatic Mode of Production: Sources, Development and Critique in the Writings of Karl Marx (Van Gorcum and Comp., Assen, 1975); Umberto Melotti, Marx and the Third World (Macmillan, London, 1977) and Marian Sawer, Marxism and the Question of the Asiatic Mode of Production (Martinus Nijhoff, the Hague, 1977).

47. Hisashi Nakamura, Accumulation and Interchange of Labor: An Inquiry into the Non-Market Economy in a South Indian Village (Institute of Developing Economies, Tokyo, 1976), I.D.E. Occasional Papers Series No. 14.

48. Certainly S.S. Sivakumar interprets Nakamura as I do. S.S. Sivakumar, "Revival of the Asiatic Mode?", Economic and Political Weekly, Vol. XIV, No. 11 (March 17, 1979), pp. 591-2.

49. Kathleen Gough, "Modes of Production in Southern India", Economic and Political Weekly, Vol XV, Nos. 5-7 (Annual Number, 1980), pp. 337-364. See also her "Colonial Economics in South East India", Economic and Political Weekly, Vol. XII, No. 13 (March 26, 1977), pp. 541-554.

50. Hindess and Hirst argue forcefully that no unique mode of production can be derived from what they term the 'tax/rent couple'. See Barry Hindess and Paul Q. Hirst, Pre-capitalist Modes of Production (Routledge & Kegan Paul, London, 1975), pp. 192ff.

51. Gough "Modes...", pp. 344-5. For Marx's analysis of the universal slavery inherent in the Asiatic Mode of Production, see K. Marx, Grundrisse (Penguin, Harmondsworth, 1973), pp. 493 and 495.

52. Gough "Modes...", p. 347, My evidence indicates that Dr. Gough is wrong in tracing the abandonment of joint tenure to this period. See below, fn. 111.

53. See Place's "Final Report on the Jagir" dated 6th June, 1799, reprinted in Bayley and Hudleston, Papers..., pp. 40 ff.

54. See the "Memorandum submitted by Col. Blackburne, resident at Tanjore, to Lord William Bentinck on the subject of Meerassee right; dated 27th. December, 1804" in Bayley and Hudleston Papers..., p. 89, Place's "Report...", and the "Replies from Mr. F.W. Ellis, Collector of Madras, to the Mirasi Questions, dated 30th May, 1816" in Bayley and Hudleston, Papers..., pp. 172-344.

55. See Place, "Report...", pp. 42ff, and S. Lushington, "Extract from Report of Mr. S. Lushington on Tinnevelly, dated 29th December, 1800" in Bayley and Hudleston, Papers..., pp. 77-85, esp. p. 79.

56. See Lushington, "Extract...", p. 79, Ellis, "Replies...", pp. 190 and 341-2. See also T. Venkasami Row, A Manual of the District of Tanjore (Government of Madras, Madras, 1883), pp. 379ff. and 400ff.

57. Madras Board of Revenue Proceedings, 15 November, 1819. [India Office Library (hereafter: IOL): Range 293, Vol.38, pp. 13,685-7].

58. For an accessible summary of the literature relating to South Indian slavery, see Benedicte Hjejle, "Slavery and Agricultural Bondage in South India in the Nineteenth Century", Scandinavian Economic History Review, Vol. XV, Nos. 1 and 2 (1967), pp. 71-126.

59. See George Travers, "Report on the Triennial Settlement", Madras Board of Revenue Proceedings, 6 May, 1811, [IOL: Range 289, Vol. 84], pp. 3785-6. See also: "Extract from Minute of the Board of Revenue, on the different modes of Land Revenue Settlement, as existing in different Districts; dated 5th January, 1818" in Bayley and Hudleston, Papers..., p. 382.

60. An anonymous author writing in May, 1777 writes that the lands of Srirangam Island "... and several other detached villages in the Trichinopoly and Tanjore countries added to them at different times by the Gifts of well disposed Naindoos of Trichinopoly and Rajahs of Tanjore have been appropriated to the use of the [Srirangam] Pagoda [Temple], and the maintenance of upwards of 40,000 Soules belonging to and depending upon it." "Some Enquiries into, and account of the State of Annacathy" May, 1777. [IOL: MacKenzie Collection, Vol. LIX, n.p.].

61. T. Clark, undated, March, 1863. Reprinted in Selections from the Records of the Madras Government Relating to the Survey and Settlement of the Trichinopoly District, Vol. L (Government of Madras, Madras, 1876), p. 443.

62. Burton Stein, "The State and the Agrarian Order in Medieval South India: A Historiographical Critique" in Burton Stein (ed.), Essays in South India (Vikas, Delhi, 1975), p. 79.

63. Ibid., p. 174-6. The incessant wars between the Southern Kingdoms and those in Sri Lanka make this evident even if we accept the force of Stein's point that the actual foci of military resources were localized groups of villages.

64. The most obvious indication of this is to be found in the state's role in adjudicating conflicting claims to mirasi property. Col. Blackburn noted in 1804 that "the right of meerassee is constantly brought into the Courts of the Collector, as it formerly was into the established Courts of the country. It is claimed, defended, and decided upon, as regularly as any questions relating to any other species of property." "Memorandum..." in Bayley and Huddleston,

Papers..., p. 90.

65. George F. Travers, "Report...", Madras Board of Revenue Proceedings [IOL: Range 289, Vol. 84, pp. 3788-9]. One cannot unfortunately be certain whether the actions to which Travers referred were those of the traditional Tamil state or merely those of the recently arrived Muslim powers. It should also be noted that Travers is the only commentator of whom I am aware to have noted this aspect.

66. Though he works with a quite different frame of reference, Burton Stein also firmly rejects the applicability of the concept of feudalism to South India. "The State...", pp. 83-88.

67. One of the first Europeans to visit the area, S.H. Showers, reported in 1768 that Garha was "...populous but very ill built, the best houses being little better than Huts". [IOL: Orme Manuscripts, Volume 4, p. 99].

68. Molony died before he was able to submit a formal report. The earliest records of what he found were contained in private letters Molony sent H. MacKenzie, then Secretary of the Bengal Revenue Department. The letter cited was dated 18 June, 1818. [Bengal Government Court of (Directors?) (to Board of Control) dated 16 August, 1827. "Extract of Revenue Letter from Bengal".] [Bengal Revenue Department Draft 83, 1830/31. "Affairs of the Saugor and Nerbuddah Territories..."] [These documents are held in the India Office Library as part of the Board of Control's Collections 1830-31 (old No. 30945) (new No. F/4/1208)], p. 10.

69. Ibid., p. 13.

70. R. Temple, Annual Report on the Administration of the Central Provinces for the Year 1861-62, Administrative Reports of the Government of India, V/10/16, p. 47.

71. C.A. Molony, "Extract...", pp. 13-17. For a description of the Maratha revenue system as it was introduced into Malwa, see Stewart N. Gordon, "The Slow Conquest: Administrative Integration of Malwa into the Maratha Empire, 1720-1760", Modern Asian Studies, Vol.II, Part 1 (February, 1977), pp.1-40, esp. pp. 20 ff.

72. Irfan Habib, The Agrarian System of Mughal India (1556-1707) (Asia Publishing House, London, 1963), p. 319.

73. Ibid., p. 317.

74. Irfan Habib, "The Social Distribution of Landed Property in Pre-British India", Enquiry, Vol. III, No. 3 (New Series) (1965), pp. 62-3.

75. Irfan Habib, "Marxist Interpretation", Seminar 39, (November, 1962), p. 37.

76. Irfan Habib, Agrarian System..., pp. 236 ff. Habib recognizes the importance of commodity production and notes that W.C. Smith was the first to draw attention to it. Irfan Habib, "Potentialities of Capitalistic Development in the Economy of Mughal India", Enquiry, New Series, Vol.III, No.3, (Winter, 1971), pp. 12 and 55. Tapan Raychauduri notes acutely that "...the village sold, but hardly ever purchased anything

from the outside world....for all practical purposes, the process of monetisation stopped at the border of village India", "The Agrarian System of Mughal India", Enquiry, N.S., Vol.II, No.1 (1965), pp. 118-9.

77. See S. Nurul Hasan, "Zamindars under the Mughals" in R.E. Frykenberg (ed.), Land Control and Social Structure in Indian History (University of Wisconsin Press, Madison, 1969). In what follows, I am implicitly extending the discussion of zamindars to the bhaiachara tenures which Fox and Stokes have shown to be linked with them. See Richard G. Fox, Kin, Clan, Raja, and Rule (University of California Press, Berkeley, 1971), Chapter 3 and Eric Stokes, The Peasant and the Raj (Cambridge University Press, Cambridge, 1978), Chapter 3.

78. Hasan, "Zamindars...", p. 27.

79. Irfan Habib, Agrarian System..., p. 111-112.

80. Irfan Habib, "Social Distribution...", p. 68.

81. Irfan Habib, Agrarian System..., p. 159.

82. Ibid., p. 114.

83. Ibid., p. 115.

84. Walter C. Neale, "Land is to Rule", in R.E. Frykenberg (ed.) Land Control..., p. 15.

85. The most famous of these is of course contained in Francois Bernier's "Letter to Monseigneur Colbert", Travels in the Mogal Empire (S. Chand and Co, New Delhi, 1972), p. 211.

86. Walter Neale, "Land is...", esp. pp. 6-8.

87. Irfan Habib, Agrarian System..., pp. 159-163.

88. Ibid., p. 165.

89. Ibid., p. 166.

90. Perhaps the best analogy we have of this is to be found in Fredrik Barth's description of Pathan society in Political Leadership Among Swat Pathans (Athlone Press, London, 1972).

91. Walter Neale, "Land...", pp. 12-13.

92. Karl Marx, "The British Rule in India", June 10, 1853; in Karl Marx and Frederick Engels, On Colonialism (International Publishers, New York, 1972), p. 41.

93. Perry Anderson traces the evolution of Marx's thinking with commendable clarity in the Lineages of the Absolutist State (New Left Books, London, 1975), pp. 462-495.

94. Karl Marx, Grundrisse..., p. 495.

95. Daniel Thorner, "Marx on India and the Asiatic Mode of Production", Contributions to Indian Sociology, Vol. IX, (December, 1966), pp. 3-66.

96. Ibid., p. 57. I have added the qualification of 'north India' to Thorner's remarks.

97. Ibid., p. 44.

98. Perry Anderson, Lineages..., p. 490.

99. Barry Hindess and Paul Q. Hirst, Pre-Capitalist Modes..., pp. 178-220. See their 'recantation' as well: Mode of Production and Social Formation: An Auto-Critique of Pre-Capitalist Modes of Production (Macmillan, London, 1977).

100. Pre-capitalist Modes..., p. 197.

101. Irfan Habib, Agrarian System..., pp. 320-322.

102. Ibid., pp. 330ff.

103. Stewart N. Gordon, "Scarf and Sword: Thugs, Marauders and State-formation in 18th century Malwa", Indian Economic and Social History Review, Vol. VI, No. 4 (December, 1969), p. 423.

104. It is this imperative which, in my opinion, explains why Mughal hegemony was re-established after crises and wars of succession. Habib, Agrarian Systems..., p. 318, notes "... the great degree of cohesion in the basic structure of the Empire", but offers no structural reason for it.

105. P.B. Mayer, "The Penetration of Capitalism in a South Indian District: The First 60 Years of Colonial Rule in Tiruchirapalli, 1800-1860" forthcoming in South Asia, Vol. III, No. 2 (1981).

106. J. Wallace, "Report on the Revenue from Trichinopoly District for Fusly 1211 (1801)" Madras Board of Revenue Proceedings, 13 September, 1802. [IOL: Range 287, Vol. 14, pp. 10458-521].

107. Ibid., pp. 10462-3.

108. Sara Braunstein, who has also examined this period in Tiruchirapalli, denies the validity of claims that there were serious economic difficulties occasioned by low market prices. She interprets them as simply the 'grievances' of a disgruntled class of parasitical Brahmin landlords, which a succession of weak collectors found it easier to endorse than oppose. "British Land Revenue Policy and Social Continuity in a South Indian District: A Study of Trichinopoly District, 1801-1924" (unpublished M.A. thesis, University of Western Australia, 1976), pp. 30-54.

109. C.M. Lushington, "General Report of the Jummabundy for Fusly 1225", Madras Board of Revenue Proceedings, 3 October, 1816 [IOL: Range 292, Vol. I, pp. 1168].

110. Sara Braunstein, "British Land..." argues, without furnishing evidence in its justification, that "in fact, mirasi lands in Trichy district were not usually held in common...", p. 77.

111. H. Dickinson, "Report on the Settlement of Trichinopoly for Fusly 1236", Madras Board of Revenue Proceedings, 3 September, 1827 [IOL: Range 296, Vol. 28, pp. 9953-55].

112. F.R. Hemingway, Madras District Gazeteers: Trichinopoly, p. 151, and R.K. Puckle, "Scheme for the Revision of the Assessment of the Trichinopoly District", reprinted in Selections from the Records..., pp. 9-10.

113. See Benedicte Hjejle, "Slavery ...", pp. 71-126.

114. See for example F.R. Hemingway, ...Trichinopoly, (Government of Madras, Madras, 1907), p. 152.

115. I find it hard, however, to accept the suggestion that areas like Tiruchirapalli and Thanjavur were developed by colonial capitalism "as monocrop rice-producing regions..." if by that it is meant that they practised a vastly more

diversified agriculture before the penetration of colonial capitalism. "Anonymous", "Class Developments in South India", Journal of Contemporary Asia, Vol. 6, No. 1 (1976), p. 35.

116. As we have seen, both of these classes existed and indeed were integral, to Mirasi Production; capitalism certainly 'freed' them, but it did not create them. For the claim that these classes were created by colonialism, see Surendra J. Patel, Agricultural Labourers in Modern India and Pakistan (Current Book House, Bombay, 1952), pp. 63-67.

117. Letter to C.M. Molony from H. MacKenzie, 13 February, 1823., In Board of Control's Collections 1830-1 [IOL: Vol. F/4/1208, pp. 101-2].

118. See the Minutes of Evidence, heard by the Indian Famine Commission (1898), especially the testimony of Lt. Col. P. Cullen, p. 164, and that of Mr. C.W. McIver, p. 175.

119. Bernard Cohen, "The Initial British Impact on India" in I. Wallerstein (ed.) Social Change: The Colonial Situations (Wiley, New York, 1966).

120. R. Low, Principal Assistant to the Commissioner Saugor and Nerbudda Territories, to F.C. Smith, dated 27 August, 1834. Bengal Sudder Board of Revenue, W.P. Proceedings, 16 September 1834 [IOL: Range 82, Vol. 6, Proceeding 36]

121. Maurice Dobb, Studies in the Development of Capitalism (International Publishers, New York, 1975), p. 120.

122. H.R. Crosthwaite, Report on the Land Revenue Settlements of the Jubbalpore District in the Central Provinces, Effected During the Years 1907 to 1912 (Central Provinces Administration, Nagpore, 1912 [1913]) p. 18.

123. A.E. Nelson (ed.) Central Provinces Gazetteer; Jubbulpore District (Times Press, Bombay, 1909), pp. 137-8.

124. Ibid., pp. 143-44. The family is said to have had a total of 300 shops in a chain which stretched from Jaisalmer in Rajasthan to Rangoon, and possession of some 800 villages in all. See Bhupendra Hooja, A Life Dedicated: Biography of Govind Das (University of Delhi Press, Delhi, 1956). I must express my gratitude to David Baker for lending me his copy of this book.

125. See Peter Harnetty, '"A Curious Exercise of Political Economy": Some Implications of British Land Revenue Policy in the Central Provinces of India 1861-c.1900', South Asia, No.6 (December, 1976), pp. 14-33.

126. A.E.Nelson,...Jubbulpore, p. 162. See also Peter Harnetty, "Crop Trends in the Central Provinces of India, 1861-1921", Modern Asian Studies, Vol.11, Part 3 (July, 1977), pp. 341-377.

127. Peter Harnetty remarks in a unpublished manuscript that "...the distinction between agriculturalists and non-agriculturalists becomes impossible to sustain in this period." Peter Harnetty "The Landlords and the Raj: The Malguzars of the Central Provinces, 1861-1921". See also Eric Stokes, The Peasant and the Raj..., Chapter 11. I am indebted

to Peter Reeves for drawing these works to my attention.

128. H.R. Crosthwaite, Report..., p. 17.
129. A.E. Nelson,...Jubbulpore, p. 144.

Chapter 4

CAPITALISM AND COMMODITY PRODUCTION IN JAVA

G.R. Knight

Introduction : 'Involution' and the Spread of Capitalism in Rural Java

There is a widely-held view that the development of world market production in nineteenth century Java was accompanied by (and based upon) a substantial degree of petrifaction of the existing social and economic structures of the countryside. Since these structures are at the same time conceived as having been essentially non-capitalist in character, the conclusion has therefore been drawn that Dutch colonialism, and particularly the sugar industry which grew up under its aegis during the nineteenth century, both stifled the development of indigenous capitalism in rural Java and set in motion a process of 'involution' whereby the traditional order drew in upon itself and ossified alongside a modern economy under western control. This has led in turn to a dualist explanation of the 'underdevelopment' of Java, in terms of the failure of capitalism to transfer itself successfully from the one sector to the other. The conclusion drawn from all this, even by writers with no apparent commitment to the theory of 'involution', has been that indigenous capitalism has been a post-colonial development in rural Java, associated primarily with developments in the countryside since 1965 under the aegis of the New Order.[1]

Despite the influential nature of the argument, and particularly of the core-concept of 'involution' as expounded by Clifford Geertz, it has not gone unchallenged as a satisfactory explanation of the course of Javanese socio-economic development. In recent years especially, there has been increasingly trenchant criticism of 'involution' by researchers sceptical of its applicability to modern Indonesia. The present paper seeks to sustain and develop that critique by focusing attention on the alleged roots of 'involution' in the nineteenth century and by developing a counter-argument for the emergence of indigenous capitalism in the countryside during the heyday of Dutch colonial rule.[2]

There are two fundamental problems involved in such an approach. The first revolves around conceptualisation of the 'old' Javanese rural society as it existed on the eve of the Cultivation System, the name given to the colonial government's drive for vastly increased world market production inaugurated in 1830 by Governor-General van den Bosch. The second relates to analysis of the nature of the change wrought on rural society by the operations of the new System in its mid-nineteenth century heyday. In discussing them, I shall be using examples drawn from the nineteenth century socio-economic history of the north coast (pasisir) Residencies of Java, particularly the small but populous Residency of Pekalongan, westward of Semarang. How far such findings are relevant to the whole of Java remains, of course, an open question. Despite assertions of the uniqueness of provincial experience during the colonial period, however, I remain convinced that discussion can usefully be carried forward by suggesting a number of common themes. In the context of the present argument, these are as follows. One: social differentiation and commodity production were sufficiently developed in the countryside of Java prior to the Cultivation System for it to make sense to speak of a potential for capitalist development. The 'old' society was not set on a road which precluded capitalist development. I am profoundly sceptical, for this reason, of the applicability here of such concepts as the 'asiatic mode of production'. Two: the changes which were taking place in Javanese rural society during the heyday of the Cultivation System in the mid-nineteenth century were of a capitalist rather than an 'involutional' kind. An embryonic indigenous capitalism was clearly evident in the rural areas, expressed in terms of generalised commodity production, wage labour and a further development of socio-economic cleavages among the peasantry. There is a fundamental error in attempts to delineate this society in non-capitalist terminology (ie. as 'feudal' or 'traditional') and to argue that the capitalist 'transformation' had yet to come.[3] Three: I reject, therefore, the idea that world market production in nineteenth century Java co-existed with an ossified 'traditional' order. On the contrary, in rejecting both old-style dualism and the modified, Geertzian variety, I want to emphasise those aspects of change during the era of the Cultivation System which clearly point to the emergence of indigenous capitalism. In short, my argument seeks to identify the beginnings of indigenous capitalism in the Javanese countryside with the very process of the growth of world market production and of the sugar industry in particular.

The Organisation of Agricultural Production in the Pasisir in the Early Nineteenth Century

Agricultural production in the north Java littoral around 1800 can be seen as organised at two, closely related levels: the peasantry and the supra-village sphere of 'gentry' (priyayi), Chinese and Dutch. It had long ceased to be geared solely to local consumption. From at least the time of the Dutch takeover of the pasisir in the mid-eighteenth century both peasant and priyayi had been drawn (however indirectly) into the business of producing for the world market. The Dutch Company, whose 'system' remained effective into the second decade of the nineteenth century, made two kinds of demand. The first was for labour, supplied primarily for the carting of goods and for operating the warehouses and port-facilities which it established all along the north coast. The second was for specified quantities of agricultural produce, principally rice, but also indigo, cotton thread and a little sugar. These were provided by 'agreement' with the local rulers, the bupati, whom the Dutch called Regents. The business of how production was organised was left firmly in the hands of the bupati. "In a word", noted a laconic report from Semarang in 1812, "the government knows nobody and treats with nobody but him".[4]

It was not, in fact, until the closing years of the eighteenth century that the Colonial authorities began to take much notice of what was going on in the countryside, and only under the regimes of Daendals and Raffles, between 1808 and 1816, that substantial and systematic inquiries began to be made into rural society and economy. The consequence is that the picture of both peasantry and gentry of north coast Java (as it emerges from European accounts) is inevitably one derived from a period when world market production under colonial aegis had already begun to make a certain impact. Only with the attempts after 1813 to implement Raffles's Land Rent, did the colonial government begin directly, systematically and as a matter of policy to involve itself in rural affairs below the level of the bupati. Not until 1823, moreover, was there instituted a system of regular annual reports from the Residencies to the central government, possessing the potential for eliciting a wealth of detail about villagers and priyayi. Even so, such inquiries were constantly frustrated by a whole number of factors, including a certain disinclination on the part of the bupati to supply information which might jeopardise their own claims on the peasantry. In this way, for instance, both land and people were often concealed from prying colonial eyes, in some cases for decades.

It is, therefore, against this background of fragmentary and often questionable information that an analysis of agricultural production in the decades immediately prior to the Cultivation System has to be made.

The Peasantry of the Pasisir

The direct producers in the north Java coastal Residencies in the early nineteenth century were predominantly rural cultivators growing rice during the wet monsoon and a variety of second crops (beans of various kinds, maize, indigo-leaf and sometimes cotton and tobacco) during the dry season. The rural population was not, however, engaged exclusively in agriculture. Handicrafts for local consumption and regional trade were widespread, and some of the 'common people' of the countryside were in fact fishermen, traders and specialist handicraft producers. The economy was nonetheless dominated by farming.

Land was held by the peasantry on the basis of labour services supplied to the priyayi, who also levied a portion of the cultivator's padi-harvest. There was some post-1813 alteration to these arrangements to bring them into line with the formal requirements of the Land Rent System introduced in that year, but the close connection between landholding and the obligation to perform labour services for the 'authorities' remained unchanged.

Not all the peasantry held land. On the contrary, the relations of production which existed among the peasantry of the early nineteenth pasisir were characterised by a broad distinction between landholders and landless. This was not merely an incidental of rural socio-economy, but an integral part of it. There are, admittedly, a number of difficulties in such a concept. In the first place, it is virtually impossible to estimate how large a proportion of the rural workforce held either no land at all or, at least, none of the sawah which formed the central resource of peasant agriculture. Equally, although it is obvious that landlessness was a permanent condition of rural life from the time of the earliest European accounts (the veteran Jan Knops, for instance, wrote in 1812 of those who "held no share in the sawah-fields") it is not clear that the landless themselves constituted a permanent, hereditary class. Indeed there is a deal of evidence that in the opening decades of the nineteenth century there was no invariable, hard-and-fast distinction between those who held land and those who did not. Possibly the clearest contemporary statement of this was provided by Resident Pieter le Clercq of Semarang, describing in 1831 the landholding situation which he believed to have prevailed in his Residency prior to the introduction of the Land Rent System eighteen years earlier. Le Clercq explained that land had been apportioned among members of the peasantry in return for the performance of labour services within and above the village. These people were called sikeps and:

> Every sikep had a djoeroe-sawah or assistant. It was these latter who, in the event of a shortage of sikeps

for labour service for the negeri* [state], were recruited to make up the numbers. The sikeps shared the produce of the fields assigned to them with their djoeroe-sawah, because they jointly shared the cost of cultivation.

When the sikeps had held their sawah for a year, they had to hand them over to the keriks, ["people who had no field"] who then in their turn worked them for a year or for one harvest.

The djoeroe-sawah or assistants had the choice of taking the place of the sikeps or of relinquishing their place to the keriks or of remaining in the service [of the landholders]. This change-over took place among the entire population, so that everyone had to take a turn at performing labour service for the negeri and as a consequence held sawah, on account of which he was called sikep.[5]

This was not an isolated statement. Similar observations had been made earlier in the century by Knops and P.H. van Lawick van Pabst in a lengthy report on the old North-East Coast Governorship dating from 1812. According to this, the "common man" only held his share in the sawah for a year before relinquishing it to another, "with a view to letting the whole mass of the village people share in the enjoyment of a part of the sawah.[6]

At the same time, there is ample evidence that the landholding patterns prevailing among the peasantry of the pasisir in the early nineteenth century were not quite as simple or egalitarian as might be inferred. In the first place, not all peasant sawah was subject to periodic redistribution in the manner described. Recently developed sawah, in particular, was excluded from such arrangements and reserved for those who had opened it up. In Pekalongan around 1820, for example, it was said that developer's rights passed from one generation to the next in the sparsely populated uplands, but in the more populous lowlands lapsed after the first generation. Resident H.J. Domis in neighbouring Semarang described a basically similar situation.[7] It is also important in this context to remember that not all peasant land was sawah. At the very least, the irrigated fields of the village were supplemented by 'dry' land of one kind or another, usually known as tegal or gogo. Knops, speaking of the situation in Semarang in 1813, said that "the Javanese who clears such land ... and renders a wilderness fit for cultivation, considers himself

---

* I have retained throughout the original Dutch spelling of Malay and Javanese words.

as proprietor of the same" and that this was also the case with land planted with fruit trees.[8] In short, there was the possibility that considerable amounts of productive land remained outside the operation of any re-distributive mechanisms which may have characterised the peasantry of the northcoast Residencies.

These mechanisms, for annual or at least periodic re-allocation of some portion of the fields, were certainly widespread, and seen through western eyes answered a number of purposes. Resident H.T. van der Werff of Rembang, for instance, explained in 1812 that:

> The lands are yearly changed, as well the poorer as the rich land, viz. those that had rich lands this year are obliged the next year to take poorer lands ... it is settled yearly in such a way that one has nothing to complain against another.[9]

Knops made the same point about the northern littoral districts as a whole: "everyone in his turn shares in the greater or lesser productivity". He indicated, however, that population pressure played a part in redistribution. Sawah had to be circulated because there was not enough to go around. In districts, where the demand for land was great (he named specifically the Regency of Semarang), claims could only be honoured on a year-and-year-about basis.[10] Periodic redistribution was also a response to the fluctuating demand for labour services from the authorities. As Raffles remarked during the period of his Governorship of the island;

> In the neighbourhood of despotic authority, it may naturally be expected that constant and undefined demands for the public service, and the corresponding demand on the land, led to continued changes in its distribution. In some cases more than one half of the inhabitants of a village were kept in constant readyness for the government employ, while the lands were divided amongst the remainder: these were alternately changed at the end of each year. In others, it was the invariable rule for the head of the village to apportion to each individual cultivator his share of the land annually, according to the instructions of the Regent ...[11]

The redistribution of land, however, took place on a basis that was far from equal. Domis noted in the early 1820's that although it was nominally based on an "equal right to the fields, yet the rank of the cultivator mostly determines the quantity."[12] It was clearly the village headmen and the 'elders' who did best out of this. Domis explained that it was they who:

Are by rotation, some for one, some for two or in other
places for three years, holders of the best land
belonging to such villages. The younger cultivators
have claim to fields of the second sort, and the widows
and strangers ... are assigned the third or poorest
category of rice-field.[13]

Knops, too, made it clear that it was the headmen who took
the prime share in the village sawah. Writing a full decade
before Domis, he reckoned that as a general rule the lurah
(headman) held between one and two jonk of land apiece,
whereas the 'common people' received only one quarter or at
the most one half of a jonk. In Semarang in particular, he
calculated that more than 12 percent of the total sawah area
was held by lurah. Given the scanty information available
even to the best informed western observers, figures of this
kind can be no more than the crudest approximation.
Nevertheless, it is interesting to see that in the same
Residency around the mid-century attempts were being made to
limit the landholding of village headmen to no more than
eight percent of the cultivable land.[14]

A two-fold picture of the peasantry of the north Java
littoral in the early years of the nineteenth century begins
to emerge. On the one hand, landed cultivators who were
themselves differentiated in terms both of the quantity and
quality of sawah which they held. On the other, an amorphous
group of landless peasants (some of whom apparently
alternated with the landed) bound by a whole series of
arrangements, including wages and share-cropping, to those
who had a right to land. In Knop's view it was usual for the
landless to take on some of the labour services falling on
the landholders, in return for which they received a share in
the sawah.[15] This roughly accords with Le Clercq's already
quoted remarks about the relationship between landed peasants
and their assistants. In Pekalongan, however, Resident F.E.
Hardy reported in 1812 on what he evidently perceived as
simple share-cropping, which was fairly common in the
villages:

... one half of the crop is the reward of the
cultivator, the other half remains to the landowner.
The seed is provided for by both, and also the
Contingent [i.e. the Regent's share of the crop] but the
cultivator bears all the charges attending his task.[16]

Share-cropping was also reported from Semarang by Knops in
the same year, in the course of his explanation of the
intricacies of land re-distribution. Those who got no sawah:

... hire them from others, either at an agreed price
according to their produce, or for a certain quantity of
the crop, or else in dividing, one gives his rice-field,

the other the buffaloes to plough it and the hands to work, another or the proprietor, the padi for sowing, the whole according to the agreements made beforehand, but which are generally at one-third for the buffaloes and working hands, and two-thirds for the proprietor.[17]

The mention of the straightforward hire of sawah is likewise a far from isolated reference (though of course not necessarily confined to the relations between land and landless). It occurs again, for instance, in two different Regencies of Japara, in the same year, 1812. Raffles said that in the Kudus Regency, the cultivators "regularly dispose of their lands for money,"[18] and Resident Doornick observed that "a rice land allotted A may be let by him in hire to B, in which case they both appear before the headmen of the dessa and inform him of the agreement they have made."[19]
As to the incidence of wage and day labour, it is obviously impossible to quantify, but it can be said to have been commonplace. In the 1820's, for instance, when Resident Cornelis Vos set out to demonstrate what the peasantry of Pekalongan could hope to earn from second ('dry' season) crops, his calculations included a quite unambiguous deduction for wages (Loonen) as well as for the hire of buffaloes.[20] The same point was made on a less specific level in the following decade by J.I. van Sevenhoven, a very experienced and senior official of the Indies Government, whose analysis of rural Javanese society accorded the lowest category to those who were known as "menoempang" and who had no fields of their own but were "people who practise a craft, engage in trade or who work as day labourers (boedjangers)."[21] It would be rash to assume, of course, that what was referred to as day-labour was necessarily paid for in cash. Then as now, harvest work at least was clearly paid for in kind.[22] Nonetheless, the economy of the countryside was sufficiently monetarised in the early nineteenth century to make a cash-wage perfectly practicable.

The Priyayi, The Chinese and the Dutch

Any analysis of the supra-village economic structure of the north coast Residencies at the beginning of the nineteenth century has to take into account not only the Javanese 'gentry', but also Chinese and 'Arab' traders and entrepreneurs and Dutch officials (there was only a handful of European planters active on the entire north coast prior to 1830). All three groups were involved in the appropriation of peasant surplus, through a variety of mechanisms, and in varying degrees of dependence on one another.
The north coast 'gentry' comprised the bupati, the

wedana or district heads and their satellite officials. These people were the successors of the tribute-collecting officials of the old Javanese state whose allegiance had been transferred to the Semarang Governor when the Dutch gained control of the pasisir in the mid-eighteenth century. Even a century later, however, according to the Resident of Pekalongan, the 'gentry' of his districts still looked upon Solo rather than Batavia as the centre of their world.[23] They were not hereditary office holders (though the Dutch generally appointed son to succeed father) and they were not properly described as landlords. In the old Javanese state, the bupati had been appointees of the Sultanate, and had been the pivot of the expropriation of peasant produce and labour for the use of the royal court. They continued, under Company rule, to fulfil a similar role for the Dutch. In short, they formed a 'gentry' whose income came from whatever they contrived to keep of the rice and labour dues owed by the cultivators to the state.

There was, according to Knops and Lawick van Pabst in 1812, a three-fold division of the peasantry for the purpose of labour requisition. They were categorised as 'front', 'middle' and 'rear' people. While the first two had to perform labour service for the state (ie. the Dutch colonial authorities), the last category was reserved for the use of the bupati. The apportionment of sawah to create labour service was, of course, an integral part of the arrangement.[24] As far as the bupati's own people were concerned, the situation prevailing in one of the regencies of Rembang in 1812 can be taken as fairly typical:

> ... the Regent of Lassum employs for his own private use 322 families, which he supports from his own rice-fields, to whom no allowance of rice-fields is made, and who are handicraft men, musicians and labourers in the field, which latter receive 1/4 of the crop. His house servants amount to 75 ...[25]

The full extent of the gentry's demands for labour is, nonetheless, virtually incalculable. The difficulties in the way of such enquiry were neatly summed up by the Resident of Japara in 1812:

> ... The Regent in the strictest sense of the word had no right to assume a prerogative over the natives in general ... But the Regents, who are well-acquainted with the temper of the Javanese, and perfectly convinced that he dare not complain lest the oppression should become unsupportable, know how far they can go, and avail themselves of numberless tricks to keep him in submission. The latter remain silent, and the most attentive Resident will not be able to discover what passes. It would not be possible, even by means of a

reward, to prevail with a Javanese to make a discovery prejudicial to his own Regent, although the latter oppresses him with labour and extortion.[26]

What portion of the peasantry's padi harvest was taken by the Regents (a proportion of which was passed on by them to the Dutch as part of 'Contingent') is likewise a difficult matter to judge. Knops and Pabst reckoned that under Company rule this had amounted to three-fifths or two-thirds of the crop, but added that there was so little system and so much local variation that any hard-and-fast figure was inappropriate. In addition to this levy on the harvest, the bupati also made a variety of other demands on peasant resources. These could be in either cash or kind. Contributions to the bupati's household had to be made on feast days (chickens, for instance), a headtax was levied and buffaloes, firewood and bamboo were requisitioned at prices below the prevailing market rate.[27]

In some cases, the bupati appear to have organised the direct exploitation of some of the districts under their control. In the Regency of Semarang in the early years of the century, for instance, the Bupati made the following arrangement for working some thirteen and a half jonk of land:

"The Regent gives the buffaloes, the implements of labour; the country, that is to say, the district entirely, gives the hands of work. During the work, the Regent furnishes the victuals. He also furnishes the seed for sowing. He has the work for nothing. All the produce of the 13-1/2 jonks comes to him; they receive the ordinary share which is given to the reaper, which is one-fifth".[28]

This was, of course, a fairly small amount of land. A much more common arrangement for exploiting the resources of the districts under the bupati's control was for villages and whole districts to be hired to Chinese entrepreneurs. In the entire Northeast Coast Governorship in 1803, 9 percent of the villages were said to be farmed in this way. The practice was far from uniform, however: in Peklongan Residency 307 out of a total of over two thousand were farmed to Chinese, while in neighbouring Tegal a mere nine villages were affected.[29]

The hire of villages to the Chinese was prohibited under the restored Dutch regime of 1816, and at the same time, as a consequence of the implementation of the Land Rent System, potentially far-reaching changes were made in the way in which peasant surplus was appropriated. Labour services remained a corner-stone of the colonial edifice until late in the nineteenth century, and the bupati continued to be the agency through which they were requisitioned. Formally, however, the bupati were forced to give up their claims to a levy of the harvest in favour of a tax levied directly on the cultivators by the state.

What actually happened no doubt varied a good deal from one Residency to another. In Pekalongan (to cite an area where the Dutch encountered particularly strong resistance from the bupati) the colonial administration was heavily dependent on the Regents and their families for the day-to-day running of the Residency. There were no alternative power-holders in the countryside to whom the Dutch could turn; no potential replacements to the incumbent bupati families waiting in the wings. Equally, most of the Dutch Residents who served there until the early 1830's were either complaisant or utterly compromised in their relations with the gentry. During the Java War (1825-30), additionally, the colonial authorities were hamstrung by the threat that anything which provoked the ill-will of the bupati would result in a disastrous spill-over of the fighting from central Java into the pasisir (this in fact happened briefly at Semarang in 1826). Consequently, there was a big gap between the appearance and reality of the Land Rent which only began to be closed in the 1830's.[30] Devices whereby the gentry continued to take a large share of the cultivator's harvest in return for a forced 'agreement' to pay his Land Rent were widespread, and greatly facilitated by the fact that many of the actual collectors of the Land-Rent (the Ondercollecteurs in colonial terminology) were themselves members of the bupati families. In Pekalongan there were unusually close ties between the two bupati and local Chinese and 'Arab' (ie. non-Javanese Moslem) traders. They were very much in evidence in the gentry's arrangements for by-passing the Land-Rent, as appears from a Dutch report from 1834:

> It is accepted that when some-one takes it upon themselves to pay the Land Rent for the cultivators that person has a right to half the crop. This does not happen here with the cultivator's consent, as in other Residencies. No! People here have opted for a different way, namely as follows.
> When the harvest has begun, a certain number of people, women as well as men, belonging to the following of the gentry, as well as Chinese and Arabs, go out to the fields, choose the sections which has succeeded best, and tell the owner that they will pay his Rent in return for half the crop. The poor peasant agrees to this, and is sometimes forced to carry the padi to the houses of these people. Alternatively, he has the [bitter experience] of seeing the requisitioned part of his crop sold on the spot for half as much again or even twice as much as the amount of his Rent. The Regent of Batang has arranged matters somewhat differently, since he assigns this privilege only to the members of his own

family and to ... Chinese and Arabs.[31]

Although prior to the Cultivation System the levy on the
padi-harvest and the requisition of labour were the main
forms in which the peasant surplus was appropriated in the
north coast Residencies, they were not the sole ones. Small
scale factories for the manufacture of indigo produced from
leaf grown on peasant land (usually only during the dry
season) and a number of sugar mills were scattered across the
lowlands. The oldest of them generally dated from the
closing years of the eighteenth century. The sugar mills
were run exclusively by Chinese entrepreneurs, using for the
purpose labour recruited in the villages which they had hired
from the Regents for cane growing. The indigo factories
appear to have been managed directly by the bupati (their
output formed part of the annual contingent payable to the
Dutch) and to have been worked by requisitioned peasant
labour.[32] The information available here is so scanty that
it is difficult to get beyond the most superficial
observations as to how production was organised. There were
changes, however, in this area of production even before the
implementation of the Cultivation System. The most important
of these concerned the indigo industry based on the
Pekalongan Residency, where a few big European entrepreneurs
set up business, in advance as it were of Van den Bosch, in
the late 1820's.

Unlike the old factories run by the bupati, the new
indigo manufactures were run with (nominally) free
day-labour in receipt of a cash wage. As far as the
arrangements for growing the leaf from which the dyestuff was
made were concerned, the general practice seems to have been
payment of the Land Rent of the households who agreed to
cultivate. Agreements of this kind could also involve the
buying-off of government-imposed labour services. Obscure as
these arrangements are, they were evidently far enough
removed from the 'old' system of production to raise the
hackles of the local Javanese authorities. Trouble with
'gentry' and village headmen was to follow the nascent
industry into the era of the Cultivation System.[33]

We are now in a position to review how rural production
as a whole was organised in the north coast Residencies in
the opening decades of the nineteenth century, prior to the
Cultivation System.

(a) Undoubtedly, the 'gentry' (and through them the Chinese
and the Dutch) got hold of a good deal of unpaid labour and
levied a substantial part of the peasantry's padi-harvest
without any cash return to the cultivator. In this sense,
the basis of a great deal of rural agricultural production
was the non-economic coercion of the direct producers by the
bupati and their subordinate officials.

(b) The purposes to which the surplus thus appropriated was put were twofold. In the first place, the rice, indigo, cotton-thread etc. which the Regents levied from their districts was in part handed-over to the Dutch (prior to 1813) and in that way entered world trade. After the changes initiated by the Land Rent System, the rural surplus increasingly found its way onto the world market through the agency of Chinese middlemen. An important role in this was still played by the gentry, who continued to use their 'influence' over the cultivators to obtain rice (in particular), often for the benefit of their Chinese or 'Arab' associates. A substantial amount of the surplus levied from the peasantry, however, was used to cover the household expenses of the bupati themselves. This included the maintenance of the Regent's often extensive families, and provision for a substantial number of retainers. The bupati of Pekalongan, for example, had in 1812 an establishment which numbered 24 pike-bearers, 22 lackeys, 22 ornament carriers, 100 domestics, 54 musicians and 20 dancers and wayang players.[34] Ceremony and chivalry clearly consumed a great deal of the Regent's substance. Van Doren's description of the installation of the new Regent of Semarang in 1822, for example, includes extensive reference to the richly ornamented horses and lavishly clad grandees, many of them from the Bupati's own family, who took part in the tournaments which accompanied the ceremony.[35] There is reason to suppose that the north coast gentry of the early nineteenth century frequently lived beyond their incomes, a position worsened in the case of the Pekalongan Regents by their gambling debts.[36] In turn, this offers a partial explanation of the hold which the Chinese had over them, and through which they were drawn firmly into the business of world market production in the interim between the end of the Company's Contingents and the beginnings of the Cultivation System.

(c) It is obvious, however, that by no means all rural surplus extraction on the eve of the Cultivation System took place on the basis of the gentry's long-standing rights to unpaid labour service and a share in the harvest. This is at once apparent from descriptions such as those of Resident Domis of Semarang, dating from the early 1820's, of "Chinese and others who, as buyers-up of produce ride round the villages."[37] This frequently led to what Domis characterised as the "improvident" disposal of most of the padi-crop by the cultivators straight after harvest. In Semarang, at least, this appears frequently to have been a cash transaction, barter being limited to the hill-country and to goods sold in very small quantities.[38] In Pekalongan, on the other hand, at about the same period, Chinese traders were said to go round the villages carrying salt, gambier, iron, coarse cloth and cotton "in order, as far as possible, to carry on a barter-trade."[39] The complexity and monetisation of relations among the peasantry has already been commented upon earlier in this paper. A further insight into them, however, was provided in 1823 by the Resident of Pekalongan's explanation of why he had not collected the statutory one-fifth prepayment of the Land Rent. This was because:

> The cultivator is shortest of cash on the eve of the harvest, as a result of which a provisional payment would compel him to pawn his farming tools to usurious individuals or else borrow money on the crop at a high rate of interest.[40]

In short, alongside and suffusing a system of agricultural production based on extra-economic coercion of the cultivators, was a production of commodities for cash and barter stimulated by the activities of Chinese and 'Arab' traders and organised within the peasantry on the basis of a broad distinction between landed and landless.

The Peasantry and the Cultivation System in the Mid-Nineteenth Century

What remains to be seen is how the rapid expansion of world market production, engineered in Java by the Dutch colonial government from 1830 onwards, affected the 'old' social and economic order in the countryside. To begin with the peasantry, the crucial point is that by the mid-century they had already been subjected to several decades of the operation of the so-called Cultivation System. This is the name given to the series of devices, inaugurated by Governor-General Van den Bosch in 1830, whereby the colonial administration itself set about organising agricultural production suitable for export. In the lowlands of the north Java pasisir, these "Government Cultivations" were largely confined to indigo-leaf (from which the dyestuff was manufactured) and sugar, with sugar predominating after 1850. For the purpose of manufacturing sugar, the colonial government provided capital to European contractors who, in little more than a decade after 1830, had succeeded in creating a network of nearly one hundred sugar factories in east and central Java. In Pekalongan Residency, the focus of the present study, there were three of them in the mid-nineteenth century : Sragie, Kalimatie and, largest of all, Wonopringo. If the manufacturers were European, however, the business of planting the cane and providing the labour force for the sugar factories fell exclusively on the Javanese.

As elsewhere in the pasisir, sugar production in Pekalongan was based on the cultivation of cane on peasant land by local labour drawn from within the ranks of the

132

peasantry itself. The burden of cultivation fell directly on the village landholders, whose land was taken at the behest of the Residency authorities and amalgamated into a complex of large 'plantations'. The landholders and their dependent labourers were then required to work the 'plantation', using their own tools and plough-animals. The notional channel through which this requisition of both land and labour took place was that of the existing local Javanese power-holders, the priyayi or 'gentry'. As we shall see later, however, their role in the actual organisation of production for the export market was changing, and by the mid-century it is doubtful whether they were any longer playing the crucial role allotted to them by Van den Bosch some twenty years earlier.

The initial argument, however, concerns the impact of the Cultivation System on the village cultivators rather than on the Javanese rural bosses, and centres on the nature of the changes brought about in the social and economic structure of the peasantry by the weight of the forced cultivations after 1830. In particular, it centres on the contention that the mid-nineteenth century saw a levelling process going on among the peasantry in consequence of the burdens imposed by the forced cultivations, resulting in the breakdown of the 'old' distinction in the countryside between nuclear, landholding villagers and their largely landless counterparts. Somewhat paradoxically, this levelling has also been taken to show that the System began that petrifaction and re-inforcement of the existing village social order which resulted in 'agricultural involution'. Either way, the effects of the Cultivation System on the peasantry have been interpreted as smothering the development of agrarian capitalism in the villages and preventing the formation of a class of 'yeomen' farmers.[43] The argument of the present paper is that quite the contrary was the case, and that the levelling-hypothesis runs into serious difficulties when tested against our growing knowledge of how the Cultivation System worked and what its effects were.

The problem can best be approached by way of the recent succinct and cautious re-statement of the case for the socially levelling effect of the System in the opening pages of Professor Fasseur's Kultuurstelsel en Koloniale Baten. Fasseur makes two basic points about peasant landholding and the Cultivation System:

(a) That land-tenure in the village was essentially determined by the so-called Dorpsbeschikingsrecht (or village right of disposal).
this finds expression ... in the village community having a certain amount of say in the disposal (vervreemding) of the cultivated land in the village. In pressing cases, this can be utilised to empower the fresh division of the sawah belonging to the dessa among

those villagers who have a share in the holding of land (the so-called nuclear villagers), whether supplemented or not by those who until then were excluded from a share in the fields.

(b) According to custom (adat), only those villagers who held a share in the cultivated village land had to perform [labour services] ... Under the pressure of the Cultivation System, the cultivated land was often divided afresh into smaller parcels, in order to increase the number of landholders and consequently the number of those subject to labour service. A fresh division of the land was also necessary when ... the village had to hand over sawah to be used for government cultivations ... The developments would have taken place primarily at the expense of the more substantial cultivators within the village.[44]

This raises a number of problems. A major one relates to the response of the peasant landholders to the increased demands made on their labour services under the Cultivation System. Fasseur speaks of the cultuurdiensten (i.e. labour-service for cultivation) used for crop-growing, and it is obvious that we need a great deal more research into the nature of peasant response to the increased weight of these. All the same, a number of recent investigators have concluded that crop-growing (sugar cane in particular) brought appreciable financial benefits to peasant landholders, especially perhaps in the later years of the System.[45] Should we conclude too hastily that these people felt an irresistable pressure to re-allocate their sawah to 'lighten the burden'? Of course, cultuurdiensten were not the only services performed by the peasantry: there were also what the Dutch called heerendiensten, under which rubric most of the Campaign (i.e. manufacturing season) labour in field and factory was performed until the 1860's. This labour burden, which could certainly be very heavy, again fell largely on the peasant landholders. Yet their response, as amply demonstrated in at least some of the north coast sugar districts, was certainly not one of spreading the load through re-allocation of sawah, and a broadening of the landholding group. Quite the contrary: labour during the 'Campaign' was organised among the peasantry on a basis which took account of the existing socio-economic differentiations in the village, rather than cut across them. "The substantial villager never performs the heerendiensten in person", reported the Resident of Pekalongan in the 1850's. Instead, he either hired somebody from within the landless group in the village or sent along one of his labourers.[46]
These points about peasant responses to the demands of the Cultivation System suggest the need to review the widely accepted arguments about the levelling effects of the System in the countryside of the pasisir. This becomes even more apparent when the historical origins of the levelling concept
134

are taken into account. Professor Fasseur cites no lesser authority than the colonial elder statesman J.C. Baud (though it is Baud's fear of what might have happened rather than confirmation of what had happened). The bulk of the supportive evidence, however, appears to originate in the well-known Eindresumé van het...Onderzoek naar de Rechten van den Inlander op den Grond.[47] (i.e. Conclusions from the Inquiry into Native Land Rights), edited by W.B. Bergsma between 1876 and 1896. As such Eindresumé needs to be looked at rather carefully.

From the outset, its findings are given a certain colour by Bergsma's determination to demonstrate that the Cultivation System had destroyed the small-holding peasantry of Java and created in its place a rural society in which village communal landholding was the dominant feature. This led him into profound misconceptions about the nature of peasant landholding in nineteenth century Java and into what Fasseur, among others, has characterised as an "illusory battle" between the claims of "hereditary landholding" and "communal possession". Nonetheless, this does not detract too seriously from the very real worth of the material which Eindresumé reproduces, mostly from Dutch investigations carried out in the late 1860's.[48]

Yet what light does this material throw on the alleged levelling effects of the Cultivation System? It is claimed, for instance, in Eindresumé (2, p. 346) that as a result of the forced cultivations, "it was not the land-holders who paid the labour-tax, but those who took on [the burden] of labour-tax who obtained thereby the right to share in the cultivated land". This in itself implies that Bergsma was aware that not all villagers were landholders. Indeed, Dutch investigations from the late 1850's onwards revealed quite significant amounts of landlessness in the countryside, of which Bergsma cannot have failed to be aware. But had landholding itself become as subject to flux as Bergsma clearly intends to suggest? Doubts arise, for instance, when Eindresumé is compared with the findings of the so-called Umbgrove Commission, dating from the 1850's. This was an official Dutch inquiry, headed by Inspector of Cultivations G. Umbgrove, into the conditions of operation of the 95 sugar factories working on government contract on the island. Umbgrove's wide sympathies, however, ensured that it became an investigation of the whole gamut of rural life in the districts from which the factories drew their cane and labour. His findings have much to tell. They make clear, for example, that in at least some of the pasisir Residencies in the late stages of the Cultivation System there persisted a "class" of peasant land-holders which was "hereditary (erfelijk) in the line of the next of kin, provided they were prepared to accept the obligations which were attendant upon that class".[49]

If the fluidity of landholding arrangements as suggested by Eindresumé is questionable, so too is Bergsma's contention that the Cultivation System brought about a significant dilution of the landholding group within the peasantry. In the opening sections of Eindresumé (1, p. 63) there appears the comment that "above all, it was as a result of the Cultuurdiensten that the admission of [land] share-holders was facilitated within many villages". Yet even within the pages of Eindresumé this contention finds only the slenderest support. In Pekalongan Residency it is based on information from only a few of the 26 villages investigated. The unreliability of Eindresumé on this score (and the difficulties inherent in colonial officials questioning Javanese village-heads?) can be gauged from its findings in the Batang district of Pekalongan. There, we are told with "the introduction of the compulsory sugar planting ... the ground was at the same time divided up among all". This may indeed have been initially the case: by the 1850's, however, the Residency archives clearly demonstrate that there had been a significant consolidation of rural landholding among the privileged few.[50]

There is a further conflict of evidence in relation to the incidence of re-allocation of sawah among the peasantry. Eindresume's verdict was that this had increased markedly in response to the demands of the Cultivation System after 1830. Some doubt is cast on this, however, by the evidence cited early in the present paper about the prevalence of land re-distribution among the peasantry of the pasisir in the opening decades of the nineteenth century. In the 1850's, on the other hand, Umbgrove's informants appear to have perceived the annual re-allocation of sawah as an innovation of recent origin, associated with the expansion of world market production by the Dutch. In Pekalongan, for example:

> Only this can be accepted with certainty, that earlier there was no annual division of the rice-fields, so that each sikep could be assured of being able to work the same piece of land each year.
> The introduction of the [forced] cultivations, and of the sugar cultivation in particular, brought about a change in this, for those villages which took part in cane planting have no alternative but to console themselves with a yearly division [of the land], while the remaining villages, either by choice or through instigation by the government, have followed suit.[51]

The essential point to grasp, however, is that re-allocation of this kind was not necessarily a levelling process. On the contrary, it appears to have been primarily an arrangement among the landholders to accommodate the demands of the sugar industry for large, consolidated plantations on which cane could be grown. This, as Umbgrove

136

shows, disturbed existing landholding arrangements. It was not, however, synonymous with the creation of a substantially homogeneous peasantry.[52] Far from it; as Umbgrove's findings make clear, the peasantry of the pasisir continued to be characterised by significant cleavages running along social-economic lines.

In Pekalongan Residency, which appears fairly typical in this respect, peasant society in the mid-1850's was intricately differentiated in terms of access to land. Dominating the village in terms of landholding were the headman and members of the village government. There was then a major division between sawah-holders (sikeps) and those cultivators who held no sawah and were designated as menoempang. They lived in the household of the landholders, and might themselves become sikep in the event of sawah becoming available. They only formed part of the landless rural workforce, however. In addition there were boedjangs, mostly unmarried men who also lived in the sikep's household and who worked as labourers for a wage in cash or kind. Likewise labourers called wong boerooh, who were generally people from outside the village. Wage labour was not the only way in which the relations between the landed and landless were articulated: various forms of share-cropping and land-rental were also known.[53] Before examining more closely this aspect of the peasant economy, however, it is necessary to attempt to clarify the issue of landlessness among the peasantry, on the basis of Umbgrove's evidence.

The problems of calculating just how many households and how much sawah there actually was in the pasisir Residencies around the mid-nineteenth century are legion, and it is quite impossible to analyse them here. Nonetheless, Umbgrove's findings related to the areas exploited directly by the sugar factories where managers and overseers (as well as Residency personnel) had a more than common interest in finding out exactly what was going on. This is not to say that they did so, but does suggest that Umbgrove's findings are likely to be superior to most available for that period. In the districts assigned to the three big sugar factories of mid-nineteenth century Pekalongan, Umbgrove found there to be 9,169 landholding households as against 2,238 which were landless. Among these landless households there were undoubtedly some which were non-agriculturalist- craftsmen and the like.[54] How many is impossible to calculate from Umbgrove's data, but it is unlikely to have been very great. The figures for the landless do not, however, include 'temporary' workers from outside the village.

The significance of the continued existence of a broad socio-economic differentiation among the peasantry was not limited, of course, to the presence in the villages of the mid-nineteenth century pasisir of substantial numbers of landless. It extended to a number of other features of peasant agricultural production which were equally capitalist in their implication. These can be summarised as follows:

<u>The Growing Concentration of Power and Wealth in the Hands of</u>
<u>a Small, 'Privileged' Group within the Peasantry.</u>   As
early as 1850 Inspector of Cultivations Van der Poel had
remarked that in many north-coast Residencies the best fields
were kept by the village headman and his cronies, and that
"the poorest fields constantly fall to the share of the most
hardworking class."[55]   A few years later, the Umbgrove
Commission found in the case of Pekalongan that the annual
repartition of sawah took place in an arbitrary fashion,
"often more in the interest of the members of the village
government and to the detriment of the sikep. They choose
the best ground, take larger shares than are due to them or
they can work themselves [and] favour their own families
..."[56]   To what lengths this could go was illustrated by
the Resident of Pekalongan's report on developments in the
Batang district in the late 1850's:

> The custom exists, to denote as shareholders in the
> sawah only those cultivators who take part in the sugar
> cultivation. The [village] heads have made it a rule
> there to assign each bouw of sugar cane to four men
> only, regardless of the number of people available. All
> the available sawah is divided among these men, and
> those not involved in labour-service for the
> cultivations have to hire sawah if they want them.
> Hence it is obvious that only the privileged have a
> share in sugar cultivation and enjoy a double advantage,
> from both the sawah and the sugar.
> These people who are involved in the labour service for
> the cultivations are the only ones regarded as
> cultivators (landbouwers), and the remaining population
> are considered pariahs, who have to make their fellow
> villagers rich through their labour.[57]

That this was not an isolated instance of the disparities in
landholding among the peasantry of the pasisir is confirmed
by evidence from Japara Residency at about the same time.
Some village heads there held between four and twenty-six (or
even more) bouw of sawah, while the 'ordinary' cultivators
held no more than one bouw.[58]

More was involved in this process of differentiation
than landholding alone. The finding of replacements for
landholders unwilling or unable to perform in person the
labour services demanded of them under the Cultivation System
also contributed to the growing wealth of the headmen and his
associates. Witness for example the observations of the
European administrator of the big Wonopringo sugar fabriek in
Pekalongan in March 1859:
"... the supply of coolies for the Fabriek gave the petty
chiefs an opportunity to use the coolies for their own

138

purposes ... There was ... a constant traffic in coolies carried on by the loerahs. Sometimes men who did not wish to work as coolies sent as much as half a rupee to the loerah, who found a replacement to whom he gave perhaps 10 doits, reserving 40 doits to his commission."[59]

Renting of Land.   According to Eindresumé, the renting of land (huur en verhuur) was widely practised among the peasantry of a number of the pasisir Residencies c. 1870. It took place on a cash basis, and usually for no more than one year.   Eindresumé   clearly   differentiated   it   from share-cropping, which was also "generally prevalent."[60] The report about landholding practices in Batang already cited makes specific mention of "the hire (verhuren) of sawah" by the landholders of the district, out of which they got enough money to buy substitutes to perform the labour services required by the Cultivation System.[61]

Land as a Saleable Commodity.   Land sale was apparently commonplace in mid-nineteenth century west Java. In central Java, however, where a wholly different set of social and economic institutions prevailed, it was seemingly rare but not unknown. Eindresumé's conclusion was that where it did take place, it was limited to cultivators within the same village, and was a result of a peasant's inability to pay the Land Rent or of old age.[62] Pekalongan evidence from the mid-1850's indicates both land-sale and devices for getting round the 'customary' prohibition of it. According to the Residency's Kultuur Verslag for 1856:

> There exists here an abuse which has crept in over the years, namely of fencing (ompaggeren) the sawah and making so-called gardens of it, which are, however, mostly still planted with padi.

The aim of this procedure, according to the Resident, was to avoid paying Land Rent and to facilitate the sale of the land,

> since the abuse has crept in here of considering house-plots (erven) and suchlike farmland as individual property, in deviation from all Javanese institutions.[63]

Wage Labour.   The existence of wage labour among the peasantry was already noted in the early years of the nineteenth century. It is amply confirmed by mid-century sources such as the Umbgrove Commission. What is of major significance, however, is the increasing use of free wage labour by the sugar factories of the pasisir by the 1860's. This was labour drawn from among the peasantry (though not always from the peasantry of the districts surrounding the mills). Its increasing availability in the final years of

the Cultivation System serves to highlight yet again the need
to consider the sugar industry and the peasantry as bound
together in one economic structure, instead of being divided
into 'modern' and 'traditional' sectors. The Javanese
village did not co-exist, ossified but in its fundamentals
unaltered by the expansion of world market production,
alongside the European-run sugar mills. To take but one
vital instance, the sugar industry's demand for water during
the dry season (both to operate the predominantly
water-powered cane-crushers and to irrigate the newly-planted
cane) played havoc with village agriculture[64] and forced a
section of the village workforce into the orbit of the mills.

As we have seen at an earlier stage of this analysis,
the existence of a landless rural labour-force was something
which had already characterised agricultural production in
this part of Java at the beginning of the nineteenth
century. Control over this workforce had been contested
since the 1830's between the sugar mills on the one hand and
the more substantial peasantry, village-headmen and priyayi
on the other. It was access to labour during the early
months of the Campaign which was the most contentious issue,
because of the conflicting interests of the various parties
who had a call on the services of the menumpangs and other
landless agricultural workers. The more substantial peasants
wanted them for work in the padi-harvest and the planting of
second crops; headmen and priyayi needed to marshall them
for laying-out the cane fields for the following season,
while the fabriek needed as many men as possible to get the
Campaign under way.[65] By the 1860's, it appears that in
Pekalongan at least the fabriek was beginning to win the
battle. One of the chief causes of this was the reduction in
the output of 'village' agriculture in the wake of the sugar
industry. Declining rice harvests, the difficulty of
expanding the existing sawah area and diminished
opportunities for second-cropping were having the effect of
'freeing' a section of the rural workforce which had hitherto
been forcibly recruited for work in the Campaign only with
difficulty and on a very unstable basis. The rural landless
who were dependent on field-work could no longer find a
living within the village, and were forced to seek work in
the sugar factories during the Campaign. This was clearly
perceived both by government officials and fabriek managers
at the time. There was a well-understood equation between
peasant food production and easy recruitment of factory
labour in the sugar industry: a good rice harvest, a fabriek
manager reported from the Kendal Regency of Semarang in 1867,
"has meant that the people have little inclination to work
..." Conversely, in neighbouring Pekalongan a decade
earlier, it was remarked by another of the factory owners
that "the people go about the work eagerly ... to which fact
the failure of the rice-harvest has maybe contributed." By
1870, at the same Pekalongan factory, workers were being

turned away daily from the factory gates, so abundantly were they pouring out of the villages during the dry season. It was, as the management so aptly remarked, "a gratifying spectacle" to see them all crowding outside the factory at the change of shift, each man trying to make sure that he would be taken on.[66] In short, a class of free labourers, dependent for a substantial part of their livelihood on wages earned in the sugar industry, was in the process of formation in the countryside of the pasisir by 1870.

Commodity Food Production.   Well-placed European observers had noted from the onset that the Cultivation System was likely to create an internal market for rice in Java. John Palmer, for example, absentee owner of the Tjikandi Ilir estate in west Java, had remarked to his Batavia agent in 1832 that however ill-advised Van den Bosch's schemes might be, they could well be to the advantage of rice estates such as his, for "rice would never want a market with an increasing population and the devotion of lands to other branches of agriculture."[67]   In fact, it was obvious by the mid-century that the Cultivation System had led to a considerable increase in the traffic in rice between one Residency and another as production was locally curtailled by the demands of the forced cultivations. The Residency of Pekalongan itself, once a major exporter of rice, had become a rice deficit area by the 1850's, in part, at least, as a consequence of the operations of the sugar industry. Population increase was a relatively minor factor here. Indeed in some of the major sugar-growing districts of the Residency it was scarcely a factor at all. In the area which serviced the big Wonopringo factory, for example, there was little significant increase in population until the eighteen sixties. It was the demands of the sugar industry which were a fundamental factor underlying the rice deficit, as the Residency authorities quite openly admitted. The situation was entirely justified in their eyes, nonetheless, by the amount of money which the peasants earned from working for the sugar industry. According, for instance, to the Resident's Kultuurverslag for 1857, the cash gains from sugar outweighed the potential earnings from main-harvest padi and second-cropping taken together, and provided more than enough money to buy rice imported from elsewhere.[68]   The self-serving nature of this analysis (the Resident enjoyed a percentage share in the profits of sugar, but drew nothing extra from the padi harvest) is quite apparent, as is its entire disregard of the elaborate relations of production existing within the peasantry and vastly complicating any realistic calculation of gain and loss. Yet it contains an essential truth: the pressure of the Cultivation System had gone a long way towards developing a generalised commodity production in foodstuffs in rural Java by the second half of the nineteenth century.

141

The Priyayi, the Colonial Authorities and the Sugar Factories

Although free wage labour was beginning to make its appearance in the sugar industry by the 1860's, the part played in the organisation of world market production by extra-economic coercion on the peasantry exercised through the 'gentry' remained considerable. Even so, in many of the north coast Residencies the power of the bupati and their hold over the cultivators had undergone a number of significant changes by the final years of the Cultivation System. As has already been indicated, the erosion of village self-sufficiency in foodstuffs reduced the importance of the priyayi in securing control over peasant land and labour. At the same time, the growth in power and influence of the colonial administration and of the sugar factories themselves meant that the bupati and their subordinates now operated in a markedly different environment than had existed thirty years earlier. To describe them as a 'feudal' class or as the 'traditional' rulers of the countryside serves less to reveal reality than to obscure the changes which were taking place.

The following analysis relates almost exclusively to the Residency of Pekalongan. It is important, therefore, to be aware that this was an area of the pasisir in which the Dutch had particular difficulty in successfully implementing the Cultivation System, not least because of the sustained hostility of the priyayi led by the Regent family of Batang. The old Bupati, Soero Adiningrat, who retired in 1836, and the son who succeeded him both proved to be intractable and very effective opponents of the extension of Dutch power. It was typical, for instance, that when in 1837 an Assistant-Resident was appointed to the bupati's court with the avowed purpose of keeping a close watch on him, the wretched man was disgraced and dismissed within a few months for apparently aligning himself with the Regent against the Residency![69] Despite the peculiarities of the Pekalongan situation, it serves effectively to highlight what was happening to the priyayi throughout the pasisir as world market production was expanded there under the aegis of the Cultivation System.

The Assumption that Expanded World Market Production Could Be Obtained through the Agency of the 'Traditional' Authorities Proves Incorrect. The bupati and their subordinates (the district heads or wedana) were supposed to be the lynch-pin of the Cultivation System. It was through the utilisation of their influence in the countryside that the peasantry were to be organised and disciplined in the business of export-crop growing. (There was a place in Van den Bosch's scheme for financial incentive to the cultivators, but it was in practice a minor one). The opposition or indifference of the priyayi was thus a major blow to the System's hopes of

142

success in the Residency. Their attitude appears to have
been based on two considerations. In the first place, the
System threatened to undermine the existing relations of
production in the countryside of which the priyayi and their
Chinese and 'Arab' connections were major beneficiaries. The
Dutch were quite reckless in their determination to squeeze
as much as possible out of the Residency's sawah, and set
about with a will the 'discovery' of people, land and even on
occasion entire villages. This of course jeopardised the
harvest levies and call on labour services (the 'old ways' as
it were) which had survived under the facade of the Land
Rent.[70] A second consideration was that the priyayi seem
to have rated the new System's chances of success fairly
low. Van den Bosch had hoped to win them over by allowing
them a percentage of the profits of the forced cultivations.
These remained singularly unalluring in Pekalongan, however,
for many years after 1830. Even in the 1850's (by which time
the System had begun to pick up in the Residency), the
cultuurprocenten accruing to Pekalongan's two bupati was
significantly lower than those enjoyed by the Regents in
neighbouring Residencies.[71]

The upshot was that the priyayi failed to provide the
degree of co-operation which the System required for its
successful implementation. In 1844, for example it was said
of the Wedana of Pekalongan that he "appears to cast to the
winds all orders concerning the government service, of
whatever character."[72] This was perhaps an exceptional
case of defiance, yet it betokened an indifference to the
forced cultivations which was widespread among the priyayi.
The Regent of Batang himself set a matchless example. An
investigation into the poor state of the sugar plantations in
his area in July 1844, for instance, produced information
that fewer and fewer peasants were turning out to prepare the
ground for sugar, that those who did come arrived late in the
morning and left early in the afternoon, and that some of the
newly planted cane was already over-run with weeds. The
problem was, the Dutch kontroleur complained to the Resident,
that the Regent would not stir himself to help. This was
despite repeated requests (and the threat of report to the
Resident), the net result of which was:

> that I have so far not been able to discern even the
> slightest improvement in the present feeble execution of
> the work which has to be performed each day, least of
> all as regards the turn-out of labourers.[73]

Faced with recalcitrance of this kind, the Dutch finally
acted in 1848 to break the power of the Regents. During the
course of the year both incumbent bupati were removed from
office, for reasons which had no direct connection with the
failure of the forced cultivations but which can only be
fully understood in the light of long-standing Dutch

143

exasperation at their inability to win over to the Residency's priyayi to the service of the System.[74] In that respect the move was a success. After the mid-century the newly-installed bupati and their subordinates were evidently a deal more responsive to Dutch pressure than previously, and were generally careful to toe the line. By 1855, for example, the Resident could report that "the extortions of the gentry are starting to become a thing of the past." A decade later, with scarcely an exception, the district heads could be described as "very suitable people", while by 1870 the Resident felt confident of saying of the bupati that "their attitude towards the government leaves nothing to be desired."[75]

The Changing Role of the Priyayi in the Organisation of Production.   After the mid-century it is obvious that the bupati and wedana began to collaborate much more effectively with the Residency authorities in the organisation of world market production than had earlier been the case. Their power and influence was nevertheless being eroded to such an extent that description of them as 'traditional rulers' becomes increasingly hollow.

The bupati were both demoralised and lacking in authority. This emerges so clearly from Residency reports of the 1850's that one of them is worth quoting at some length. In 1857, for example, it was remarked that the Regent of Pekalongan himself had retreated into opium-taking, while his counterpart in Batang was utterly pre-occupied with financial and household problems.

> On the other hand, it must not be forgotten that neither of the Regents followed their fathers in the correct line of succession, but that, in consequence of the dismissal or transfer of the former [Regents], were chosen for the post by the government. Hence they have, in a manner of speaking, nothing with which to establish themselves, and the moment of their appointment also signalled the beginning of their insolvency ... There is no need to mention that their authority has suffered as a result of this. Outward show and splendour are still one of the firm supports of the authority of the native rulers ... their power is consequently ... nihil, and both are accounted no higher than any other native official by the ... population of this province. Their prestige as leader is wholly lost.[76]

The weakening of the position of the bupati was paralleled among the priyayi as a whole. In the eyes of the common people they were salaried officials, doing a job: "generally speaking, hereditary prestige does not exist here."[77] Even allowing for some degree of exaggeration in this account (subsequent Residents were a little more sanguine in their

144

analysis), it can scarcely be doubted that the character of the 'traditional' rulers of the countryside was changing to a significant degree under the impress of colonial rule.

The process was considerably assisted by increasing Dutch pressure to reduce the amount of labour services requisitioned by the priyayi from the peasantry and to ensure that the Land Rent functioned as intended, instead of being subverted by the bupati and district heads. This had, of course, the consequence of beginning to remove the priyayi from their position as direct expropriators of the peasant surplus. Equally obviously, it could only proceed in measure with Dutch knowledge of the precise extent of the land and labour resources of the countryside. This left a large area of doubt as to how effective were Dutch intentions. In 1859, for instance, the Resident was inclined to believe that only one of the district heads was still levying rice from the peasantry in return for Land Rent payment,[78] but attempts in the same decade to 're-organise' labour services were frustrated by the lack of reliable population statistics.[79] Still, the Dutch persevered and by the late 1860's a major Opname had been completed in the Residency.[80] By 1870 the colonial authorities there were sufficiently confident to speak of a "major contraction of heerendiensten, especially of the personal services for the native officials" as having taken place.[81]

The position of the priyayi in the organisation of world market production in Pekalongan after 1850 was undoubtedly both changing and complex. On the one hand, as long as the cultivation of cane continued to be carried out on the basis of forced labour (ie. until well after the 'end' of the System in 1870), they appeared to be a vital part of the operation. An extract from the dagboek of the kontroleur of Pekalongan for the 6th May 1858, for example, shows very clearly how directly instrumental even the bupati themselves were in the running of the plantations:

> Rode with the Regent to the Wonopringo fabriek. Surveyed the land for the new [cane] planting. Took this opportunity of pressing the Regent to instruct the Wedono and Mantries to ensure that the ploughing of the ground is done deeper than before. The Regent complied with this immediately.[82]

Even in this sphere of production, however, reservations about the role of the priyayi creep in. By 1870 the owners of this same factory at Wonopringo could seriously contemplate the 'free' planting of around 400 bouw of land, "by arrangement with the landholders" and "without the intervention of the Native Chiefs."[83]

For the Campaign itself (the manufacturing season lasting from May until September/October) there are much clearer indications that by the later years of the

Cultivation System the priyayi were no longer indispensable. In any event, the position which they held in the process of world market production had undergone a significant transformation. In Pekalongon in 1856, one of the wedana felt confident enough to tell the administrator of the Wonopringo sugar fabriek that it was useless for the factory to attempt labour recruitment on its own account. The "orang ketjil" (the 'common people') would obey only him.[84] Yet within little more than a decade, workers were massing outside the factory gates waiting to be taken on. Here the vital point was that by the mid-sixties the supply of forced labour recruited by the colonial authorities to work during the Campaign had largely been phased out in Pekalongan.[85] Some controversy surrounds the 'free' labour which replaced it.[86] There is some evidence, for example, that priyayi and headmen continued to supply labour to the factories as before, with the difference that this was now the result of private arrangements made directly and discreetly with the fabriek, with the possible connivance of the Residency authorities. "I need hardly inform you", wrote Wonopringo's administrator to his employers in Batavia in 1863, "that here almost everything is compulsory".[87] Yet within only a few years there had been significant changes, both in Pekalongan and in neighbouring Semarang. As has already been mentioned, the growing inability of the peasantry to provide for their own livelihood from village agriculture alone was forcing sections of the rural workforce directly into the orbit of the mills. In this, the role of the priyayi seems to have become one of disciplining labour rather than recruiting it. Their authority was vital in keeping peasants to the contracts.[88] To be sure, both priyayi and headmen were in receipt of cash payments from the sugar factories. Arguably, however, these payments were as much to compensate for the labour lost to them as to encourage them in their role of labour broker. In the Kendal division of Semarang Residency in the 1860's, for example, the difficulties experienced by the sugar manufacturers in getting labour during the 'Campaign' were said to relate to:

> The arbitrariness and opposition of the Native Chiefs, who attempt as much as possible to suppress the free development of labour-power among the Javanese on account of it conflicting with their own interests and prestige, while to date they have seen in the people's compulsory labour services a source of authority and considerable income.

By 1866, however, it was remarked that "perseverance, good management and generous payments" had put an end to the opposition of the local Javanese authorities. Recruitment of free labour could now proceed without hindrance from either headmen or priyayi[89].

The Sugar Factories Begin to Involve Themselves in Cane Production. It was not, however, simply that the priyayi were being forced to relinquish some degree of control over the organisation of production. In the sugar-growing lowlands of Pekalongan, as elsewhere in the pasisir, there was a new factor in the situation: the European-run sugar fabriek, which was becoming an ubiquitous feature of the countryside. The putative arrangement of the sugar industry under the Cultivation System was for cane to be grown by the peasantry under the supervision of village headmen and priyayi, and for the business of harvesting and milling the cane (and that alone) to be in the hands of the fabriek, run for the most part by European contractors.[90] This dichotomy of production caused a lot of problems for the mills and was soon abandoned in practice. The output of sugar, and hence the contractor's profit, was closely tied to the quality of the cane. Factory technology was only a secondary consideration.[91] In these circumstances, it was not long before the fabriek began to take a hand in the organisation of cane cultivation. At Wonopringo, the biggest of the three major Pekalongan sugar mills in the mid-nineteenth century, the fabriek's administrator was already by the early 1850's making regular, monthly inspections of the cane-fields with evident confidence that his recommendations would be acted upon. The fact that the Dutch kontroleur of the district dined at Wonopringo each week presumably facilitated this. By the close of the decade the fabriek had installed some overseers of its own in the plantations, had introduced deeper ploughing and new planting methods and was discreetly suborning the wedana.[92] In short, the fabriek did not stand apart from the arrangements for cultivating cane. On the contrary, long before the close of the era of the Cultivation System, it had become deeply involved in all aspects of production.

Conclusion: Capitalism in Rural Java

The bulk of this paper has been devoted to discussion of the society and economy of rural Java as it existed in the mid-nineteenth century prior to and during the era of the Cultivation System. As I see it, the fundamental argument revolves around two major issues. The first concerns the kind of socio-economic structures which characterised the countryside of Java in the early nineteenth century, and the second relates to the nature of the changes which took place with the acceleration of world market production after 1830. My contention throughout has been that potential for development of a capitalist kind existed in rural Java in the opening decades of the nineteenth century, and that subsequent developments, far from representing the petrifaction of 'pre-capitalist' structures, revealed a pervasive growth of capitalist relations and purposes.

It is, of course, precisely in the area of the relations and purposes of production that the nub of the dispute is located. If I understand it correctly (and the argument is certainly susceptible to varying emphases of interpretation) Agricultural Involution's position is that peasant production remained predominately subsistence, while world-market production was confined to the 'modern', western-controlled sector. At the same time, the relations of production among the peasantry remained 'traditional' and best comprehended in non-class terms. In a celebrated passage, Geertz spoke of a rural society which had contrived to maintain a "comparatively high degree of social and economic homogeneity by dividing the economic pie into a steadily increasing number of minute pieces." There can be little doubt that in Geertz's view this pie was a non-capitalist one. There is, to be sure, an incipiently capitalist woof to the warp of Agricultural Involution : a nascent 'rural bourgeoisie' is shown in the making, as major landholders and agents for the sugar mills in their dealings with the peasantry at large. It is clear, however, that Geertz sees this development as a short-term aberration from the overall pattern of 'involution', and one which was aborted by the Depression of the 1930's.[93] Far more characteristic of his Javanese society in the long-term was the continued and strengthened existence of a series of re-distributive mechanisms which formed the basis for "shared poverty". The consequence of these, according to Geertz, was that any disparities in land-holding which may' have existed within the peasantry were no real guide to socio-economic differentiation. The emergence of classes within the peasantry was militated against by essentially benign arrangements for share-cropping, harvest-work and so on, which resulted in a peasantry composed of "just enoughs and not-quite enoughs" rather than "haves and have-nots". In short, the 'involuted' peasantry of Java was depicted as something other than capitalist, both in terminology and in concept. The view is by no means unique to Agricultural Involution, however, and finds expression in a number of writers whose debt to Geertz is otherwise by no means obvious. In a recent paper reviewing Javanese political economy, for example, Dr. Dick Robison argues (inter alia) that with the acceleration of world market production in the mid-nineteenth century, "pre-capitalist modes were frozen" and that in consequence the "existing Javanese agrarian relations of production" had been consolidated.[94] As will be obvious, the argument here is that quite the contrary took place. On the one hand, the stimulating character of Geertz's writings about Java over the last twenty-five years is something which can scarcely be overestimated. Yet a brilliant hypothesis is precisely what Agricultural Involution remains, and it would be a pity if it were mistaken for something more. I have attempted to demonstrate in this paper that a rather different view of what was happening in nineteenth century Java can be maintained, supported by the historical data which is increasingly becoming available.

I have been led to this conclusion by a number of considerations. The first arises from a rejection of 'dualist' explanations of economic development in colonial Java. The argument presented here asserts the indivisability of the relations between peasantry, 'gentry' and sugar industry. A highly significant instance was the undermining of peasant self-sufficiency in foodstuffs as a result of the industry's demands for land, water and labour. The consequences of this, as well as many other important developments relating to both villagers and priyayi, have been outlined in the foregoing analysis. The outcome, far from representing petrifaction of the existing organisation of production, represented the drawing of the rural economy and society firmly into the orbit of capitalist enterprise. In the process, they became an integral part of a capitalist system of production.

The extent of this integration becomes even more apparent when the effects of accelerated world-market production on the social and economic relations existing within the peasantry are examined in greater detail. I have already indicated how deceptive is the picture of a largely homogeneous 'traditional' village world of peasant farms worked more-or-less exclusively by familial labour. An historical account of the 'traditional' society of the rural pasisir can only with difficulty be pushed back as far as 1800. What it reveals is that even in the opening decades of the nineteenth century agricultural production was organised among the peasantry on the basis of a broad differentiation between landholders and landless. Although this differentiation may have been called into question by the pressures exerted by the colonial authorities in the early years of the Cultivation System, there is every indication that in the long-run it was confirmed and strengthened by the profits which the System brought to the 'privileged', larger landholding groups within the peasantry. The 'big peasantry' did not disappear from the countryside of nineteenth century Java as a consequence of the alleged levelling effects of the Cultivation System. On the contrary, it was precisely this group who were among its beneficiaries.

As a result, agricultural production continued to be organised among the peasantry on the basis of share-cropping, land-rental and day-labour arrangements between the landholders and the landless. It was the rural landless who were also drawn on an increasingly 'voluntary' basis into the sugar industry as cane-cutters and factory "coolies". To be sure, in neither case could they be described as fully proletarianised. The relations which existed between them and the peasant landholders were clearly characterised by something more than a purely economic nexus. Clientage, for instance, had a multiplicity of extra-economic dimensions. Likewise (as Geertz observed) the majority of Javanese workers in the sugar industry were seasonal only, returning to the village after the Campaign.

Yet to view the Campaign workforce as fundamentally a 'part-time peasantry' is to ignore the fact that the rural landless were becoming increasingly dependent on what they could earn as labourers in the sugar industry. The diminished returns of 'village' agriculture under the impact of export crop production (taken together, after the mid-century, with growing numbers) meant that those who had formerly found their livelihood largely within the village could no longer do so. They had been brought, by one route or another, to a marked dependency on the sugar factories. In the circumstances, the contention that they were not 'fully proletarianised' runs the risk of becoming a merely pedantic device. A similar charge might be levelled at insistance on the paramountcy of extra-economic factors in determining the relationship between landholder and landless among the peasantry. Both arguments for the non-development of capitalism in rural Java during the colonial period are founded on a paradigm of what constitutes capitalist development that is profoundly misleading. It is a paradigm that might fit, let us say, the relations between General Motors and its factory workforce, but is totally inadequate to describe the complex relations, both past and present, which are generally accepted as being capitalist. Forms of clientage, for example, existed and continue to exist within the framework of capitalist production. It can only serve to obscure understanding of what was taking place in colonial Java to insist that their demonstrable presence rules out the simultaneous possibility of capitalist development.

NOTES

1.   The concept of 'involution' is, of course, primarily derived from Clifford Geertz, Agricultural Involution: The Process of Ecological Change in Indonesia (University of California Press, Berkeley and Los Angeles, 1963). The widespread acceptance of Geertz's hypothesis can be judged from a number of recent attempts at synthesis, eg., P.R.B. Carey, "Aspects of Javanese History in the Nineteenth Century", in Harry Aveling (ed.), The Development of Indonesian Society (University of Queensland Press, St. Lucia, 1979), pp. 84-5 and Susan Abeyasekere, "Social and Economic Effects of Increasing European Penetration in the Nineteenth and Twentieth Centuries", in Elaine McKay (ed.), Studies in Indonesian History (Pitman Australia, Melbourne, 1976), pp. 130-1. That this acceptance has extended to major scholarly research is demonstrated by Onghokham's Ph.D thesis on 'The Residency of Madiun: Pryayi and Peasant in Nineteenth

Century Java', Yale, 1975. For a discussion and further reference concerning the argument for the late, post-colonial appearance of capitalism in the countryside, see Frans Husken, "Landlords, Sharecroppers and Agricultural Labourers: Changing Labour Relations in Rural Java", Journal of Contemporary Asia, Vol. 9, No. 1 (1979), pp. 140-51, and Alec Gordon, "Some Problems of Analysing Class Relations in Indonesia", Journal of Contemporary Asia, Vol. 8, No. 2 (1978), pp. 210-218. I have been greatly assisted in the writing of this paper by many discussions with my colleague Dr. Doug McEachern, who was also kind enough to provide me with a copy of his paper on "Colonialism and Colonial Modes of Production". I am deeply grateful also to my colleague Dr. P.L. Burns, without whose constant encouragement this paper would have remained unwritten.

2.   For criticism of 'involution' from (primarily) the standpoint of twentieth century developments, see William L. Collier "Agricultural Evolution in Java: The Decline of Shared Poverty and Involution", mimeo. Bogor [1976] and Declining Labour Absorption (1878-1980) in Javanese Rice Production, (Bogor, 1979). I am grateful to Dr. Collier for providing me with copies of these papers. A most useful summary of this and similar criticism is Hiroyoshi Kano, "The Economic History of Javanese Rural Society: A Re-Interpretation", The Developing Economies, Vol. 18, No. 1 (1980), pp. 3-22. A notable critique of Geertz's picture of nineteenth century Javanese development is R.E. Elson, The Cultivation System and Agricultural Involution, Monash Centre for Southeast Asian Studies, Working Papers, No. 14 (1978). Likewise, see Jennifer & Paul Alexander, "Labour Demands and the 'Involution' of Javanese Agriculture", Social Analysis, No. 3 (1979), pp. 22-44 and the extensive bibliography therein.

3.   Although terms such as 'feudal' and 'traditional' appear to be falling into disuse in the context of discussion nineteenth century Java they are still in evidence in a number of important and influential works eg. W.F. Wertheim, Indonesian Society in Transition (Van Hoeve, The Hague/Bandung, 1959), pp. 133, 156 & 159 and (with considerable qualification) in D.H. Burger, Sociologisch-Economische Geschiedenis van Indonesia, Vol. 1 (Wageningen, 1975), pp. 104-5 & 124-5. Despite this, it must be said that Burger's work still represents one of the very few significant attempts to grapple schematically with the problems of Javanese development. A recent plea for the applicability of the 'asiatic mode of production' in this context is Alec Gordon, "Stages in the Development of Java's Socio-Economic Formations, 700-1979", Journal of Contemporary Asia, Vol. 9, No. 2 (1979), pp. 129-39. F. Tichelman, The Social Evolution of Indonesia: The Asiatic Mode of Production and its Legacy (Nijhoff, The Hague, 1980) arrived too late for incorporation into this paper. Tichelman's

remarks about the Cultivation System ("pre-capitalist methods of appropriating agrarian surplus, whether in kind or in labour") form a valuable counterpoint to the present argument, but do not appear to be supported by the sort of historical evidence which is increasingly becoming available.

4.   "Provisional ... View of the Regency of Samarang and its Dependencies [By Mr. Knops, 1812]". India Office Library, London (hereafter cited as IOL), Mackenzie Collection (Private) 79, p. 195.

5.   Le Clercq expanded on keriks: "they were people who had no field ... the keriks were free men ... [who] worked the fields of the loerahs or hired them from them. See "Bijdragen tot de Kennis van der Inlandsche Huishouding op Java", Tijdschrijft voor Nederlandsch-Indie, Vol. XXIV, No. 1 (1862), pp. 75-6.

6.   J. Knops & P.H. v. Lawick v. Pabst, "Java als het is ... 1812". IOL Mackenzie (Private) 56, pp. 81 and 128-9.

7.   "Statistiek Pekalongan [1823]", C/1. Algemeen Rijksarchief, The Hague (hereafter cited as ARA), Collectie Schneither 90; "Algemeen Jaarverslag Samarang 1823," pp. 265-6. ARA Schneither 91.

8.   Knops, cited in T.S. Raffles, Substance of a Minute Recorded by the Honourable Thomas Stamford Raffles ... (London, 1814), pp. 30-2.

9.   "Statistic Report on the District of Rembang". 1812, IOL Mackenzie (Private) 7, pp. 264-5.

10.   Knops & Lawick, "Java als het is". IOL Mackenzie (Private) 56, pp. 22, 81 & 205-6.

11.   Raffles, Substance, pp.80-1.

12.   See note 7.

13.   "Statistiek Samarang [1822]", C/1. ARA Schneither 91.

14.   [W.B. Bergsma], Eindresumé van het ... Onderzoek naar de Rechten van de Inlander op den Grond op Java en Madura, Vol. 2 (Batavia, 1876-96), p. 144.

15.   Knops & Lawick, "Java als het is". IOL Mackenzie (Private) 56, pp. 113-31.

16.   "Extract Replies ... by Mr. Hardy, Landrost of Pekalongan." 1812. IOL Mackenzie (Private) 7, pp. 46-8.

17.   "Provisional ... View of the Regency of Samarang [1812]", IOL Mackenzie (Private) 79, pp. 205-6.

18.   Raffles, Substance, pp. 80-1.

19.   "Memoir and Answer of Dr. Doornik, Landrost of Japara". 1812. IOL Mackenzie (Private) 7, pp. 179-80.

20.   "Statistiek Pekalongan [1823]", B/1. ARA Schneither 90; A decade later, when the Dutch official P.F. Clignett reported on a Land Rent investigation which he had carried out in several pasisir Residencies, including Pekalongan, he too left a strong implication that the peasant farm worked exclusively with familial labour was a rarity, at least in the lowlands. See S. van Deventer, Bijdragen tot de

Kennis van het Landelijk Stelsel op Java, Vol. 3 (Zalt-Bommel 1866), p. 49.

21.   J.I. van Sevenhoven, "Java: ten Diensten van hen die over dit Eiland Wenschen te Reizen", Tijdschrijft voor Nederlandsch-Indie, Vol. I, No. 1 (1838), pp. 29-30.

22.   "Algemeen Jaarverslag Japara' 1823", p. 48. ARA Schneither 92.

23.   "Solo is immer de Negari", "Politiek Verslag Pekalongan. 1857", p. 7 Arsip Nasional Republik Indonesia (hereafter cited as AN), Jakarta, Pekalongan Residentie Archief. (Pekalongan) 1.

24.   Knops & Lawick, "Java als het is". IOL Mackenzie (Private) 56, pp. 113-31.

25.   "Points of Inquiry Concerning the District of Rembang". 1812. IOL Mackenzie (Private) 7, p. 99.

26.   "Memoir and Answer of Mr. Doornick, 1812". IOL Mackenzie (Private), 7, pp. 174-5.

27.   Knops & Lawick," Java als het is". IOL Mackenzie (Private) 56, pp. 131-47.

28.   "Provisional ... View of the Regency of Samarang [1812]". IOL Mackenzie (Private) 79, p. 201.

29.   S.v. Deventer, Bijdragen tot de Kennis ven het Landelijk Stelsel, Vol. 1, p. 8. In 1808 the Dutch Landrost Van Middelkoop reckoned that out of a total annual income of Sp. Dollars 9,696 enjoyed by the Regent of Pekalongan, some 6811 Sp. Dollars came from the hire of villages to the Chinese. See: "Bijlagen behoorende tot de Memorie van ... J.A.v. Middelkoop, 1808". Bijlagen, no. 6, AN Pekalongan 48.

30.   This is too complex an issue to enter into here. Some useful preliminary remarks by B.J. Elias (Director of Cultivations between 1833 and 1836) are to be found in his Report of 31.3, 1833 no. 2875. ARA Collectie Baud 454.

31.   "Copie Verslag ... van den Inspecteur der Kultures L. Vitalis over zijn Regeling van de Kultures in de Residentie Pekalongan, 29.10.1834", p. 5. ARA Baud 460.

32.   W. Beeckman," Verslag Pekalongan ... 1803". AN Pekalongan 48. Beeckman's account, which only mentions Javanese in the running of the indigo factories, implies that the workforce were assigned sawah by the Regent on the strength of their involvement in indigo production. In the Ulujami district (leased by Chinese) there was mention of "paying" and "hiring" people to work in the indigo factory.

33.   See G.R. Knight, "Estates and Plantations in Java, 1812-1834", unpublished Ph.D. Thesis, University of London, London 1968, pp. 297-310.

34.   "Extract Replies ... by Mr. Hardy, Landrost of Pekalongan". 1812. IOL Mackenzie (Private) 7, pp. 43-4.

35.   J.B.J. van Doren, Reis naar Nederlands Oost-Indie, of Land-en-Zeetogten Gedurende de Twee Eerste Jaren Mijns Verblijfs op Java, Vol 2, (The Hague, 1851), pp. 257-9.

36.   See eg. Vitalis's remarks about the Regent of

Batang being in the "leading strings of the Chinese woman Oeij Thaijlo", to whom he was forcing the peasantry to deliver rice. "Verslag Vitalis Pekalongan", 1834, pp. 35-6, ARA Baud 460.

37. "Statistiek Samarang [1822]," C/3. ARA Schneither 91. Domis also pointed out that a considerable trade in rice also took place between the plains and the hills, on account of the difference in harvest times.

38. "Statistiek Samarang [1822]", G/3. ARA Schneither 91.

39. Rapport Van Beusechem/Pekalongan c. 1832, p. 47. ARA Archief Ministerie van Kolonien (hereafter cited as Kolonien) 3050.

40. "Algemeen Jaarverslag Pekalongan 1823", pp. 67-8. ARA Schneither 90.

41. C. Fasseur, Kultuurstelsel en Koloniale Baten, (Universitaire Pers, Leiden, 1975), pp. 25-7 & 57-9.

42. "Politiek Verslag Pekalongan 1866", p. 3. AN Pekalongan 2.

43. The thesis is to be found stated with varying degrees of emphasis in: W.F. Wertheim, Indonesian Society in Transition, (Van Hoeve The Hague/Bandung, 1959), pp. 139-41; D.H. Burger, Sociologisch-Economische Geschiedenis van Indonesia, Vol. I, pp. 113-5; J.S. Furnivall, Netherlands India, (Cambridge University Press, Cambridge, 1939, pp. 140-1; G.H. van der Kolff, "European Influence on Native Agriculture", in B. Schrieke, The Effect of Western Influence on Native Civilisations in the Malay Archipelago, (G. Kolff en Co., Batavia, 1929), pp. 110-11. The most influential recent re-statement, of course, remains that of Clifford Geertz in Agricultural Involution. The overall impression left by Geertz's work of Javanese society homogenised and ossified by its contact with the sugar industry/colonial rule is not always borne out by a close examination of his text. For instance, as regards the alleged social levelling brought about by land re-distribution under the Cultivation System, Geertz recognizes that "periodic rotation" only occurred among the "qualified families" (Involution, p. 91). Yet the implications of this for his argument are quickly submerged in the development of the main theme: that rural Java "maintained a comparatively high degree of social and economic homogeneity by dividing the economic pie into a steadily increasing number of minute pieces" (p. 97).

44. Fasseur, Kultuurstelsel, pp. 13-14. I have used Professor Fasseur's discussion of this issue both for its recent origin and because he states the case so moderately and with such careful reference to the historical origins of the idea. This is clearly far from the full-blown Geertzian position. Professor Fasseur has re-iterated and supported his argument in "Organisatie en Sociaal-Economische Betekenis van de Governments Suikerkultuur in Enkele Residenties op Java Omstreeks 1850", Bijdragen tot de Taal-, Land- en

Volkenkunde, Vol. 133 (1977), pp. 270-4.

45. Eg., Dr. Elson's findings, in "The Impact of the Government Sugar Cultivation in the Pasuruan Area, East Java, during the Cultivation System Period", Review of Indonesian and Malay Affairs, Vol. 12, No. 1 (1978), pp. 51-5. My own conclusions from research in Pekalongan also point to the fact that some landholders did relatively well out of the Cultivation System. See above, p. 138.

46. "Kultuurverslag Pekalongan 1857". ARA Collectie De Vriese 59; "Kultuurverslag Pekalongan 1864" [Fragment: Heerendiensten]. AN Pekalongan 99.

47. E.g. Professor Onghokham's valuable recent study of the Residency of Madiun makes extensive use of the findings of Eindresumé. See 'The Residency of Madiun: Priyayi and Peasant in the Nineteenth Century', Ph.D. Thesis, Yale University, 1975, especially pp. 177-8 & 185-97. A bibliographical note on Eindresumé appears above, footnote 14.

48. Eindresumé, 1, pp. iii-xi; 2, pp. 294-5 & 302-5. Fasseur, Kultuurstelsel, p. 13.

49. "Monographie Fabriek Wonopringo". III/C p. 20. ARA Kolonien 1181. A general introduction to the Umbgrove Commission's findings in Fasseur, Bijdragen tot de Taal-, Land- en Volkenkunde, Vol. 133 (1977), pp. 261-93.

50. Eindresumé, 2, p. 84.

51. "Monographie Fabriek Wonopringo". III/C p. 21. ARA Kolonien 1181.

52. Dr. Elson has reached similar conclusions for the Oosthoek. See Review of Indonesian and Malay Affairs, Vol. 12, No. 1 (1978), pp. 51-2.

53. "Monographie Fabriek Wonopringo". III/C pp. 18-23. ARA Kolonien 1181. The reports from the other two government-contract factories in Pekalongan tell a more or less identical story.

54. This information is taken from sections III/B & C of the Umbgrove reports on the sugar factories Sragie, Kalimatie and Wonopringo, all for the mid-50's. ARA Kolonien 1181.

55. Van Deventer, Landelijk Stelsel, Vol. 3, pp. 266-7.

56. "Monographie Fabriek Wonopringo". III/C p. 21. ARA Kolonien 1181.

57. "Politiek Verslag Pekalongan 1859", p. 3-4. AN Pekalongan 1; Resident Pekalongan to Director of Cultivations 21.3.1869/1. AN Archief Cultures (hereafter cited as AN. A/C), 458.

58. Fasseur, Bijdragen tot de Taal-, Land- en Volkenkunde, Vol. 133 (1977), pp. 267-8.

59. Extract from a Letter of the Administrator of Wonopringo, 19.3.1859 in Factory to A'dam, 26.3.1859/2583. ARA Archief N.H.M./Tweede Afdeeling B (hereafter cited as NHM).

60. <u>Eindresumé</u>, 1, pp. 79-81.

61. See note 57.

62. <u>Eindresumé</u>, 1, pp. 45-51.

63. "Kultuurverslag Pekalongan 1856". AN A/C 1624.

64. See, e.g., the comments of the Director of Cultivations on how vital an issue water rights were to the peasantry, and on the effects on peasant agriculture of a sugar industry still dependant primarily on water-power. Advies D.C. 4.8.1860, Exh. 3369/2. AN A/C 463 & Advies D.C. 1.5.1862, Exh. 2093/2. AN A/C 481.

65. I have followed in this the analysis of the difficulties in getting 'free' labour written for his employers by the administrator of the Wonopringo fabriek in the early 1860's. One point at least needs further clarification, and this concerns the role of women in the rural workforce. It may well be that, then as now, most of the harvest work was carried on by women, in which case the concurrent demands on peasant males may have been somewhat reduced. Of course, the padi-harvest was also a time of important rural festivals, which again competed with the mundane demands of the sugar manufacturers. See Factory to A'dam, 29.12.1864/1315. ARA NHM.

66. "Nota over de Suikerfabrieken Wonopringo, Pegoe, Gemoe en Tjipiring," in Factory to A'dam, 27.6.1867/1576; Factory to A'dam 25.8.1857/577; Van Gennep, "Nota Betreffende de Suikerondernemingen" in Factory to A'dam, 17.7.1869/1764. ARA NHM.

67. See my "John Palmer and Plantation Development in Western Java during the Earlier Nineteenth Century", in <u>Bijdragen tot de Taal-, Land- en Volkenkunde</u>, Vol. 131 (1975), pp. 332-3.

68. "Kultuurverslag Pekalongan 1857", ARA Collectie De Vriese 59.

69. Gouverneur-Generaal Buiten Rade (GGBR) 3.1.1837/4. ARA Kolonien 2566; GGBR 7.9.1837/16. ARA Kolonien 2574.

70. See, e.g., Vitalis's difficulties with the Regent of Batang over the expansion of indigo cultivation in 1834, and a similar dispute between the Regent and a newly-arrived sugar contractor over land-use, three years later. See footnote 31 above and Inspector of Cultivations to D.C., 10.8.1837 Exh. 2261/2. AN A/C 379.

71. See, e.g., the comments of the Director of Cultivations in GGBR 22.4.1849/8 ARA Kolonien 2717 and Director of Cultivations to G.G. 26.4.1855 in Exh. Kolonien 24.10.1865/21. It appears that c. 1850 the Regent of Batang was drawing f. 2,142 annually from the cultuurprocenten, and the Regent of Pekalongan f. 3794. In neighbouring Tegal, the Tegal bupati himself got f. 4872. The Regent of Cheribon further along the coast, got f. 6311.

72. Kontroleur Afdeeling Pekalongan to Resident of Pekalongan, 23.7.1844. AN Pekalongan 106.

73. Kontroleur Afdeeling Batang to Resident of Pekalongan, 20.7.1844. AN Pekalongan 106.

74. GGBR 8.2.1847/1. Kolonien 2691; Geheim Besluiten GG, 10.9.1848, Lett E/2. ARA Kolonien 4513.

75. "Politiek Verslag Pekalongan 1855", p. 7. AN Pekalongan Archief 1; "Politiek Verslag Pekalongan", 1865 & 1870, AN Pekalongan 2.

76. "Politiek Verslag Pekalongan 1857", pp. 41-4. AN Pekalongan 2.

77. See note 76.

78. "Politiek Verslag Pekalongan 1859", p. 15. AN Pekalongan 1.

79. Resident of Pekalongan to Director of Cultivations, 1.5.1861/884. Exh. 2344/17. AN A/C 1398.

80. "Politiek Verslag Pekalongan 1869". AN Pekalongan 2.

81. See note 80.

82. "Extract uit het Dagboek van den Kontoleur der Afdeeling Pekalongan". [6.5.1858]. AN Pekalongan 99.

83. Ven Gennep, "Nota Betreffende de Kultuurondernemingen", in Factory to A'dam, 17.7.1869/1764, ARA NHM.

84. Factory to Director of Cultivations, 31.1.1857, in Factory to A'dam, 11.3.1857/533. ARA NHM.

85. "Jaarverslag Batavia Factorij NHM, 1869-70", 45, pp. 95-104; Factory to A'dam, 27.7.1866/1479. ARA NHM.

86. See, e.g., Fasseur, Kultuurstelsel, pp. 129-49.

87. Quoted in Factory to A'dam, 14.10.1863/1197. ARA NHM.

88. The sugar factories (e.g., in Semarang Residency) evidently found that the giving of cash advances was unavoidable in the business of free labour recruitment. The 'problem' then remained of ensuring that the contracts were honoured. This was evidently giving the factories a good deal of trouble c. 1869. Factory to A'dam, 18.6.1870/1880; Nota van den Heer Morbotter (n.d.) in Factory to A'dam, 14.12.1867/1627. ARA N.H.M.

89. "Jaarverslag Batavia Factorij NHM, 1865-6", pp. 225-7; Factory to A'dam, 27.7.1866/IA79, ARA N.H.M.

90. On the development of the sugar industry under the Cultivation System, see Fasseur, Kultuurstelsel, passim.

91. In Pekalongan by 1847, for instance, the contractor Louis Vitalis (the former Inspector of Cultivations) was already claiming "the right ... to keep an eye on the work of cane-planting". Vitalis to Resident Schiff, 2.9.1847. AN Pekalongan 74.

92. I am at present preparing a short monograph on the Wonopringo Fabriek which will, I hope, demonstrate this and related points about the mid-nineteenth century development of the sugar industry in some detail. On the question of the relations between the Fabriek and the priyayi, see e.g. Factory to A'dam 24.10.1857/594. ARA NHM.

93.	The most interesting example of this is to be found in Geertz's The Social History of an Indonesian Town (M.I.T. Press, Cambridge, Mass., 1965), pp. 40-42. What clearly needs a great deal more attention from scholars than it has yet received is Geertz's interpretation of the fate of the 'big-peasants' during the Depression and the War Years which followed. Far less attention is paid to this "genuine rural middle class" (Social History, p. 42) in the pages of Involution, presumably because in the overall pattern of 'involution' Geertz perceived it as a developmental cul-de-sac.

94.	Dick Robison, "Culture, Politics and Economy in the Analysis of Indonesian Political History." Paper presented to the 3rd National Conference, Asian Studies Association of Australia, Brisbane (1980), p.17. A revised version of this paper has subsequently appeared in Indonesia, Vol. 31 (1981), pp. 1-29.

Chapter 5

CAPITALISM AND THE MALAY STATES

P.L. Burns

Much of the discussion in the proceeding essays has focused
on the problem of how capitalism came to be established in
societies where production of commodities for the
international market was largely located in agriculture. As
we have seen, in some cases the colonial state often played a
critical role in initiating the process of transformation in
the mode of production, in others, trade and expanded
production of agricultural commodities set in motion a
pattern of change which the colonial state helped to deepen
and consolidate. The case of the Malay States - those which
were the principle producers of tin in the nineteenth
century, Perak, Selangor and Sungei Ujong - offers a very
different context for examining this process of
transformation. Here, in the Malay States, the
transformation of the social relations in production
underwent a profound change during the nineteenth century.
This is most clearly apparent in the tin industry. In this
case, the colonial state did not initiate the process, it was
the Malay chief as owner of the mines who, with unintended
consequences, rendered the change. Merchants intervened in
the process of production to insure their control over the
commodities which, on the one hand, helped to sustain the
expansion of tin production and, on the other, insured their
control over the marketing of the mineral in the
international market place. In all of this, peasant
surpluses, in terms of agriculture produce, were not
immediately critical to the new mode of production which
emerged before the establishment of the colonial state. The
Malay States' case allows us to see how capitalist production
can occur before direct colonial rule is established and how
it can set the conditions under which agricultural production
is eventually incorporated into the new mode of production.

There exists for Malaya an extensive body of literature
of high quality on the period before and after the
establishment of British rule, on the colonial state, and on
the development of the economy under colonialism. There is a

wide measure of agreement about the broad dimensions of this experience and remarkably little controversy of the kind found in Indonesian historiography and especially in that on India, about the nature and character of these changes. In many of these works, 1874 - the year Britain established its control over the tin-producing states of Perak, Selangor, and Sungei Ujong - is often taken as the point of departure. For those who have adopted this periodisation, it has rested uneasily as they acknowledge the continuities in the history of tin and planting, which were well launched by the time the first British Resident was appointed to the Malay State, and, as well, the persistence of elements of 'traditional' Malay society represented by the aristocracy and peasantry.[1] What has been unclear about all these accounts is what was central to the changes of this period; indeed there is no single causal explanation. The difficulty of characterising the changes has been thoughtfully weighed up by Khoo Kay Kim who has argued that the period 1850 to 1874 saw 'the pressure of extraneous forces' direct Malay society 'towards a new course of development'. Yet, for him it was a period of 'confusion', and he concludes that

> If change in the early post-1874 period was largely political in nature, in the third quarter of the nineteenth century the significant developments were basically economic in content: the growth of the Chinese community, the expansion of tin production to meet the growing demand of the tin-plate industry, the surrender of economic control by the Malay chiefs to Straits merchants and, most importantly, even the very basic causes of political turbulence.[2]

This thorough, richly documented study is quite the best account of the intimate 'commercial' links which were forged between the Straits Settlements merchants and the Malay chiefs in nineteenth century Malaya. Nevertheless, it is a study about the politics generated by these changes, not of the deep social and economic changes themselves. We are still left with a need for a comprehensive explanation of why and how the transformation of society occurred in the tin producing states of Perak, Selangor and Sungei Ujong. The growth of the tin industry, the migration of Chinese and the extension of Chinese and European capital to these states, do not in themselves constitute an explanation of why the Malay chiefs were unable to sustain their 'traditional' social and political institutions, or why 'capitalist' forms of economic activity necessarily emerged. Khoo Kay Kim characterises the period prior to British intervention as one of 'little constructive change'; it will be argued here that, on the contrary, it is a period which marks the break into the 'modern' world, a period of profound structural change, one

160

which saw the emergence of a capitalist mode of production, at least in these three states.

Pre-colonial Society and State

While the scholarship of recent years has done much to deepen our understanding of pre-colonial Malaya, conceptually, that concerning the structure of society has not gone much beyond the functionalist assumptions of J. Gullick's Indigenous Political Systems of Western Malaya (1958).[3] What is still wanting is an account of the social basis of production and power in these societies in which the class relations are more clearly discernible prior to British rule. It is necessary, therefore, briefly to attempt such a general account, which, while carrying the weaknesses of any general statement, is applicable to the three states central to this chapter, Perak, Selangor and Sungei Ujong.

All three states were built around the major river systems which afforded navigable means of communication, access to areas in the interior where sedentary agricultural communities arose and allowed for the exploitation of the natural wealth of the forests and land itself. The three states had been forged out of a long struggle for control over the area by numerous rivals, both European and Southeast Asian. Perak was built on the extensive river system which bears its name. Selangor which became a Bugis Kerajaan (kingdom) in the eighteenth century was built upon the three rivers, the Selangor, Klang and Langat, which by the mid-nineteenth century all served tin mines in the interior. Sungei Ujong was populated largely by Menangkabau originally from Sumatra and formed one of the several states which comprised the confederacy of Negri Sembilan. It shared a boundary with Selangor and reached the straits of Malacca by the Linggi River.

All three states shared political systems which invoked notions of a centralised polity, political authority vested in a singular ruler (yang di-pertuan), custodian of the faith, Islam, but in practice displayed a dispersal of power and variety in forms of control. In fact, the yang di-pertuan, while the head of a system of status, maintained his position through alliances with other territorial chiefs (orang besar or dato) - his own effective control seldom running beyond his district. Although the territorial chiefs held their districts (daerah or jajahan) nominally at the ruler's pleasure, in reality power turned on their ability to control the human and material resources of their districts. How this was achieved is best understood by observing how production was organised and in particular what were the social dimensions of this activity. From this account the class relations that emerge will indicate the interdependence between individuals and in turn reveal the structure of these societies and the social context in which power was exercised.

The village (kampong) under the headman (penghulu or ketau) with its mosque, burial grounds, houses, orchards and padi-fields provided the usual composition of settlement. The peasant producers sought a livelihood through the cultivation of food crops, especially padi, the harvesting of fruit orchards and jungle produce, and worked where possible, the streams and adjacent land for alluvial tin, but always with the necessity of meeting the demands of the chief or his agents. This is clearly seen in the ownership and access to land. Land was nominally held in the ruler's name. Access to it was bound by conventions (adat) which gave the direct producer - a freeman (orang merdeka) - control on the basis of usufruct when in production and for three years thereafter. At the same time, the producer was liable to the demands of the district chief for a share of his labour time and produce. For his part, in order to enforce these demands, the chief had to enter the process of production at three points: first in his control of the labour resources of the community; second, in his access to a portion of the produce of his district; and third, in his participation in production on his own account.

The chief's control over the labour of his district took two forms: corvée labour (kerah) and labour in servitude (hamba). His right to kerah was sanctioned in customary law (adat). Kerah gave the chief the labour to work his padi fields, occasionally to work his mines, and labour on 'public' works necessary for the reproduction of the community of which the chief was the principal beneficiary. On the same authority, the chief could call 'free' men to arms. There were, nevertheless, limits to the chief's ability to command the labour of the peasantry or orang merdeka. Kerah, taxes and even direct plunder might be used to appropriate surpluses of the population, but in a non-capitalist society the capacity of the non-producers to extract surpluses from the producers is limited as long as the latter retain some measure of control over the means of production. In this case, it was land, held on the basis of usufruct, with use-rights which made it difficult for the chief to secure a portion of the produce. By contrast, slavery, in its several forms provided the most effective means of separating the direct producer from the means of production. Labour in servitude gave the chief unfettered control over the object and product in the process of production.

In general, slaves, subordinated for life (abdi), not surprisingly were drawn from outside the community and were most often drawn from non-Muslims captured in war or purchased from the extensive trade in them in Southeast Asia.[4] Debt-bondsmen (orang berhutang) were drawn from within the local population and, given that their condition was conceived of as compensatory, they were, at least in theory, made over to servitude temporarily. In fact, the two

162

categories tended, on the one hand, to dissolve into a number of others and, on the other, coalesce as few bondsmen were able to redeem themselves. One eighteenth century legal digest suggests how the debt-bondmen might become a slave. It declared that,

> if the period within which payment has to be made is exceeded even by a single day the debtor may be sent to work in the tin-mines of the creditor and if he runs away he forfeits his status of a freeman and becomes the slave of the tin-miner.[5]

Evidence for the period prior to British intervention in the Malay States indicates that a freeman, or woman marrying a person in bondage, assumed the same burden of debt, as often did their off-spring. In other cases, debts were simply fabricated.[6]

Labour in this form came to perform a wide range of activities, most common in domestic service, but commonly necessary to agriculture and mining. Indeed it, along with kerah, was critical to the mode of production in these Malay States in the nineteenth century. One estimate for the 1870s had one sixteenth of the population of Perak in bondage and significantly it was most prevalent in the two major mining centres of Larut and Kinta.[7] In slavery, unlike kerah, the direct producers were separated from the means of production. By the period under study, slaves had assumed the character of a commodity in that they had a monetary value and could be transferred.

This then was in general the way production was organised and surplus extracted by the chiefs in these states. It reveals how the chief's control of manpower enabled him to enter the process of production. The main form of surplus extraction turned on slavery and kerah. To these must be added the judicial fines, usury - as the presence of debt-bondsmen attest - and plunder. Two other forms of surplus extraction became very important to the rulers and chiefs especially by mid-nineteenth century. These were taxes on commodity production and exchange. The chiefs levied taxes (chukai) on trade passing through their districts and raised a royalty (chabut) on the produce of mines within their districts.[8] Commodities for export ran from ivory, rattans, damar, and of course, to tin. Imports, especially in regions where mining was widespread, included a wide range of foodstuffs such as oil, salt, salt fish and rice, spirits and, as well, opium.[9] The appropriation of a portion of the commodities in circulation did not in itself alter the existing mode of production. Nevertheless, it did expand the size of the chief's surplus and allow the process of primitive accumulation to occur. At this point, where the opportunity presented itself, the chief entered into production on his own account, most commonly during the mid-nineteenth century, in tin-mining.

The consequence of this process at the political level was to intensify the efforts of the ruler and chiefs to control the most lucrative mining areas, or at least the points at which taxes could be levied on trade. The pre-colonial state was therefore always delicately poised on the edge of turbulence, driven by the contradictions of a system whereby loyalty to the ruler could only be sustained if the ruler could contain the capacity of the chiefs to grow rich, while the chief in turn could only maintain his position by the thorough expropriation of the surpluses of his district. Trade in itself could disturb the political stability, but could not transform the relations of production in some direct way. The crisis of the 1860s and 1870s in these tin producing states was not the result of some single external intrusion - either mercantile or imperial - but of an internal metamorphosis in the relations of production.

Trade, Tin and the Transformation of the Relations of Production

The growth in the demand for tin began to widen in the eighteenth century as Dutch, British and Southeast Asian merchants used the metal in local and inter-Asian and increasingly European trade. But if the commodity was important in the interregional trade, especially with China in the latter part of the eighteenth and early nineteenth centuries, its value in the composition and character of trade in the third quarter of the nineteenth century gave it a new importance. The demand for tin was directly associated with the expansion of the industrial base of the British economy. The industrialisation of British capitalism, and the growth of the tin-plate industry in Wales and England, enhanced the value of alluvial tin ore which the Malay states, especially Perak, Selangor and Sungei Ujong, could supply. The reduction and eventual abolition of restrictions on the importation of tin into Britain by 1853 gradually saw 'Straits tin' supercede both Cornish and Banka (Indonesia) tin by 1880s for many purposes but especially in the tin-plate industry. In the Malay states old fields were worked more intensively, new ones were opened as the search for the mineral widened to meet the demand. The old patterns of production were stretched and forced to give way to new forms. Malay society - the Malay ruling class - was faced with a profound crisis: how could the existing forms of labour be transformed to allow for continuous and expanded production? The peasant producers could not immediately, and except by force, be transformed into workers. Only those in servitude or 'free labour' - those freed from ownership of the means of production and freed from customary obligations - could be locked into a form of labour which would allow for sustained production of the mines. It was at this point that Malay chiefs contracted to work the mines with imported labour. The ethnic composition of this labour force was eventually to become predominantly Chinese, but as we will see it was by no means the only ethnic group to work in the tin mines of the Malay states. We will return to this question later; what is of utmost importance here is to comprehend the full dimension of the change in the relations of production. In a short space of time, the direct producers, crucial to the most lucrative sector of the economy, the one area capable of expanded commodity production, were to become labourers whose surpluses were extracted by a purely economic means, means which assumed several forms, but eventually emerged as a wage contract. This new dimension in the relations of production in Perak, Selangor and Sungei Ujong was to constitute a critical juncture in the history of these societies, one which in its total complexity was to insure the eventual dominance of a capitalist mode of production in the Malay Peninsula.

Tin mining in this expanded form began in earnest from about the 1840s in Perak, Selangor and Sungei Ujong. By the 1870s tin was being worked in areas of Perak besar, widely in the Kinta valley, but most extensively in Larut - an area remote from the heartland of Perak - where between 20,000 to perhaps as many as 40,000 Chinese labourers were at work in the early 1870s.[10] In Selangor, the three rivers Selangor, Klang and Langat had several mining settlements, and by 1873 after serious fighting some 15,000 Chinese were at work in the Klang valley. A similar number was estimated to be working in Sungei Ujong at about the same time. Wong Lin Ken's study on the history of this period is as admirably thorough as it is clear about the structure of the expanding industry. Still, his exposition of much of the history of the industry is in terms of 'Chinese' and 'Western' mining operations; while this approach is valuable at one level, it tends to obscure the nature of the transformation of production. In fact, the picture is somewhat more complex in its historical dimensions. There is a good deal of evidence to show that chiefs, as well as rulers, opened mines themselves with capital advanced from surpluses drawn from other areas of the economy, especially from taxes on trade. This was true of the mines opened in Selangor, and in Larut and the Kinta valley in Perak. Moreover, the ethnic composition of those who advanced capital does not necessarily explain why Chinese eventually came to constitute the largest component of the labour force in the mines. As well, not all the Straits merchants who advanced funds for mining ventures were Chinese, some were European, others Eurasians, Arabs, and Jawi Peranakan. Everyone who could afford to, dabbled in the rapidly growing industry. What eventually gave the Chinese a considerable edge in this area was first, that they simply formed the largest and most prosperous ethnic group among the merchants. Second, they played a role in the commodities trade which left them predominant in the local trade. The Europeans relied on them for the acquisition of local and regional produce and the retailing of imported manufactured goods from Europe and South Asia. In the 1860s, when labour was required for the expanding tin industry in the Malay Peninsula and plantations of Sumatra, it was the merchants of the Straits settlements who provided people able to work. At the China end of the trade, and in the movement of labourers, European merchants played an important role. But retailing this scarce commodity within the Malay States was controlled entirely by Chinese merchants. In this, as is well known, they utilized the institutions of clan association and secret society as mechanisms for the movement and control of labour in the mines.[11]

If the merchants of the Straits Settlements had ever merely confined their capital to spheres of circulation, by the middle of the nineteenth century, some, at least, had invested their capital in production.[12] This move into production was most evident in the widespread planting industry which was carried on within the colony and had spilled over into the neighbouring Malay States of Johore and Negri Sembilan. Merchants invested in the tin mining industry by providing the working capital to a mine leasee (towkay lombong). The towkay lombong recruited the labour from 'coolie-brokers' and organized the mining operations. To the 'advancer' (towkay labur or towkay bantu, depending upon his financial relationship with the towkay lombong) the towkay lombong had to repay not only the interest and principal on the capital advanced, but also one-tenth of the output and as well the remainder of production at a rate below the market value. The 'advancer' also retained the option to purchase the mining lease itself. The towkay lombong, in the words of one colonial official was, 'a ganger advanced to for tin. The towkay lombong is a form of middleman. He receives the advances and supplies the coolies.'[13] His income was earned on the advance of provisions, especially opium, to the workers on credit at exhorbitant interest rates. The 'advancer' would in fact probably invest in several mines on these terms to more than one towkay lombong in the hope of finding a profitable mining field. Clearly, the activities of the 'advancers' went well beyond mere money lending. Investment was in production to control the destination of the produce.

The forms of labour varied, but tended towards two types; the kongsi and the hun systems.[14] The former was based on wages, the latter, often called the 'tribute system', rested on the towkay lombong securing his labour on a profit sharing basis, the towkay lombong holding a number of shares. The towkay lombong extracted a surplus through provisioning the miners. The hun system tended to become

166

widespread especially during times of labour scarcity. Nevertheless, while it was a variation on the wage contract form of surplus labour, surplus was extracted from the worker on the basis of an economic sanction, not by force, or some extra-economic form of coercion as had previously occurred. Thus, wage-labour and commodity production gives us social relations in production which were capitalist.

Whilst the structure of the industry in the 1860s and '70s is seen most clearly in the major mining areas of Larut, Klang, and Sungei Ujong, it is clear that it did not differ substantially in areas where Chinese did not necessarily constitute the bulk of the labour force. One example in the Kinta valley illustrates the point. In the late 1860s, Kuloop Rheo had two mines in operation in the Gopeng region, one worked by Chinese labourers, the other by Malays, though these appear to have been mostly Mandalings.[15] A brother and cousin oversaw the Malay mine to which Kuloop Rheo supplied the provisions. The other mine was managed by a Chinese headman, but was funded by two Penang merchants Wee Chin and Haji Slaiman. Kuloop Rheo received one-tenth in kind of the output from each mine, but he gave half of the 'tenths' (hasil tanah) or tax from the Chinese-worked mine to the two Penang merchants. The tin taken by the Chinese headman was either sold to traders at Kota Lumut or taken directly to Penang; Kuloop Rheo usually sold his tin in Kota Lumut. His success with these mines led him to open others, one of which he purchased from a reported agent of Raja Muda Abdullah, and for a time he worked Sultan Ismail's mines at Papan. Political events forced him out of the Kinta valley mines until after the Perak War. What is of interest in this account is the way the mines were worked by the non-Chinese mine owner, that is with labour evidently brought into Perak from Sumatra (or drawn from Mandaling communities elsewhere, possibly from the Klang region in Selangor). Nearly four hundred were employed at Kuloop Rheo's mine. The numbers in the mines worked with Chinese labour eventually rose to about 3000. While there would have been differences in the way in which the labour was organised and applied to the task of working the mines, the social relations in production were the same. The form of surplus extraction was by economic means; the direct producers had been freed from the ownership of the means of production; and their labour power was now directed to commodity production.

Although the evidence does not make this clear, it is possible that the Mandaling labourers were slaves, or at least so perceived by the beholders and were treated by their owners as chattels. Even if this were so, it would still be wrong to assume that somehow two different modes of production existed in some articulated way. Slavery can of course exist under capitalist mode of production and is often most prevalent where 'free' labour is scarce. Where labour is plentiful and the technological levels still constitute a minor component in production, then slavery is soon dissolved in more efficient forms of exploitation.

More broadly we may conclude that although in theory the land and the mineral rights belonged to the ruler (indeed many of the Kinta mines were opened by Sultan Jaafar, 1850-65), by the 1870s the mining rights had acquired a value and could be transferred by others than the ruler. In Kinta we see the extent of the transformation in the relations of production. Moreover, those who worked the mines were no longer involved in the simple reproduction of the social formation where the surpluses were consumed by the ruling class or dispersed by some formalised redistributive mechanism, but as we see in Kuloop Rheo's case, the surpluses were now applied to expand capital accumulation with a concomitant expansion of the material basis of the productive process. This is evident in accumulation through improved technology represented by the introduction of the chain link pump by Chinese miners. One of the few mining leases (surat chap) in existence issued by a chief, recognized and encouraged these innovations when allowing a Chinese headman to work a mine.[16]

This account of Kuloop Rheo's mining operations relates to the late 1860s and early 1870s. The Kinta valley was the centre of the tin mining for Perak besar. At the time of British intervention, Sultan Ismail and his closest political allies controlled most of the important mines in the valley. Indeed, his village was situated there. Malays - regardless of their precise ethnic derivation - along with Chinese provided the labour for these mines well into the 1880s. Ownership of the mines remained in Malay hands, until the 'rush' of capital and labour in the 1880s. In 1884, of the five hundred mines registered in the Kinta valley, some three hundred and fifty were held by Malays.[17] In short, to characterize the growth of this industry, as Wong Lin Ken does, as one which saw the 'penetration of the indigenous economy' by Chinese because of the 'lack of requisite capital, skill and labour' obscures the nature of the process at work and the character of the structure of this society.[18]

In Selangor and Sungei Ujong the new form of relations in production did not differ significantly from that of Larut in Perak. In Selangor, it was perhaps more comprehensive in the extent of its hold on the society of that state. The civil war, which ended about 1873, helped to disrupt and depopulate much of the state. Among the peasants, as Raja Bot noted, 'it followed of course that the raiats of Selangor forgot altogether about planting padi, preferring to engage in buying and selling.'[19] By the end of the fighting the triumphant faction - that led by Tengku Dzaiuddin and Yap Ah Loy - controlled most of the important mining areas. At a rough estimate, two-thirds of the population was locked into the mining industry one way or another. In Perak perhaps thirty to forty per cent of the adult population were similarly involved. In Sungei Ujong some 15,000 miners in the early 1870s outnumbered the small Malay population, but more significantly these numbers give some indication of the relative scale of the mining industry in that society and the impact it had in dissolving the old mode of production.[20]

Allowing for the different chronologies in the three states, a profound change in relations of production occurred in the 1860s and 1870s giving rise to a new mode of production. 'Freed' labour was now applied to the alienated means in the production of tin - a commodity which was to form the staple of the economy of the three states for many decades. The surpluses generated in this production were re-invested in a process of extended and expanded reproduction. By the 1870s a capitalist mode of production was dominant since it was clearly determining the direction of social relations in production and, as has been extensively recorded, conditioning the pattern of politics in the tin producing states and Straits Settlements. Everywhere the old social formation - 'Malay society' - persisted, most extensively evident in Perak besar and in the areas peripheral to the mining industry, but the context of its existence was radically different in the 1870s to the 1840s. Yet, even in remote areas old ways were giving way to new ones. Most simply illustrated, the padi producer who abandoned his crop to collect rattan did so because this product was now a commodity of value which surpassed that of rice.[21] The new mode of production now provided the context for the dissolution - often very gradually - of the old institutions.

The Dissolution of the Pre-colonial State.

As these changes brought about a profound transformation in the structure of society, the form that the exercise of power assumed had to alter. The existing literature speaks of the 'disintegration' of the Malay state,[22] 'the sweeping away of the feudal framework' and 'liquidating the old structure'[23]. In fact, the process was more complex than simply an inability on the part of the rulers and chiefs to manage the influx of Chinese miners as suggested by many writers.[24] The old political system was being dissolved by the erosion of the social base upon which it had rested for so long. This was most advanced in Larut, in Perak, in the early 1870s, and in Selangor, particularly in the Klang valley by about the same time. The Orang Kaya Menteri, Ngah Ibrahim, who controlled Larut, allocated the land to be worked by the miners, collected a land tax (hasil tanah)[25] and levied a duty on the tin exported (estimated in 1872 at $180,000 per annum). He also controlled the bullock cart transport and coastal shipping.[26] He had done his best to centralize his control of the 'state apparatus' in the collection of revenue, the organisation of production, and the enforcement of 'law and order' through the system of mining headmen and the recruitment of a paramilitary force from India under a European officer.[27] In short, the Menteri was attempting to build in a crude, and perhaps haphazard way, the elements of the state structure which we associate with 'modern' government. It is in this sense that we see the alliance of class forces, the chief of Larut, who owned the land, the mine lessees and investors constituting the new 'ruling class' of the district. It has been often noted that there was an alliance between chief and Straits merchant, some writers seeing the Malay chief as the 'sleeping partner' and Khoo Kay Kim arguing that the Malay chiefs surrendered 'economic control' to the Straits merchants.[28] At this point we find instead the chief critically locked into the process of production.

The same may be said of the Tengku Dzaiuddin in Selangor, who in alliance with Yap Ah Loy at Kuala Lumpur won the civil war, or at least appeared to have done so by the end of 1873. As Viceroy, (wakil matluk) his position was never strictly comparable to that of the Menteri of Perak. He legally governed in the Sultan's name and in fact by early 1874 he and Yap Ah Loy controlled the Klang valley and the Selangor river to the Kanching hills. Langat, the domain of the Sultan and his 'sons eluded his effective control, but elsewhere it is clear that before British intervention Tengku Dziauddin was attempting to centralise his control through his headmen in the principal regions under his authority while leaving the direct control of production in the interior to Yap Ah Loy.[29] Likewise, in Sungei Ujong, the Datuk Bandar dominated the area where most of the tin mining occurred, farming the principal sources of revenue and receiving a royalty on all tin exported.[30] One finds, throughout this period, forms of political organization emerging which were compatible with the new mode of production.

Perak besar was a different story. By the early 1870s the Raja Muda Abdullah (the heir apparent) was isolated at the mouth of the Perak river while Sultan Ismail controlled the heartland of the negeri. Ismail and his chiefs dominated the tin producing districts, most importantly those in the Kinta valley. Ismail himself owned a number of mines. From the produce of these, and a royalty on the minerals exported from the state he derived a considerable revenue. Although the number of people involved in tin mining increased throughout the 1860s and early 1870s, the old forms of production, especially in agriculture, persisted. Nevertheless, deep inroads had been made into it as the account of Kuloop Rheo's activities indicates. The contradictions emerging were nicely revealed in the course of the political events in the early 1870s. On one occasion, at the height of the last outbreak of fighting in Larut between rival Chinese factions, before British intervention, the Menteri asked Sultan Ismail if he would allow 15,000 miners to enter Perak besar. The yang dipertuan reportedly 'ridiculed the idea'.[31] On another, Ismail confronted Kuloop Rheo and asked him, as the latter reported,

> if I was a Raja [empowered] to make roads and introduce people into the country. I shewed the Sultan an authority in writing under the seal of Toh Nahra [Ismail's ally by] which I had authority to introduce people into the Country. I also reminded him that I had opened the place under his authority. He replied I gave you leave to bring five or ten men into the country but you brought hundreds. I said it is impossible to get Tin without collecting people together. He got angry and said I was very proud, and that he had a mind to kill me; adding that if the White people knew that there was so much tin to be got they would come and take the Country. He said already the White people are fighting in Klaang. The next thing would be they would come and fight here. I replied I knew nothing about affairs of state. I only understood mining matters. Sultan Ismail said that is just so, you only know about mining and I shall have to pay afterwards; if you do not send all these Mendaling men away I will kill you.[32]

Later Kuloop Rheo's tin was seized and one of Ismail's men was ordered to go to Penang and purchase provisions for the Chinese miners and drive Kuloop Rheo out of the area. The old concerns about the rise of independent chiefs are here, but in this tale we see Ismail consolidating his hold over the more lucrative mines. Ismail and his closest chiefs were locked into the production of tin with 'freed' labour. Where the process would have led, and into what form the old political institutions would have dissolved in Perak besar, is an open question. Its development was to be cut short by Britain's intervention in the affairs of these three states in 1874.

The Colonial State and the Consolidation and Extension of Capitalism

The rise of a capitalist mode of production in the tin states of Perak, Selangor and Sungei Ujong and the deepening involvement of the Straits merchants in production in the expanded mining industry, gave the politics of these three states and the Colony a new dimension, one which eventually led Britain to assert its control over the Peninsula. Using the chiefs allied to some of the principal merchants of the Straits Settlements, and the force of arms, Britain levered its officials, British Residents, into Perak, Selangor and Sungei Ujong in 1874. When British Residents found in the

Langat district of Selangor, and Perak besar, that their
'advice' was not being implemented the Colony's Governor, Sir
William Jervois, moved to break the authority of the last
vestiges of the pre-colonial state. In a nice piece of
rhetoric before the Legislative Council, following his
ultimatum to the Perak chiefs to abandon their power in
return for a pension, Jervois asked, why the Malay Peninsula
should not prosper like Ceylon:

> Why should not a large labouring population of immigrants
> be imported into or voluntarily enter the states? Why
> should not English capital be invested as readily in
> these rich states as it is in the other parts of the
> world, to feed the labour so imported and to aid the
> general development? The answer can be given in two
> words: Malay rule.[33]

A few days later J.W.W. Birch, the British Resident to Perak
was assassinated. The Perak War followed, 'pacification' of
ulu Perak was eventually completed, and the alleged
perpetrators of the crime hanged.[34] Raja Abdullah, whom
the British had made Sultan, the orang kaya menteri and
Sultan Ismail were all exiled along with four other principal
chiefs. Earlier, the power of Datuk Bandar in Sungei Ujong
had been broken by a band of mercenaries led by a British
official and he too was forced into exile. In Selangor,
where the Viceroy was the principal collaborator in Britain's
ambitions, the Sultan had acquiesced, and the disaffected
chiefs had been successfully contained.[35]

What was left of the aristocracy and chiefs was pensioned
off. Only a few individuals found a role in the colonial
state. The sultanates remained as a device to enable Britain
to legalise as well as legitimize its control. By 1876,
Malay rule was indeed broken. Thereafter, the authority of
the colonial state was secure. Over the following decades it
busily set about dissolving the remaining elements of the
pre-colonial social formations and consolidating the basis of
a new system of surplus extraction and accumulation in its
distinctive 'imperial' context.

With the coming of pax Britannica, the colonial
administrators established the legal basis for this new and
now dominant mode of production and set about providing the
infrastructure for its expansion. The history of these
developments in Perak, Selangor and Sungei Ujong, along with
the rest of Negri Sembilan and Pahang which came under
British rule in the mid-1880s, forms a rich area in Malaysian
historiography.[36] Still, to conclude my argument it is
necessary to single out a number of developments.

At first, little was done to disturb the existing system
of production, rather the efforts of the colonial officials
were directed to strengthening it and providing the legal
basis for what they found. Thus, the consolidation of the

172

employer's hold over labour was expressed in a number of enactments assuming what became known as the 'Discharge Ticket System' in Selangor and Perak in the early 1880s.[37] The state's role in improving the physical infrastructure was nicely expressed by Swettenham when he wrote that the colonial administration had a responsibility for 'liberal but prudently-directed expenditure of public funds, especially when they are invested in high-class roads, in railways, telegraphs, waterworks, and everything likely to encourage trade and private enterprise.'[38]

Breaking the authority of the old ruling class allowed the colonial administrators to reconstitute the negeri with the yang di-pertuan as a constitutional monarch legalizing British rule in laws enacted by a state council. More importantly, it destroyed the nexus of chief and producer at the point of production. Depriving the chiefs of ownership of the means of production and destroying their ability to exercise political power, removed them from participation in the most lucrative sector of the new mode of production, one which, ironically, they had done much to bring into life. Moreover, the colonial state brought about a restoration of ownership of land in the state and emergence of a system of land tenure on a leasehold basis. In the mining areas, therefore, the 'ownership' of the mines passed from the dispossessed chiefs to those who held leases to work the mines prior to British rule. This was generally true of the three states, but in Kinta where many Malays worked the mines - and wherever peasant producers existed - separate categories of tenure were initially devised.[39]

Moreover, in those areas which generally fell outside the principal towns and tin mining areas, such as Larut, the system of pre-colonial governance was ostensibly retained through the retention of the office of penghulu (headman) at the mukim (embracing one or more villages) level. Renumeration of these officials, who were often mineowners, took the form of a percentage (chabut, a royalty) of the legally collected revenue. By the 1880s, as the rush to the tin fields of Kinta began, many penghulus were receiving handsome incomes, two at least earning more than the European collector.[40] Swettenham, the Resident of the time, moved quickly to dissolve this final area of Malay, or chiefly, participation in the expanding capitalist mode of production. The number of 'ancestral mines' - as they were designated - were sharply reduced to apply to members of families 'of the original grantee'.[41] (Among these most interestingly was Sultan Idris. In 1875 he struck a deal with the British, when Jervois was struggling to secure the agreement of the Perak chiefs to his demands, whereby Idris and his descendants would retain control of the rich mines he claimed at Kampar.[42]) At the same time, Swettenham prevented the penghulu from receiving chabut and converted them into salaried civil servants thereby depriving them of the old forms of surplus extraction and binding them to the colonial bureaucracy.

In the case of Kinta, we see how the context set by the new mode of production determined the way class interests, in this case specifically mining towkays, were served by the colonial state. Other aspects of the pre-colonial social formation were also modified and eventually done away with. Slavery and debt-bondage of course continued to exist even after labour was being imported to work the mines for the simple reason that freed labour was a scarce and valuable commodity. With colonial rule the necessity for these forms of slavery for the old ruling class lessened and slavery was eventually abolished by the British officials. Kerah, or corvée labour, continued for the same reason well into the colonial period, but in much reduced and regulated form.[43] Its attractiveness to the colonial state lay in its usefulness in rural areas where wage labour could not be easily contracted.

Finally, how do we accommodate the peasant producers in this analysis? Unlike India and Indonesia, peasant surpluses in the three states were not critical to the colonial economy. This is not to say that they were unaffected by the emergence of a new mode of production. Indeed, it is clear that the pattern was in broad terms similar, but the time span quite different. The capitalist mode of production created the context within which changes in the relations of production occurred, with a resulting pattern of social differentiation which at one end saw producers separated from the means of production and at the other, a landlord class emerge. The conditions which made this possible were laid earlier than most students of the Malay peasantry are prepared to consider.[44] The introduction of a system of land tenure - however haphazardly and unevenly implemented at the formal administrative level - transformed land into a commodity. The essential feature of this change was that land acquired a value, it could be transferred and was taxed (though in the early years of British rule at a very low level). Moreover, the taxation, whether in kind or cash likewise transformed a portion of the produce of the land into a commodity. Taxation in cash shifted the burden of maintaining revenue levels to the peasantry. As the elements of a capitalist economy began to make themselves felt in the kampong through exchange forms in cash, markets and credit arrangements conditioned by a world transformed in its mechanisms for surplus extraction, the peasant was drawn relentlessly into commodity production which exposed him increasingly to the vagaries of market fluctuation, seasonal variations and fiscal crisis. This becomes clearer, as Lim Teck Ghee has shown in his work, when the plantation industry gets underway in earnest at the turn of the century, but the context for these developments was set by a profound change in the societies of these states in the latter half of the nineteenth century.

It is the argument of this chapter that a capitalist mode of production was in existence in the tin producing states at the time of British intervention in 1874. In such a system, the social relations in production were characterised by the separation of the producers from the means of production while these were increasingly controlled by a class which, by virtue of other forms of accumulation of capital, had invested in the mining industry. The colonial state confirmed these developments and provided the administrative and infrastructural conditions which permitted the escalation of the process of capital accumulation. Finally, the widening of this mode of production at the level of production and by means of the colonial state helped to dissolve, unevenly, the old social formations. Elements of this new mode of production were in evidence throughout the West Coast Malay states by the 1870s: commodity production in agriculture especially rice in Kedah, gambier and pepper in the Straits Settlements and Johore, sugar in Province Welleseley; labourers with no control over the means of production had existed in agriculture and mining from the end of the 18th century. Merchants seeking outlets in production, or seeking to control production, have a continuing presence in the history of the Straits Settlements. But, it was in Perak, Selangor and Sungei Ujong that the process of expanding tin production on the basis of new forms of labour overwhelmed the old mode of production and gave capitalism a foothold in the Malay States.

NOTES

1.   For a discussion of some of the recent literature on the problems see, J. Drabble, "Some Thoughts on the Economic Development of Malaya under British Administration" Journal of Southeast Asian Studies, Vol. no. 2 (Sept. 1974) and P.J. Drake, "The Economic Development of British Malaya to 1914: An Essay in Historiography with some Questions for Historians", Journal of Southeast Asian Studies Vol. X, no. 2 (Sept. 1979).

2.   Khoo Kay Kim, The Western Malay States, 1850-1873: The Effect of Commercial Development on Malay Politics (Oxford University Press, Kuala Lumpur, 1972), p.226.

3.   J.M. Gullick, Indigenous Political Systems of Western Malaya (London School of Economics, Monographs on Social Anthropology, University of London, The Athlone Press, 1958) Chapters 3-5, gives an account of the workings of the political system.

4.   On slavery, see W.E. Maxwell, "The Law Relating to Slavery Among the Malays", Journal of the Straits Branch, Royal Asiatic Society, No. XII (1883), pp. 247-297; and V. Matheson, "Categories of dependency and compensation from

Malay texts" (Unpublished manuscript).

5.   W.E. Maxwell, "The Law Relating to Slavery Among the Malays", p. 286.

6.   For example, see P.L. Burns (ed.), The Journals of J.W.W. Birch, First British Resident to Perak, 1874-1875 (Oxford University Press, Kuala Lumpur, 1976).

7.   W.E. Maxwell, "The Law Relating to Slavery Among the Malays", p. 249.

8.   On the use of these terms see J.R. Wilkinson, A Malay-English Dictionary, (1959).

9.   Perak Enquiry Papers, Vol. I, Kulup Mahrouse, 19-21 July, 1876 and P.L. Burns, The Journals of J.W.W. Birch, Appendix III.

10.   The authoritative account on the history of tin for this period, Wong Lin Ken, The Malayan Tin Industry to 1914 (Association for Asian Studies : Monographs, no. XIV, University of Arizona Press, Tucson, 1965).

11.   "Report of the Committee appointed to consider and take evidence upon the Condition of Chinese Labourers in the Colony, 3 November 1876", Straits Settlements Legislative Council Proceedings, Appendix 22; E. Thio, "The Singapore Chinese Protectorate: Events and Conditions leading to its establishment 1823-1877", Journal of the South Seas Society Vol. XVI (1960); and A. Reid, "Early Chinese Migration into North Sumatra", in J. Ch'en and N. Tarling (eds.) Studies in the Social History of China and South-East Asia (Cambridge University Press, Cambridge, 1970).

12.   G.   Kay's   influential   Development   and Underdevelopment : A Marxist Analysis (Macmillan Press, London, 1975) has very narrowly confined merchant capital to trade alone.   This raises serious difficulties in understanding how merchants become involved in the control of production in the Third World. It is clear from the evidence in Malaya that merchants were involved in much more than money lending or mere buying and selling; they invested directly in the process of production and received directly the produce of the object of their investment. On merchant investment in the cultivation of agricultural products in Malaya, see R.N. Jackson, Planters and Speculators, (University of Malaya Press, Kuala Lumpur, 1968) and R.D. Hill, Rice in Malaya (Oxford University Press, Kuala Lumpur, 1977).

13.   M. Lister, Mining Laws and Customs in the Malay Peninsula (1889), p. 12.

14.   On the kongsi and hun labour systems see Wong Lin Ken, The Malayan Tin Industry to 1914 and Yip Yat Hoong, The Development of the Tin Mining Industry of Malaya (University of Malaya Press, Kuala Lumpur, 1969).

15.   Perak Enquiry Papers, Vol. III, Kuloop Rheo, 24-25 and 31 January 1877.

16.   P.L. Burns, The Journals of J.W.W. Birch, p. 142.

17.   A. Hale, "On Mines and Miners in Kinta, Perak",

Journal of the Straits Branch, Royal Asiatic Society, No. XVI (1885).

18.   Wong Lin Ken, The Malayan Tin Industry to 1914, p. 235.

19.   Raja Bot letter, 22 Aug., 1902 enclosure in Swettenham to Sec. State, 11 Dec. 1902, Colonial Office Original Correspondence (Public Record Office, London) CO 273/284.

20.   W.A. Pickering, "Journal, 4 Oct. - 29 Nov. 1874", Swettenham Papers, Arkib Negara Malaysia.

21.   Raja Bot letter, ibid.; R.D. Hill, Rice in Malaya, pp. 156-7.

22.   J.M. Gullick, Indigenous Political Systems of Western Malaya, p. 11.

23.   Wong Lin Ken, The Malayan Tin Industry to 1914, p. 238.

24.   For example, ibid.

25.   Khoo Kay Kim, Western Malay States, 1850-1873, p. 133.

26.   P.L. Burns, The Journals of J.W.W. Birch, p. 13, fn. 2.

27.   J.M. Gullick, "Captain Speedy of Larut" Journal of the Malayan Branch, Royal Asiatic Society, Vol. no. XXVI, 3 (Nov. 1953); Khoo Kay Kim, Western Malay States, 1850-1875, pp. 124-140.

28.   Khoo Kay Kim, Western Malay States, 1850-1873, p. 226.

29.   See Khoo Kay Kim, Western Malay States, 1850-1873 and Introduction to P.L. Burns and C.D. Cowan, (eds.), Swettenham's Malayan Journals, 1874-1876 (Oxford University Press, Kuala Lumpur, 1975).

30.   Ibid.

31.   Perak Enquiry Papers, Kuloop Rheo, 25 Jan. 1877.

32.   Perak Enquiry Papers, Kuloop Rheo, 29 Jan. 1877.

33.   Straits Settlements Legislative Council Proceedings, 29 Oct. 1875.

34.   For a history of this event, see P.L. Burns, The Journals of J.W.W. Birch.

35.   For an account of these events see P.L. Burns and C.D. Cowan (eds.), Swettenham's Malayan Journals, 1874-1876.

36.   See for instance, the best of these studies. E. Sadka, The Protected Malay States, 1874-1895 (University of Malaya Press, Kuala Lumpur, 1968).

37.   Wong Lin Ken, The Malayan Tin Industry to 1914, p. 95 passim.

38.   Perak Annual Report, 1894, p. 370 in Perak Government Gazette, No. 332, 19 July 1895.

39.   D. Wong, Tenure and Land Dealings in the Malay States (Singapore University Press 1975), pp. 65-73.

40.   A. Hale, "On mines and miners in Kinta, Perak", Journal of the Straits Settlements Branch, Royal Asiatic Society, No. XVI (1885); and Wong Lin Ken, The Malayan Tin

Industry to 1914, p. 92-97.

41.   Perak Mining Enactment, 1889, cited in D. Wong, Tenure and Land Dealings in the Malay States, p. 64.

42.   P.L. Burns, The Journals of J.W.W. Birch, p. 327, fn. 2.

43.   E. Sadka, The Protected Malay States, pp. 296-7.

44.   See for instance Lim Teck Ghee, Peasants and Their Agricultural Economy in Colonial Malaya, 1874-1941 (Oxford University Press, Kuala Lumpur, 1977).

178

Chapter 6

COLONIALISM AND CAPITALIST PRODUCTION: A CONCLUSION

Doug McEachern

A number of problems characterise the debate over the mode of
production created by colonisation and/or relations with
capitalist and industrial economies in the Third World.
There are those who are too eager to extend the term
'capitalist' to include the diversity of social and
production relations that predominate in these countries and
there are those that are far too reluctant to see that there
are central and common features within this diversity that
can only be understood if they are treated as part of a
dominant capitalist mode of production. There is little that
needs to be said about the first position. Notions of
'contact', 'incorporation' and 'world market' are not enough
to establish the character of the social relations within
particular countries. Similarly, it is not enough to show
that a surplus is generated, centralised and exported. If it
is the intention to show that the 'new' mode of production is
a capitalist one, then it is necessary to be precise about
the relations that are generated in the production process,
the nature of production and the process of surplus
extraction. It is important to argue about the changes that
have occurred and about their significance. To overcome the
doubts of those who do not see capitalism in most Third World
countries, it is necessary to consider a number of
questions. These include problems in the analysis of the
labour process, the level of technical development and
capital investment and the apparently unchanged villages in
the rural areas.
     Most problems in the analysis of modes of production
arise from mistaking the labour process for the mode of
production. The term 'labour process' refers to the way in
which work is organised in particular circumstances or
processes of production. It includes both patterns of work
division and characteristic forms of payment for work done.
It is from this latter aspect that most problems arise.
Since capitalism has a distinctive form of payment for labour
performed, the wage, the absence of this from the labour

179

process is often taken to mean that the relations of production and surplus extraction cannot be those of a capitalist mode of production. This position has strength as it is through the form of payment that the process of surplus extraction operates and the direct producers experience the class character of society. The form of payment may decisively shape the direct producers' response to class relations and exploitation. Nonetheless, a simple and absolute correlation between the wage-form and capitalism is not the surest foundation upon which to construct the analysis of class relations of Third World countries affected by colonial domination and relations with industrialised capitalism.

In a related way, some remain fascinated by the notion that the labour force in capitalist society is a free, waged-labour force. This is sometimes taken to mean that the ability to work is sold without being constrained by any other than economic forces. Thus, when such analysts examine the Third World and find force used against the rural workforce of tenants and hired labourers, or that the possibility that workers can choose their employers appears illusory, they treat this as evidence of unfreedom and assert that the labour must exist in some non-capitalist mode of production. Again, it should be noted, the experience of extra-economic forms of coercion shape the environment in which direct producers relate to the experience of production and exploitation. But that is not sufficient to show that the mechanisms of surplus production and extraction are based on these forms of force and that they do not in fact operate on the basis of equally coercive and compelling economic arrangements. The crucial dimension of the freedom of the labour force in societies dominated by a capitalist mode of production is that the labourer is freed, precisely in the sense of being separated from the ownership and control of the means of production. To survive, people must enter into a relationship with means and materials of production and this only happens to the extent that they enter into 'contracts' with those that do own, control and dominate those means of production. There is no transcendent element in the sense in which the labour force of capitalism is free, nor is there an absence of all extra-economic forms of coercion in even the most developed of capitalist societies.

The solution to these difficulties does not lie in taking labour processes, forms of payment or the forms of coercion present in production as the given determinants of the mode of production. Rather, it is necessary to consider the characteristic forms of the production process, what is produced, how, and the way in which surplus is extracted before it is possible to consider the significance and status of given aspects of the particular labour process.

Another problem raised by the consideration of the labour process concerns the related questions of the level of

180

investment and the nature of the technology employed. The potential for this to produce a misleading characterisation of the mode of production rests upon two points. Firstly, there is the assumption that capitalism either goes along with or unleashes a characteristic expansion of the productive forces and the use of increasingly 'productive' technologies. This is linked to a second assumption, that high levels of investment, of capital accumulation, are characteristic of a capitalist mode of production. It is assumed that in a capitalist environment, expanded reproduction will manifest itself in increased levels of investment, symbolised by new and improved applications of technology. This position derives its force from the 'revolutionising' of industrial production that was so obvious in nineteenth century Britain. Again the industrial analogy leads to misunderstanding. As argued in the debate on Indian agriculture, the level of technology does not prove the existence of any particular mode of production. It is quite possible to have capitalist relations of production with many different levels of technology. Once the mode of production has been identified, however, a different flavour is given to the interpretation of the significance and consequences of the technology employed in production. On the question of investment, a similar qualification needs to be made. High or low levels of investment do not indicate the existence of any particular mode of production. For capitalism to exist it is necessary to show that surplus is extracted in a particular form and on the basis of a characteristic set of class relations. On the basis of those class relations it is possible to show that the surplus extracted will be accumulated in expanded reproduction. It is not possible to argue that if that surplus is accumulated in some other sector of the economy or some other capitalist country, that the class relations that produce the surplus cannot be capitalist in character. That matter can only be resolved after a detailed consideration of what happened and arguments about the character of the class relations generated in the process of production.

A further extension of these problems expresses itself in a set of assumptions about an unchanged reality in the 'traditional' rural sector. Villages appear to be unchanged - the patterns of production would seem to be timeless - the rituals and rhythms of social life seem constant. Like so many romanticised views of the lives of those in Third World countries this is wrong. Villages and village life may appear unchanged but this cannot be sustained after a detailed study of what has happened in these areas since the colonial period. If the catalogue of modifications, new procedures, crops, purposes of production, new relations of production and forms of work organisation are considered, then the only aspect that would seem unchanged is the appearance of being unchanged. The nature and purpose of production in the 'traditional' sector have been transformed completely as one mode of production has given way to another.

These then are the common problems that have dominated arguments about the impact of colonialism on various non-capitalist modes of production. In our work we have tried to avoid these and to show that, in many countries, the end-product of colonial domination was the creation of a distinctive form of capitalism, one that embraced both industry and agriculture in a unified capitalist economy. Our general arguments and case studies reveal that not only was a surplus extracted or 'creamed off' by capitalist trade but that the very production relations were changed in ways that were either directly capitalist or forms of capitalist class relations. Despite the unavoidable ambiguity of the evidence, it has been possible to identify the main stages of such a process of capitalist development and to show the many areas in which a reinterpretation of colonialism can prove rewarding.

In reinterpreting the significance and consequences of colonialism we have worked with certain assumptions. To be clear about the interpretation of circumstances that were either changed or remained constant, it was important to argue about the mode of production that came into being as a result of colonial domination. To make this possible, it was useful to produce a list of significant changes that would lead to the appearance of a capitalist mode of production in a colonial context. Thus it was necessary to the practice of 'reading out' the mode of production from the most apparent features of the labour process, the way in which work/production is organised. Production involves three processes simultaneously: the production of use values, the production of a surplus and the extraction of that surplus from the direct producers. It is not enough to take the way in which work is organised and match it against some uncomplicated model of capitalist work organisation and judge the mode of production accordingly. There is more to the concept of a mode of production than that.

The capitalist mode of production has as its central defining characteristic the extraction of surplus value and its consumption in a process of capital accumulation, that is, in reinvestment in some process of expanded capitalist production. Surplus value is generated from the basic class and production relations because of the distinctive character of labour in a capitalist system. Here it exists as a commodity, labour-power, whose value is less than the use values that it creates. The basic form of class and production relations under capitalism is that of the wage-labour/capital relationship. This relationship is only effective on the basis of a process that systematically separates the direct producer from the means of production. As a result, direct producers must hire out their ability to work to those who possess the means of production and it is

182

on this basis that the labour/capital relationship is established.

The problem in interpreting capitalist development in countries subject to imperialist domination lies in the centrality of that wage relationship between labour and capital. In most Third World countries, colonial domination did not create wage-labour relations as the dominant form throughout the economy. In particular, other forms of work organisation and payment predominated in agricultural production. Tenancy, with variants on 'share-cropping', remained common. The interpretation of the rent relations in agricultural production is central to the characterisation of the mode of production that comes into being in these countries. As the case studies show, it is possible to identify several distinctive changes in the process of agricultural production. The process is not left unchanged as a result of colonial domination, capitalist penetration or imperialist incorporation. The very character of the production process is altered as a result of colonial conquest and administration. The very purpose of production is changed. Sometimes goods are produced that were not produced before and there is a marked increase in the production of goods as commodities and this marks an end to any pattern of self-contained or localised economy. Most basically, the social character of the means of production is transformed into the legal property of private owners and then into commodities. Land became saleable. Linked to this is, of course, a process whereby the direct producers (who frequently remain direct producers) are separated from their ownership and control of the means of production. The new rent relations generated, along with landless labour hiring out for wages, are a symbol of the changed situation.

The problem is how to interpret these changes and to this question there are several different answers. The simplest, and one which we argue is wrong, is to treat agriculture as either feudal, semi-feudal or traditional because of the presence of these rent relationships. The core of that proposition is the assumption that rent relations in agriculture are incompatible with a capitalist mode of production. As has been argued, this is not so. Rent relations can and do combine with a capitalist mode of production. Most often what is treated as being capitalist is some rearrangement of the labour process so that it closely resembles that of industrial production. This treatment misses one of the distinctive features of agriculture. In agricultural production the most important means of production is land. Tractors, chemical fertilizers and other industrial inputs are secondary. As a result, quite substantial investments and improvements in productivity can occur before agriculture achieves the same level of technical development as industry. This can not be used to argue that capitalist class relations have not been generated in circumstances where land is the major means of production.

In our response to this problem we have sought to show that, under certain conditions, the changes in agriculture are of such a kind that they form a system in which the labour process, the way in which production and exploitation is organised, may take several different forms but that they all exist as forms of capitalist class relations. What for Bernstein was only a possibility, the interpretation of rent relations as forms of the wage-labour/capital relation, has proved to be viable for the three countries considered in this study. It is possible to see that as a result of colonial domination and administration, agriculture becomes organised on the basis of the separation of the direct producers from the means of production, that for the direct producers to live they need to come into a relationship (rent or wage) with those that dominate the means of production and that, in doing so, the surplus is extracted, not just through the sale of agricultural products as commodities but on the basis of the class relations that underpin the organisation of agricultural production.

To understand the pattern of capitalist development, it is necessary, as these different case studies have shown, to consider the basic history of how capitalism came to be established in societies where such would not have been the normal consequence of their development. In other words, capitalism does not express the internal logic of the mode of production that existed prior to colonial domination. Hence it is important to establish, often in rather broad terms, the character of the mode of production that preceded colonialism. Even if it is not possible to be precise, it is useful to provide a sketch of the production process and the pattern of relations to the means of production, land. Only on that basis is it possible to assess the extent of the transformation engendered by colonial domination and capitalist trade. It is possible then to trace the rise of the new relations to the means of production and the production process and to see if they conform with the basic class relations of a capitalist mode of production. Because of the logic of the circumstances in which this form of capitalism comes to exist, it is impossible to ignore the significance of global patterns of capital accumulation.

At this point it is necessary to leave the very general features of the process by which capitalism comes to exist in countries subjected to colonisation by industrialising capitalist countries and to turn to the regional variations revealed in the substantive discussions of this volume. In no country has the situation developed in the uncluttered and straightforward manner suggested by these general observations. The comparative dimension is also important because it raises the problem of how to explain the revealed patterns of regional variations. This is possible, at least

184

for those areas covered in this volume, by reference to three major features. Firstly, there are those that concern different products, different labour processes and the problems of identifying a common mode of production amidst such variations. Secondly, there is the question of the relationship of (or a measure of the degree of compatibility, or the distance between) the non-capitalist modes of production and the capitalist mode of production. Thirdly, there is the question of the stage at which commercial or colonial domination occurs. How far, for example, has the colonising country become capitalist or been industrialised? Though these three features fail to deal with the important dimensions of cultural and social affairs (which give each considered situation a distinctive flavour and appearance), the combination of these aspects does provide a framework within which variations can be approached.

The differing character of the products and the labour processes through which they are produced engenders much of the variety and most of the confusion in the attempt to analyse the mode of production created as a result of the colonial process. If Alavi's more general argument about the transformation of India is left aside, then the regional case studies are concerned with three different types of products. In the areas of India analysed by Peter Mayer, the main object of production are the food grains, rice and wheat. Roger Knight's account of Java focusses on the production of sugar, an agricultural product but one which does not have the same food status as rice. Peter Burns' examination of the transformation of the Malay states concentrates on tin production, a thing which can neither be eaten nor produced by agricultural methods. The different natures of the products affects the different ways in which production is organised: each product gives some distinctive characteristics to the particular labour process or the way in which the work is organised. It would be wrong to construe these differences in product and labour processes as being so great as to preclude the possibility that they could all form parts of capitalist modes of production. The differences in the labour processes are so marked that they help to underline the importance of distinguishing between a particular labour process and the relations of a mode of production that exist both in and through that form of organisation. What is common to the production of these products is something more basic than the labour process, it is the social form of the product, the social relations of the production process and the form of the surplus. The clearest indication of the nature of the social relations of production can be seen in the form of the product, not just as an object of immediate utility to the direct producer but as a commodity that is owned by someone else who is involved in production to acquire goods that can be sold. The separation of the direct producers from the ownership and control of the means of production also indicates that commodity production has been generalised and that the ability to work has itself assumed the form of a commodity. As the several discussions on share-cropping and other kinds of tenancy systems have revealed, the form of payment may be divided between wage and rent-product exchange systems. It is clear that the case studies of particular regions concentrating on different products does not exhaust the monographic analyses that need to be done. The variety of food products in each society needs to be analysed. In the case of Malaya this is to supplement the account given of a product which can only be significant as a raw material consumed in other processes of production. In Java, the cultivation of rice, the subject of Clifford Geertz's analysis - a partial critique of which is included in Roger Knight's examination - could easily be subjected to a detailed investigation along the lines proposed in this book. India has a variety of food crops apart from rice and the methods of cultivation and the forms of the labour process vary greatly. Further analysis would serve to reinforce the points made by both Peter Mayer and Hamza Alavi. Those non-food agricultural products which form such an important part of India's colonial history, such as indigo, tea, jute and cotton, could all be subjected to a similar treatment. The model for the interpretation of the way in which non-agricultural raw materials, minerals, are produced is given by Peter Burns.

If the abstract features of colonisation and modes of production are considered, then it is clear that the nature of the changes needed to create a capitalist mode of production, in an environment where this would not have been a predictable product of historical development, will depend on the nature of the mode of production that existed before this process of transformation commenced. Some non-capitalist modes of production would be more compatible with elements of a capitalist mode of production, others would be more starkly opposed. In each case the way in which the transformation occurs would be conditioned by the situation that prevailed before colonialism or commercial contact opened up the process. That is why all of the studies included in this volume have given some attention to characterising the mode of production and production relations that existed prior to transformation. This is also one of the most difficult areas as there are no clear theoretical precedents for an adequate characterisation of non-capitalist modes of production. Nonetheless, some progress has been made in this direction. Peter Mayer's examination of what he describes as 'Mirasi Production' and his contrast with 'Mughal Production' shows how the different levels of compatability between the existing mode of production and the capitalist mode of production affected the political accomodations that were possible between the old

society and the new. Hamza Alavi's account of developments
in North India utilises a model of transition from feudalism
to capitalism but still concentrates on establishing the
changes and the impetus for those changes that turned one
mode into another. Peter Burns' account of tin production
shows quite clearly the way in which the new ways of
producing tin, within a new mode of production, grew out of,
undermined and transformed an existing mode of production.
Roger Knight's analysis of Java undermines a number of common
assumptions about the nature of traditional society, either
when this term referred to the situation that existed prior
to substantial Dutch colonial and merchant initiative or to
the kind of society produced by that initiative.

Another source of variation is derived from the
different stages at which industrialising capitalism came to
exert its transforming effects upon the existing
non-capitalist modes of production. This can be clearly
illustrated by reference to the contrast between the
situation in India with that of either Malaya or Java. In
India the period of contact had been long and the
significance of that contact varied. In the earliest stages
the emphasis was almost exclusively on defence, limited moves
towards conquest and trade in exotic goods gathered from
existing production. The process of industrialisation and
capitalisation occurred earlier in Britain and transformed
the logic of the imperial exercise and gave a new impetus to
the changes imposed by the colonial state. The
transformation of production in India was then subsumed under
a logic of serving rather broad raw material requirements of
industrialisation in Britain. The plantation production of
cotton, tea, jute, indigo then had the effect of transforming
the relations of production in surrounding areas, especially
where labour was torn from the previous pattern of social
relations.

The contrast to the situation in Malaya is quite
strong. In Malaya the pattern of labour recruitment was not
so immediately effective in dissolving the social relations
in the areas surrounding the tin mines as the labour was
drawn from other countries, symbolising a transformed set of
production relations there. The pattern behind the increased
production of tin is only comprehensible when the level of
technology in the industrialising country is considered.
That explains why the pressures on Malayan tin production
turned into imperatives at the time that they did. But the
most noticeable distinction lies in the fact that the
transformation of the mode of production in the three tin
producing states of Malaya preceeded the imposition of
colonial power and in fact the transformation urged forward
the moves to colonise by undermining the positions of the
traditional political and ruling forces, turning them into
obstacles to the substantial development of the new expanding
productive forces. In this way, it can be seen that the

stage of industrial and capitalist development in the imperial country has a very marked impact on the pattern of transformation of existing non-capitalist modes of production. If case studies were extended to include the so-called 'scramble for Africa', the massive, violent destruction of the existing social and production relations, the full consequences of this aspect would be revealed even more blatantly.

If we were to bring together the various strands of the initial argument about the framework of analysis with the specific accounts of how capitalism came into being in the three countries considered, we would get a schematic view of capitalist development as a result of colonial domination. Prior to colonial domination, or the expansion of trade to serve the rise of industrialised capitalism in the colonial power, these societies were dominated by distinctive non-capitalist modes of production. Though these exhibited certain tendencies towards growth, trade, the development of money, centralisation of state power and authority and an incidence of commodity production, it is against the balance of probabilities that they would have developed a capitalist mode of production if it had not been for their contact with capitalised economies from other parts of the globe. The result of colonial domination and/or increasingly regularised trading contacts was that the modes of production in these societies were completely transformed. It was not a process of transition but of transformation in which acts of state or mercantile policy gradually created the prerequisites for capitalist development by separating the direct producers from the means of production, by promoting the generalisation of commodity production and by linking the economies of these societies to global patterns of surplus extraction and reinvestment. As a result urbanisation, industrialisation and rent relations acquired a new character and meaning. A form of capitalism characteristic of this particular pattern of historical creation and conditioned by its place within global circuits of capital accumulation came into being.

The argument of this book then represents a substantial challenge to the ways in which colonialism has been interpreted. It combines a concern with the analytical questions of the interpretation and identification of modes of production with detailed historical studies. The link between these two is necessarily close. The initial account of the questions to be considered did not seek to solve all the various problems by the use of pure reason. Rather it sought to set out the parameters within which a reinterpretation of the process of a colonial transformation could be undertaken. The case studies were important, not just because they clothed a skeleton of theoretical speculation with the flesh of historical detail, but because they showed up the dynamic of the process by which colonial domination produced capitalist class relations in ways and in areas where other analytical perspectives had concealed them. As such, this stands as an invitation to reconsider the available evidence with a view to discerning a different pattern in the development of the capitalist mode of production and capitalist class relations in the context of the process of colonial conquest, domination and administration.

194

India 1927

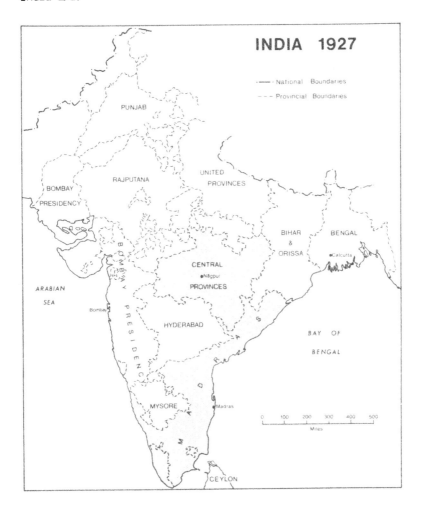

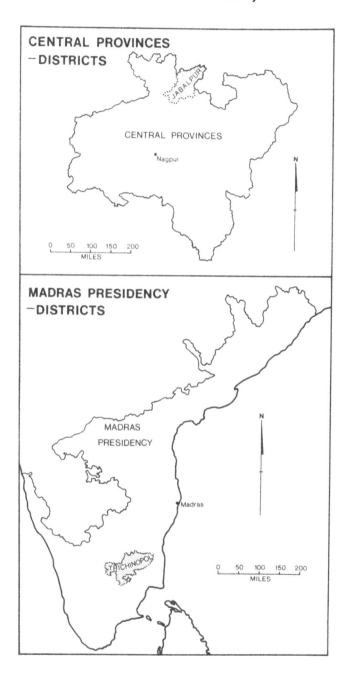

Pekalongan Residency 1870

PEKALONGAN RESIDENCY, 1870
showing the 3 major
sugar factories
JAVA
SEA
PEKALONGAN
BATANG
Kalimatie
Sragie
Wonopringo
BATANG REGENCY
PEKALONGAN
REGENCY
Djakarta
Pekalongan
Semarang
Surabaja
Jogjakarta
JAVA

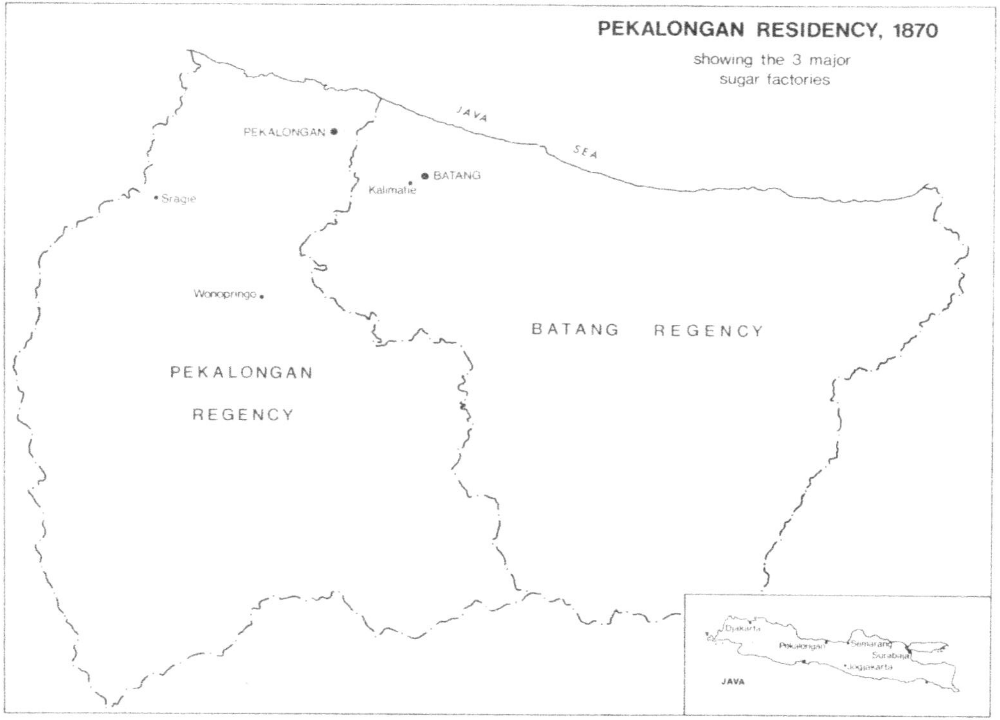

For Product Safety Concerns and Information please contact our EU
representative GPSR@taylorandfrancis.com
Taylor & Francis Verlag GmbH, Kaufingerstraße 24, 80331 München, Germany

www.ingramcontent.com/pod-product-compliance
Ingram Content Group UK Ltd.
Pitfield, Milton Keynes, MK11 3LW, UK
UKHW021828240425
457818UK00006B/116